Akira Kurosawa and Intertextual Cinema

James Goodwin

The Johns Hopkins University Press
Baltimore and London

The Johns Hopkins University Press
2715 North Charles Street
Baltimore, Maryland 21218-4319
The Johns Hopkins Press Ltd., London

LIBRARY OF CONGRESS CATALOGING-IN-PUBLICATION DATA

Goodwin, James, 1945–
    Akira Kurosawa and intertextual cinema / James Goodwin.
        p.   cm.
    Includes bibliographical references.
    ISBN 0-8018-4660-9 (acid-free paper). — ISBN 0-8018-4661-7
(pbk. : acid-free paper)
    1. Kurosawa, Akira, 1910–   —Criticism and interpretation.
2. Intertextuality.   I. Title.
PN1998.3.K87G66   1994
791.43'0233'092—dc20   93-15618

A catalog record for this book is available from the British Library.

Frontispiece: Akira Kurosawa, Tokyo, June 1991.
Photograph by James Fee/Shooting Star

Akira Kurosawa and Intertextual Cinema

For Lonnie, in shared esteem for *Sensei*

Contents

Preface

Accepting a Career Achievement award at the 1990 Academy of Motion Pictures Arts and Sciences annual ceremonies, Akira Kurosawa commented that the honor comes too early in his career, for he is still in the learning stages of his art. In conclusion, he pledged, "I will continue to devote my entire being to understanding this wonderful art." The statement, made without false humility at age eighty, expresses Kurosawa's conviction that his personality remains unformed and that this incompleteness motivates an uninterrupted search for knowledge through filmmaking. The present book, it is my hope, will contribute to our understanding of that search, which takes compelling and memorable form in Kurosawa's films.

This inquiry into matters of form and meaning in Kurosawa's cinema is charted directly through his film texts rather than through the previous findings of Kurosawa's other critics. My general critical practice is not to annotate each point of contact, convergence, or divergence between my study and the body of published scholarship on Kurosawa. After a survey in the Introduction of the Kurosawa criticism available in English, I note only the principal counterparts to my ideas in the secondary literature. The books on Kurosawa by Donald Richie and David Desser have stimulated my thinking and have spurred me to raise further critical questions. The new, thoughtful book by Stephen Prince, which pursues some of the same issues engaged here, had not been published at the time I drafted my analyses of the films discussed in the following pages. Though not acknowledged at each step in my inquiry, I remain grateful to the translators and critics who are listed in the Select Bibliography. With the use of Japanese terms and names here, in a work of film and cultural study for a general audience, I have omitted the system of macrons used among specialists in Asian studies. I have rendered Japanese names according to the Western custom of given name followed by family name. The translations made from French sources are my own.

Long and frequent discussions on Japanese film history and on Kurosawa films with Michael Baskett and with Professor Mikiro Kato of Kyoto University have contributed significantly to my knowledge of these subjects. Michael Baskett also provided valuable and resourceful research assistance. Help with matters of Japanese language and culture was kindly extended by Matthew Bills, Saori Hirata, and Hiromi Kinjo. Professor David Desser generously supplied editorial suggestions, his expertise, and much constructive advice after reading a draft of my study. Ronald Gottesman, a valued colleague and friend, has contributed greatly to my general understanding of film. My wife Andrea and my daughter Lonnie have been a constant source of encouragement and support.

I am grateful for research funds and a travel grant from the Committee on Research of the Academic Senate, University of California at Los Angeles. The Center for Japanese Studies at UCLA has substantially supported my work on this book through the Sasakawa Fund. My research with published materials was facilitated by librarians and staff at the Theater Arts Library and the University Research Library at UCLA, the Academy of Motion Picture Arts and Sciences Library, the University of Southern California libraries, the Museum of Modern Art Library, and the Film Library at the Japan Society. Sharon Farb of the UCLA Theater Arts Library and Akira Tochigi and Kyoko Hirano at the Japan Society were particularly helpful. The Museum of Modern Art has granted permission for the use of photographic illustrations from their Film Stills Archive. Frame enlargements have been made from prints distributed by Audio Brandon Films. Production companies for the films shown in the illustrations were as follows: Daiei for *Rashomon* (1950); Shochiku for

The Idiot (1951); Toho for *Ikiru* (1952), *The Lower Depths* (1957), and *Throne of Blood* (1957); and Greenwich Film/Herald Ace/Nippon Herald for *Ran* (1985). My research with film materials was aided by the UCLA Film and Television Archive and the UCLA Instructional Media Center. Carol Prescott at the UCLA Media Center and Robert Silber provided much technical assistance.

Akira Kurosawa and Intertextual Cinema

Introduction: Film Text, the Intercultural Film Text, and an Intertextual Cinema

As a foundation to the discussion of films directed and scripted by Akira Kurosawa that follows, an exposition of the concepts and critical terms that underlie my approach is necessary. It is useful to start with a few key ideas in the general theory of semiotics for preliminary definitions. Each instance of communication, in any medium, actuates a system of signs. This system constitutes a *text* that intertwines layers of content and levels of discourse. The text is thus a composite of particular codes of communication, of the processes of their combination, and of the resultant commutation of forms and messages. While a text is constituted through conventions, norms, and limits, it communicates across the boundaries of individual codes.

Codes are structures that, through their coherence, make a text perceptible and comprehensible to its audience. The principle of coherence within a code may be logical, mechanical, relational, differential, formal, or a combination of such factors. The comprehension of codes is determined by their context—that is, by their textualization. This determination ranges from a culture's institutionalized meanings and forms at one end of the context to the idiosyncrasies and idiolects of the text's producers at the other. The projection of a text toward a receiver and its organization there as communication further establish context.

An *aesthetic text* initiates a diverse system of communication acts that can elicit an original response in a member of an audience. To evoke its response, an aesthetic text *overcodes* its expressive means and its content; such a text produces a surplus in both form and meaning. Overcoding occurs at a threshold between convention and innovation in the means of communication. Umberto Eco describes this process as one that "threatens the codes but at the same time gives them strength; it reveals unsuspected possibilities in them."[1] An aesthetic text thus enlarges culture and advances knowledge.

In developing a theory of semiotics for cinema, Christian Metz starts from a categorical differentiation between *cinema*, the codes specific to this medium, and *film*, the textual system constructed of codes specific to the medium and of codes that derive from other media, other cultural forms, and other institutional modes. An active process of placement, interrelation, and restructuration among both kinds of codes constitutes the *film text*. In defining the film text, Metz concludes: "The system of a film is, among other things, a unique utilization proper to this film of the resources provided by the cinematic language system, but it is also a certain vision of the world, a certain thematics, a combination of obsessive configurations which are no less proper to the film."[2] The film text thus is not a static or inert sum of its contributing codes.

The material and codes nonspecific to cinema in a given film text are potentially vast and can readily span national cultures. Intercultural codes are a distinguishing feature of many significant films within European cinema. Representative among countless examples that can be cited are Jean Renoir's *Grand Illusion* (1937) and *Rules of the Game* (1939), Alain Resnais's *Hiroshima Mon Amour* (1959), Luchino Visconti's *Death in Venice* (1971), and Michelangelo Antonioni's *The Passenger* (1975). The presence of foreign characters or settings is no guarantee, however, that a film text is significantly intercultural, as evidenced by films produced in the Hollywood studio tradition that involve non-Western subject matter.

Two readily apparent examples of intercultural codes within the cinema of Kurosawa are a key French phrase that characters repeat in *Stray Dog* (*Nora Inu*, 1949), and the American music and song lyrics used in varied dramatic contexts within *Ikiru* (*Ikiru*, 1952). David Desser identifies Kurosa-wa's genius as his consistent ability to "adapt Western modes in a deliberate manner so as to explore the nature of Western ideals as they impact upon Japan."[3] In his critical study of the Kurosawa samurai films, Desser traces intercultural dynam-ics between West and East with particular attention to the function of American popular formulas in Japanese contexts.

To enumerate a representative set of specific cinematic codes, we can consider the codes of visual iconicity, which make the recorded subject matter recognizable to a viewer. The determinants at this level of signification include the spatial distribution and relative scale of compositional ele-ments within a geometry of the frame. Compositional ele-ments within the screen can further frame the subject. These properties have much in common with the codes of photog-raphy, as do lighting, contrast, tone, color range, and image texture. More fully media-specific codes include cinemato-graphic treatment of a subject matter in motion (or at least with the potential of motion), encoded through the camera's distance, angle, perspective, movement, and the focal length of its lens.

Codes of represented movement within the motion pic-ture image — such as real-time events, time-lapse processes, fast motion, and slow motion — comprise another cinema-specific category. Additionally, there are codes to the sequen-tial order of shots and the chronology or causality that can be conveyed through these constructions. Among the codes that pertain to this sequencing of shots are editing devices and transitions (such as the fade-in, black-out, lap dissolve, and wipe) and the constructive principles of the film text as a whole (such as the continuous sequence shot, montage, or "invisible" editing).

With projection of the motion picture another category of codes is at work, that of sound. In the silent era these codes entailed music that could vary from the repertory of an ac-companist on piano or organ to an original orchestral score. In some cases they entailed the narrative, sound effects, and impersonations provided by an interpreter such as the *benshi*, common in urban Japanese movie halls into the 1930s. On the motion picture soundtrack, audio codes encompass the sound effect, speech, voice, music, and noise as well as the represented source of these sounds, whether onscreen, off-frame, or by conventions of soundtrack accompaniment.

As in the case of nonspecific codes, the codes of the cinematic language system at work in the film text can readily span national cultures. Within film history, it is common practice to identify stylistic movements according to national film cultures, as in the cases of the Soviet montage school and the French New Wave. In truth, however, the two film movements thus designated are self-consciously intercultural in their origins and identity.

In a well-known summation of the montage system, "The Cinematographic Principle and the Ideogram," Sergei Eisenstein bases his explication in Japanese poetics, Kabuki theater, and traditional woodblock prints. In justification of his early montage experiments, Lev Kuleshov cites the irresistible influence of story forms and editing schemes found in American films. Indeed, Kuleshov attributes the original montage practices to a condition of cultural "Americanitis," as he termed the attraction of Soviet audiences and filmmakers to the formulas of imported detective serials and chase films and the styles of Griffith and Chaplin.[4] A similar cultural condition inspired the French New Wave, a movement that can be defined in part by its member cinephile directors' homages to certain American auteurs. Jean-Luc Godard indicates that in his first feature, *Breathless* (1959), he deliberately adopted the stylistics of George Cukor and Otto Preminger in giving direction to the camera crew and actors for some shots.[5]

The category *text* is relevant to units other than the release print of a single film. Within the "work of a cineast," as Metz terms it, each released film is a subsystem to the great textual system of the filmmaker's complete work. Such a system is a network of intersection and incorporation among traits, codes, and signifying units that lend identity to the individual filmmaker.[6] In the case of writer-directors like Kurosawa and John Huston (to take a Hollywood example), scripts written by the cineast but directed by others are potential components of the cineast's textual system.

Significant in this respect is Kurosawa's exclusion of a collective film production from his own filmography. For one week in 1946 Kurosawa was involved as codirector with his mentor Kajiro Yamamoto and with Hideo Sekigawa on *Those Who Make Tomorrow* (*Asu o Tsukuru Hitobito*, 1946), a pro-labor story commissioned by the filmworkers' trade unions. The production process on this film excluded Kurosawa from two phases vital to his filmmaking—the script (written by Yamamoto and Yusaku Yamagata) and the final editing. Kurosawa refers to the released film as a work made by committee under extrinsic ideological imperatives, and as such it lacks a coherent *cinematic* identity in relation to his own films.

By the conventions of film studios, filmmakers, reviewers, critics, and audiences alike in Japan, a general distinction places a Japanese film release into one of two categories: the *jidai-geki*, period drama, or the *gendai-mono*, story of modern life. The historical dividing line in this periodization is 1868 and the restoration of the Emperor Meiji, whose administration went on to modernize Japan and to adapt Western technology and material culture. Rather than genres or textual systems in their own right, *jidai-geki* and *gendai-mono* are designations that indicate the historical era (feudal or modern) in which the film story is placed.

A *genre* such as the samurai film can be treated as a vast, continuous textual system. A film genre privileges some cinematic codes (camera work that accents the *katana*, or long sword, and its deployment, for example) and selected noncinematic codes (*bushido*, the warrior's code of honor and duty, and dramatic resolution through *chambara*, or swordplay).[7] While traits associated with the *bushi* or warrior may be emphasized in modern stories, strictly speaking the samurai genre falls completely within the *jidai-geki*, since the legitimacy of this feudal class ends with the Meiji Restoration.

Other genres, such as the *haha mono*, or "mother story," are not limited to one era. One such modern story is Mikio Naruse's *Mother* (*Okasan*, 1952), while Kenji Mizoguchi utilizes pronounced elements of the *haha mono* in his period films *Ugetsu Monogatari* (*Ugetsu Monogatari*, 1953), in which attributes of a warrior culture are treated with great irony, and *Sansho the Bailiff* (*Sansho Dayu*, 1954). In studying genre, films are grouped as an ensemble that forms a homogeneous textual system whose unity is both cinematic and cultural.

The textual system of genre is not static or permanent, however, since it is subject to the permutations brought by new works in the genre and by works that mix genres.[8] Such is the case with Kurosawa's *Yojimbo* (*Yojimbo*, 1961), a samurai film that incorporates traits of the Hollywood gangster and Western film genres with the Japanese *yakuza* film, a *gendai-mono* that features the underworld activities of gamblers and criminals.[9] In its turn, *Yojimbo* contributed to an influential variation on the classic Hollywood Western through its inspiration of Sergio Leone in the creation of the "spaghetti Western" subgenre. The celebratory violence of Leone films like *A Fistful of Dollars* (1964) and *For a Few Dollars More* (1965) influenced further permutations to the genre in Hollywood productions such as Sam Peckinpah's *The Wild Bunch* (1969).

In Eastern and Western criticism alike, there has been a persistent mystique of the "otherness" and purity of Japanese cinema as an alternative to compositional and narrative norms that dominate film in Western cultures. In *To the Distant Observer: Form and Meaning in the Japanese Cinema*, the study that has provoked much valuable debate on the issue, Noel Burch claims that definitive traits of the aesthetic uniqueness of Japanese cinema are directly traceable to cultural achievements of the Heian period (794–1185). Among non-Western nations, Burch concludes, "only Japan has developed modes of filmic representation that are wholly and specifically her own."[10]

Directors Yasujiro Ozu and Kenji Mizoguchi are offered by Burch and other proponents of this argument as models of an ideal cultural autonomy. Through company policies that seem to confirm these two directors' special status, Tokyo and Kyoto studios long neglected foreign distribution of their films in the belief that they were "too Japanese." Both film-makers, however, were widely versed in and manifestly responsive to Western sources. When their careers began in the 1920s, Hollywood influences were extensive in the Japanese film industry.[11]

As David Bordwell has amply demonstrated, Ozu throughout his career included in his films prominent citations and reworkings of story forms, motifs, codes, and the data of Western movie culture. The Bordwell study documents that Ozu remained a cinephile since childhood and had, by his own admission, a persistent case of Americanitis.[12] Mizoguchi studied at age sixteen in a Western-style art school led by Seiki Kuroda, the first Japanese to adopt European realist and Impressionist techniques in landscape painting. The director's interests in realist and naturalist literature from Russia, France, and the United States also date from this period. Over the course of a thirty-five-year career, Mizoguchi freely drew on eclectic Western sources. In the silent period he adapted Eugene O'Neill's *Anna Christie* and imitated in another production the expressionism of the Robert Wiene film *The Cabinet of Dr. Caligari* (1920). With the advent of sound, he embarked on a serious study of Beethoven as a resource for film music.[13]

Since the Meiji Restoration of 1868 and the ensuing engagement in world trade and politics, Japan has undertaken a deliberate and selective assimilation of Western technology, institutions, business practices, customs, and styles. Intensified in the early decades of the twentieth century, the process of assimilation since defeat in World War II has redefined Japan as a global rather than an insular society. In public statements over the course of his career, Kurosawa has indicated that for educated Japanese of his generation it is common to be as well-versed in European classics as in Japanese ones. For a young man living in Tokyo in the 1920s, familiarity with the art of Shakespeare, Balzac, Turgenev, Schubert, and Beethoven was not a cultural anomaly. For at least three decades now, urban Japan has been far more westernized than any quality to be found in Kurosawa's films over the same period. In another ironic twist to his identity, filmmakers such as Masashiro Shinoda, Nagisa Oshima, and Shuji Terayama had come by the 1960s to consider Kurosawa a canon of Japanese traditionalism that retards new thinking and innovations in style. While he reiterates in interviews, "I can think only like a Japanese," at the same time Kurosawa recognizes "the world today is an interplay of Eastern and Western cultures." He does not share the belief advanced by critics like Noel Burch that traditional culture defines the film practices of Japan's most important directors. In weighing such issues in regard to his own cinema, Kurosawa has concluded: "Film is a new art. Even I am not aware of all the possibilities it offers. In certain aspects of my approach to this art I am doubtless Japanese and it is apparent. But I think that this new art is not the continuation of a Japanese tradition."[14]

With artists like Kurosawa in mind, the novelist Yukio Mishima once observed that "there is nothing more Japanese than being un-Japanese about being Japanese."[15] Mishima had also pointed out that for many Japanese artists since the 1860s, national recognition came only after international acclaim. Kurosawa has made a similar observation about Japan's lack of appreciation for the woodblock prints of Utamaro, Hokusai, and Sharaku until they had been cultivated first by foreign collectors. With the currently avid market in Japan for Impressionist and Post-Impressionist masterworks—European art influenced by discovery in the 1860s of Japanese prints—this circuit of intercultural exchange is reversed.

As evolved from theorists of culture and language like Mikhail Bakhtin, Claude Lévi-Strauss, and Jacques Derrida and elaborated by critics like Julia Kristeva and Roland Barthes, the concept of *intertextuality* designates a multidimensioned relation through which a particular text is intelligible in terms of the other texts that it cites, reiterates, revises, and transforms. In its most restrictive sense, intertextuality is limited to the relation between a given text and only the other texts from which it directly derives. In its more generally current sense, which arises in poststructuralist and deconstructionist thought, intertextuality encompasses any signifying unit in relation to the forms of communication, cultural codes, and social customs that endow it with meaning.[16]

From the perspective of Eco's general theory of semiotics, intertextuality is a function of overcoding that facilitates the social exchange of signifying units.[17] With the exception of its manifest level in the aesthetic text, however, Eco consigns this function to a deep structure of cultural meaning that remains largely undetected by the receiver. A more incorporative sense of intertextuality attributes to every communication, and to each component of socially mediated reality, a textuality that is absorbed and transformed by other texts. Such processes of social mediation can be in units as small, say, as a spot radio announcement or as large as a long-running primetime television series.

Following Bakhtin (who will be examined in my subsequent discussion of Kurosawa's Russian intertexts), Kristeva approaches culture in all its aspects as a vast aggregate of texts and intertextual relations. Every cultural unit of signification from a colloquial phrase or a social custom to a work of art is embedded in processes of inscription, absorption, and dissemination with other units and thus its meaning is not discrete but intertextual.[18] From Kristeva's perspective, culture exists at the intersection of various textual systems and within a dialogue between textual practices.

In elaborating a theory of the text that is equally a theory of intertextuality, Barthes sets poststructuralist concepts of *text* against classical concepts of a culture's *work* of science, art, philosophy, literature, and so on. The work functions as a source of institutionalized value and orthodoxy within culture and it assures a canonical, definitive meaning. The text is a differential system that functions plurally and it creates a field or texture of signification where many possible—and often contradictory—meanings converge. Beyond language and style, taken traditionally to constitute the literary work, *écriture* ("writing") is the text's third dimension: writing activity. A term that derives from the commentary on literature by Jean Paul Sartre and Maurice Blanchot, *écriture* for Barthes is a totality greater than the sum of language and style. Linguistics, stylistics, psychology, culture, and history converge through *écriture* and activate the text.

By Barthes's definition, a text is the field wherein codes and textual systems are redistributed: "Any text is an intertext; other texts are present in it, at varying levels, in more or less recognizable forms: the texts of the previous and surrounding culture. Any text is a new tissue of past citations."[19] While intertextuality is thus a condition of every text, it cannot be reduced to a matter of acknowledged sources and influences. An encyclopedia of codes can enter the text through processes of dispersion and permutation. The text is equally a methodological field for its receiver, who may encounter it in a fixed form such as a billboard advertisement or the release print of a film but who experiences it through a productive and interactive exchange of meanings.

By the definitions of Kristeva and Barthes, then, a text is inherently a plurality, or *intertext*, that operates within any given text. The intertext is a discursive space for the dissemination, rearticulation, interrogation, and recontextualization of cultural materials. Intertextuality is not simply a procedure of interpreting one text by way of another but a principle that each text is already the meeting place for materials from many texts. Godard films of the 1960s and 1970s, to take one conspicuous example, are tirelessly experimental in their investigation into the multiple textuality of the medium. His filmmaking brings writing, print, painting, music, still photography, video, and motion picture images into constant interaction.

In a general statement on filmmaking, Kurosawa has acknowledged the medium's plural textual structure: "Cinema resembles so many other arts. If cinema has very literary characteristics, it also has theatrical qualities, a philosophical side, attributes of painting and sculpture and musical elements."[20] Painting is just one prominent constituent of such intertextuality among media within Kurosawa's filmmaking. The climactic fight between two gangsters among paint buckets in *Drunken Angel* (*Yoidore Tenshi*, 1948) becomes an action painting. The slum environment of *Dodeskaden* (*Dodeskaden*, 1970) is reflective of a world conceived through children's drawings. The utopian fantasies of the impoverished father and son in the film are projected in the form of painterly images. The dreamscape of the nightmare vision in *Kagemusha* (*Kagemusha*, 1980) utilizes the color values and compositional conventions of Surrealism. In *Dreams* (*Yume*, 1990) famous Van Gogh paintings are transformed into dramatic space.

Within his semiotics of cinema, Metz recognizes in a general sense the aggregate, plural property of the medium as a vast system of intersecting texts:

> Consciously or not, films are determined in large measure in relation to each other. . . . They react to one another, they *cite* one another, they parody one another, they "surpass" one another, and all these plays of *contexture* (this word is to be taken in a strong and precise sense) contribute in a very central way to advancing along an uninterrupted development the production of the indefinite and collective text that cinematography offers us.[21]

But Metz limits his application of the term intertextual to two primary situations.

The first situation involves the critic or scholar who constructs "intertextual paradigms" to analyze one film text by establishing direct or contrastive relationships to elements found within other texts. This analytic procedure is characteristically *extrinsic* to a film's textual system in Metz's opinion. The second situation follows from an unusual capacity within a film's paradigmatic codes. According to the standard of linguistics, a paradigm is based on terms taken from the same code. In a film, certain textual paradigms can borrow their terms from different codes. These unique intercodical paradigms are, however, intrinsic to only a specific category of film: "The inter-codical paradigms as textual paradigms represent a less common case, reserved for films which are in some manner transgressive and develop to a greater or lesser extent in the direction of a metatext (films containing a commentary on the cinema)."[22]

Metz identifies two principal kinds of metatextual films: one hybrid in its conspicuous mixture of genres, the other self-conscious in its representation of the cinematic processes themselves. Godard's *Alphaville* (1965), an example of the first metatextuality, borrows specific codes from divergent genres (hard-boiled detective fiction, science fiction) while remaining outside determination by any single genre. Ingmar Bergman's *Shame* (1968), a metatext of the second type, reflexively explores the presence of a cinematic apparatus and matters of impersonation and acting.

Stephen Heath, in broadening the perspective on textual paradigms, usefully proposes that the film text be approached not as a fixed system but as a process "*involving* system, [as] systematic activity." The individual film text in its inevitable heterogeneity presents "a certain originality of system" in its "*movement* of relations" among textual factors.[23] Furthermore, within the film text cinematographic images invariably exceed the sequential and regulative uses to which narrative puts them. Heath concludes that at the same time that narrative strives to contain the film's textual activity it discloses the incapacity to finally do so.

In an examination of novels and films of the postmodern movement, Bruce Morrissette finds in them a shared generative textuality. Postmodern works in the two media mobilize situational, proliferative generators to produce combinatory patterns. One structuring principle of this kind is interior duplication, or *mise en abîme*, which is prominent in the writing of André Gide, Michel Butor, James Joyce, and Vladimir Nabokov, and in the written and film fictions of Alain Robbe-Grillet, Alain Resnais, and Marguerite Duras. This process entails the internal reproduction and replication of a text's own language, images, and situations.[24] Such duplication and interpenetration of a text's components is obviously intertextual. While Morrissette's focus is on writers and filmmakers associated with the *nouveau roman* and on specific instances of the "cinema novel," manifest intertextual structures are to be found in the films of directors like Alfred Hitchcock, Orson Welles, Stanley Kubrick, and Woody Allen.

Intertextuality in cinema is not by definition a matter of the adaptation into film of a literary text, though there are notable film adaptations that create intertextual relations analogous to the intertextuality found within their literary originals, such as Robert Bresson's *Diary of a Country Priest* (1951) and Karel Reisz's *The French Lieutenant's Woman* (1981). Bresson's film, to pursue only the first example here, adapts the novel by Georges Bernanos, published in 1936. The film seems austere in its formal means but proves dense in its intertextual implications. In regard to personal interactions and conversations recorded in the curé's diary, the film abstains from conventions of screen adaptation that would enact or dramatize material from the novel.

Bresson's *Diary of a Country Priest* maintains an intertextuality of reported experience and speech in depicting the priest. One factor that contributes to this quality is the interchange among three primary tenses of experience—recorded thoughts and actions recently completed, those that immediately accompany the act of diary-writing, and the anticipated future. Bresson also employs an intertextual technique of voice-over to superimpose the consciousness of the diarist onto dialogue and action in the dramatic present of events onscreen. In reaction to these properties, André Bazin has commented: "When you compare the two, it is the film that is literary while the novel teems with visual material."[25] Furthermore, its intertextuality occupies a diacritical position in relation to the two media.

Bresson's film enables the spectator, according to Nick Browne, to "see on what terms film continues its affinities with and proclaims its discontinuity from literature."[26] Dudley Andrew identifies the Bresson text with the formative concept of cinematic *écriture* as distinct from theatrical conventions of filmic construction.[27] Within film studies, Marie-Claire Ropars-Wuilleumier has rigorously applied the concept of *écriture* in order to analyze filmmakers for whom cinema is a problematic activity, particularly in matters of representation and narration. According to Ropars-Wuilleumier, the modernist and postmodern novel has generated within European cinema the *écriture* that is apparent in the complex narrativity of films by Antonioni, Bresson, Godard, and Resnais. Their films "break the immediate and univocal data of filmic communication in order to release the freedom, and ultimately the creative activity, that characterizes the experience of the reader" of intertextual fiction.[28]

Hiroshima Mon Amour presents the case of an original screen collaboration, between Marguerite Duras as scriptwriter and Alain Resnais as director, that was transformed into a print text after release of the feature film. In addition to intertextuality in the plotting of narrative events and in the disclosure of characters' perceptions and affects throughout both forms of the text, there are extensive intercultural paradigms of both an intimate contact and a historical distance between its protagonists, a European woman and a Japanese man. In many respects the properties of intertextuality within both book and film are coextensive with these intercultural dynamics.

T. Jefferson Kline, in *Screening the Text*, a study of intertextuality in the French New Wave cinema, identifies *écriture* as the model for a cinema of reflexiveness, discourse, rupture, and discontinuity. For French filmmakers of the 1950s and 1960s such as Bresson, Godard, and Resnais, the literary text, in relation to or represented in the film, is a primary means through which to explore the textuality of cinema. In their films, the library and the book stand as the textual unconscious to cinema: "French cinematography seems always to reach outward (or inward) toward other texts that both liberate and encapsulate its deeper levels of signification. . . . We can discern in the French new wave a tendency toward the 'dark scripting' of intertexts from its own and many other literatures."[29] The sources for such intertexts, as Kline's detailed commentary on individual films demonstrates, range widely across national literatures and cultures.

Seymour Chatman proposes in his recent criticism a useful addition to an understanding of intertextuality. Chatman identifies three basic kinds of text-type: narrative, description, and argument. Any one text-type can function in ways subordinate to another, dominant text-type. This flexible, mutable schema is proposed as a more accurate account of the actual plenitude of types within a given text, although many earlier theories place narrative at the top of a hierarchy wherein the other two types are always subordinate. Thus, narrative can be seen to serve the ends of description in a particular passage or segment, even within a text whose encompassing purpose is itself narrative.[30] The dynamics of interaction between narrative and argument text-types will be investigated in my analyses of *Rashomon* (*Rashomon*, 1950) and *Ikiru*.

Adaptation from a literary text to the screen or the appearance of a cinema novel in relation to a film release is no warrant of a film's intertextuality. John Huston's 1956 film adaptation *Moby-Dick* fails to impart even a suggestion of the encyclopedic intertextuality of the Melville novel. A similar criticism can be made of Huston's 1987 adaptation from a more subtle and indirectly intertextual source, the James Joyce story "The Dead." While a textual system such as the work of the cineast John Huston can be analyzed according to a *critic's* intertextual paradigms, in the case of these two films such a system is not significantly defined by any intertextual structures of the director's own design.

While by the definitions of Barthes and Kristeva any film text can be termed equally an intertext, the term *intertextual cinema* is reserved in the present study for films and the work of cineasts that exhibit conscious, marked, or dominant uses of intertextuality. In this designation of intertextual cinema, *cinema* is used in accordance with Metz's definition of the cinematic language system: the codes specific to the medium of cinema that particular films work into texts. While cinema is not in itself a text, a group of texts, or a textual system, cinema is what makes textuality in film possible.[31]

Noel Burch argues that through intertextuality Japanese films in their Golden Age (from the 1930s through the early 1940s) embody a cultural autonomy from the West that originated in Japan's feudal arts. The Heian sources for this autonomy are characterized by self-conscious textuality and deliberate polysemic practices among all the arts. As a result, traditional culture became a boundless text. Moreover, it contains dimensions of reflexive intertextuality:

> It is this inscription of the signifying process in the "text" which is such an essential characteristic of the traditional Japanese arts and which was to influence the development of Japanese cinema in this century. . . . This awareness is in sharp contrast with traditional Western attitudes which tend to close off the text, not only from other texts but, above all, from the social "text" in which it is nonetheless inevitably inscribed. This *presence of the context* is a permanent feature of the Japanese *difference*, in both Heian culture and modern film practice.[32]

In making this assessment of the traditional arts, Burch follows the suggestive speculations made by Roland Barthes in *Empire of Signs*, a meditation on the semiotics of Japanese culture.[33]

Interestingly, the American architect Frank Lloyd Wright,

who first visited Japan in 1906, made a similar assessment. Wright treasured the Japanese woodblock print for its simplification, techniques of elimination, organic character, and democratic sensibility. Writing in 1912, Wright remarked that the print's material processes are "confessed" in the art's forms, and this confession becomes "a poetic circumstance of the art."[34] Without the terminology of semiotics, Wright identified the same reflexive structure.

The claim of an absolute structural difference between Japanese culture and the West, on the grounds of reflexive and other intertextual properties, overlooks numerous parallel examples among the Western arts. The European novel, as Mikhail Bakhtin amply demonstrates, has been defined as a cultural form by its intertextuality since its emergence in the writing of Rabelais and Cervantes on through the writing of nineteenth-century masters like Dostoevsky and Flaubert. In such respects, the claim in Burch's book of complete cultural polarity between Japan and the West cannot be finally supported.

Burch esteems Kurosawa's work, in particular that of the 1950s, for its "de-construction" of textual codes, especially those from Western cinema that he had mastered early in his filmmaking career. *To the Distant Observer* maintains that Kurosawa's textual innovations in the use of cinematic codes exhibit "a specifically Japanese approach to space-time."[35] By insisting that Kurosawa's sensibility is uniquely Japanese, Burch limits the intertextuality of his films to intracultural textual operations. As a corrective to such a thesis, film historian J. L. Anderson has cautioned: "In our effort to understand Japanese insularity, we must not ignore their equally strong ties to non-Japanese sources, for much of Japanese art is more cosmopolitan than Westerners imagine."[36] Analysis that follows in the present book will examine the intercultural dynamics that animate the intertextuality of Kurosawa's cinema.

When film is approached in terms of textual system and intertextuality, old concepts of creative genius and the *au-*

teur are replaced by the contemporary critical category of
author-function. Romantic myths of art propose, in their
most popularized form, that the work rises full-born from
artistic genius. The work is thus valued as an autonomous,
singular, and perfected creation expressive of the artist's subjectivity. Auteurism places these values on the aggregate of
works, the *oeuvre*, by a director. At its most insistent, auteurism has argued that the truly artistic director devotes a
career to creating variations on one film work.

As initiated by critics like François Truffaut, Eric Rohmer,
and André Bazin in *Cahiers du Cinéma* during the 1950s,
and elaborated by Andrew Sarris in *Film Culture* in the early
1960s, auteurism identifies the director as author of a film
work through the persistence and consistency of his sensibility, visual intelligence, and compulsive themes.[37] A cult of
personality in some respects, auteurism gives priority to the
coherence and uniformity produced by the director's central-
izing subjectivity. In Sarris's application of these standards to
works of the Hollywood studio era, only those directors gain
the status of auteur who imprint their films with a personal
worldview in the face of the dictates of production chiefs,
writers, and movie genres. Resolution to all the contradictions inherent in the collaborative process and business of
moviemaking is achieved through the auteur's style, which
functions as both a private vision and a professional virtuos-
ity. By French standards of auteurism—with emphasis on
artistic individuality, self-referential expression, and idiosyncratic beauty—Kurosawa's great films of the 1950s were
largely unvalued. In the period 1954–68, of the thirty-five
active directors to receive most attention as auteurs in the
pages of *Cahiers du Cinéma*, only one was Japanese—Kenji
Mizoguchi, who died in 1956.

In his important, comprehensive study on Kurosawa, Donald Richie provides a skillful auteur treatment that identifies
bushido, the way of the samurai, as the primary unifying
principle in his life and work.[38] Accordingly, Richie discusses each film in terms of the shared attributes of an ethos

of action, a humane recognition of man's imperfections, a passion for reality, and an intolerance for illusion. From the perspective of the present study, however, the principles of *bushido* are opposed by other biographical, artistic, and cultural factors to form the textual complexes that lead Kurosawa to treat both film characters and his own personality as incomplete and in process.

With *The Warrior's Camera*, Stephen Prince greatly extends and deepens our understanding of the ethos within Kurosawa's cinema. Prince treats the film work over Kurosawa's career as a cultural project influenced by the social forces of Japan's transformations since World War II. The structural principle that underlies the evolution in visual form and narrative treatment among the films over this career is the development of a cinema that is both politically engaged and popular. In distinguishing the particular qualities of political commitment within Kurosawa's cinema, Prince draws analogies to the cultural practices of German playwright Bertolt Brecht and Soviet filmmaker Sergei Eisenstein and to the principles of Zen Buddhism. In this fashion his book does much to promote intercultural understanding of the Japanese director. With the four films released in the period 1970–85, Prince locates the permutation to a style "strongly marked by a tone of despair and renunciation."[39]

Several other prominent critics approach Kurosawa as an auteur and identify his film work with humanism and individualism. Audie Bock defines Kurosawa's worldview in terms of "humanitarianism" and "socially responsible individualism."[40] She judges the qualities of this humanism in the best films to be existential, transcendent, and inspirational. In Bock's estimation, since *High and Low* (*Tengoku to Jigoku*, 1963) Kurosawa's films have lapsed in moral power and have become by turns formulaic, remote, or dispassionate.[41] She concludes that his humanism has lessened into simplistic preachment.

For Tadao Sato, Kurosawa's imprint as an auteur is his creation of a new ideal of Japanese manhood derived from ideals of samurai strength. While qualities of physical strength may be a component of this ideal, they are not a necessity, given the human spirit's superior strength. Spiritual strength is dramatized by Kurosawa, according to Sato, in two recurrent patterns: the hero's sense of responsibility toward other people and an unwavering persistence in the face of death. Sato finds that the habitual thesis in Kurosawa's films is to endorse the cultural necessity of individualism for Japanese by presenting a protagonist whose pursuit of virtue is solitary.[42] Where Bock and Sato find in Kurosawa's films a persuasive heroism and a superior humanity, the present study finds irresolvable paradox and destructive compassion, intertextual properties many Kurosawa films share with Dostoevsky's problematic humanism.

In a study of three major films, Keiko I. McDonald focuses on the expression of Kurosawa's abiding social and moral concerns. She considers these individual films to be representative of the director's two principal alternatives in approaching such issues: to "explore man's choice of action in [a] fragmented world" or to present "the moral exposition of the central problem of man's inner nature."[43] Through her study of characterization and visuals, McDonald finds that where *Red Beard* (*Akahige*, 1965) prescribes heroic altruism as a course of human action, *Rashomon* ends with the implication that humanity is mutable and unpredictable and *Throne of Blood* (*Kumonosu-jo*, 1957) charts an inexorable process of moral decline. In her treatment, McDonald approaches character as the embodiment of Kurosawa's themes, while here character will be considered as the textual site of dynamic contest and exchange among ideas and values.

Joan Mellen has traced in Kurosawa's cinema a projection of the issue of moral commitment onto an epic plane. Her sense of the modern epic derives from Brecht's dramaturgy, where epic is a dynamic form that demonstrates a potential for individual and social change. The outcome of moral struggle for Kurosawa's epic heroes, Mellen finds, most often brings change at the individual level while failing to change society.[44] In an evaluation of the representation of women in Kurosawa films, Mellen detects for the most part stereotyped personalities and a simplification of social issues.[45] Her conclusion that the female characterizations in films after *Rashomon* fall flatly into two summary categories—angel and demon—disregards the extensive interchange of attributes in personality among principal characters, male and female alike, in films such as *The Idiot* (*Hakuchi*, 1951) and *Red Beard*.

Comparing New Wave.

women of the dines.

Though he has enjoyed great independence in his selection of projects and collaborators and in his control over script and final cut, Kurosawa exercises this artistic freedom to renew a lifelong inquiry into the problematic nature of society and humankind rather than to perfect a personalized style or to develop the same themes. This is not to say that Kurosawa's filmmaking is without an identifiable dramaturgy and visual style. Both his dramaturgy and style, however, are less a means of fixed exposition and final resolution of habitual themes than a means of investigation and speculation into abiding paradoxes such as humanity's capacity for inhumanity. Asked by Donald Richie about the intended meaning of a scene, Kurosawa responded, "Well, if I could answer that, it wouldn't have been necessary for me to have filmed the scene, would it?"[46] The answer indicates that Kurosawa's directorial incentive is to pursue and discover meaning through the production of a film text, not to replicate there what he already knows.

As this introduction has argued, a text does not derive exclusively from an author's individuality; it is replete with usages from elsewhere. It is a texture, a tissue for the articulation and distribution of various social discourses, cultural codes, and image systems. Any new text entails a recuperation of previous texts. A film text is a network of language practices, narrative modes, dramatic codes, acoustic signals, and visual motifs, many already produced and already received in the culture at large. From the perspective of the author-function, the text is a relational construct. The text is an intersection for many disciplines in the culture; it is an interdisciplinary site. The author-function thus involves a multiplicity of contexts within the text, as an intertext, while auteurism limits relational attributes to the closed system of a film creator's own work.

Conventional belief treats the author as an autonomous, unified voice, while concepts of the author-function indicate a plurality of voices and subjective relations within a cultural text even while produced by an individual (whether it be an artwork, a social policy, a scientific finding, a theory, a school of thought). Furthermore, knowledge is a function and a result—not a *prior* source or cause—of textuality. As elaborated by Michel Foucault, Roland Barthes, and Jacques Derrida, concepts of the author-function bear no resemblance to authorship's fixed, consolidated identity, from which the work issues and to which it in turn conforms.[47] In mass society's cult of artistic genius, the past is the unique antecedent of the work: after family, childhood, education, and the struggle to become an artist comes Art. By contrast, the author-function is a locus for circulation and exchange among the cultural materials of a given social environment and historical era.

Following these poststructuralist principles, Kurosawa's life and films are to be treated here as texts in which discourses, image systems, other texts, and cultural inflections are inscribed and interwoven. In their investigation of an application of Derrida's concepts and methods to the study of film, Peter Brunette and David Wills assert that "the auteur is a construction that can only be located provisionally at the 'head' of a series of shifting marks; it is a series of texts that retrospectively creates an auteur, rather than an auteur who creates texts."[48] Creative intention does not fix an itinerary of sense or meaning in a text. Intentionality is an effect constructed by the interpretation of a text and cannot be reconstructed as a principle prior to production of the text. Conceptions of an auteur, which posit individualism and cultural autonomy and which assume a stable and singular origin for the film, cannot adequately serve the purposes of intertextual analysis.

By the criteria of many of the characteristics outlined thus far, Kurosawa's approach to filmmaking can be identified as intertextual. In explanation of his own working practices, Kurosawa describes the completed film as the result of continuous dialogue of the director with writers to prepare a script, with actors to rehearse and present roles, with designers and crew to shoot footage, and with a composer to determine a soundtrack: "Talk, talk: that's all I do. You know how I work: get the writers together and talk the script, get the actors together and talk acting, get the photographers and crew around and talk production. I spend all my life talking."[49] Kurosawa's informal explication of method accords in a number of ways with Bakhtin's description of the dialogic process within each intertext, a process of unresolved interchange among varied discourses, values, and forms.

Kurosawa has enjoyed long productive relationships with collaborators such as the art directors So Matsuyama (over the years 1948–54) and Yoshiro Muraki (from 1955 to the present), sound specialist Fumio Yanoguchi (from 1949 until his death in 1984), principal production assistant Teruyo Nogami (1950 to the present), and composer Fumio Hayasaka (1948–55), followed after Hayasaka's death by his pupil Masaru Sato (1955–65). In the years 1948–65, Kurosawa frequently cast both leading and character roles from the same company of actors, at times reverse-typecasting from one film to the next. On occasion, the director could not proceed successfully with a script unless he had a specific actor in mind for each main character. This repertory situation for both cast and crew resembles the production unit that Jean Renoir led in making a succession of masterworks in the 1930s.

In 1945, after writing his first four films alone, Kurosawa began a practice of collaborating with other scriptwriters that continued until *Dreams*, whose personal nature led him to write alone again. In a period of forty years a core of five writers—Eijiro Hisaita, Ryuzo Kikushima, Shinobu Hashimoto, Hideo Oguni, and Masato Ide—has worked, in various combinations, on nineteen of the twenty-three films released up through *Ran* (*Ran*, 1985). Kurosawa characterizes the collaborative writing process as a competition between ideas and versions, as each writer's individual re-vision of the other's scenes and characters. The effectiveness of this dialogic approach has depended upon a degree of contradiction and antagonism to give life to the material, and it has often progressed through shifts in storyline and characters from their anticipated direction.

Creative dialogue over a script has not always taken the form of conventional collaboration. Kurosawa often consulted the composer Fumio Hayasaka in originating story ideas and in solving script problems. The functions of Hideo Oguni were sometimes literally those of an interlocutor. On *Ikiru* he was middle man between Kurosawa and Hashimoto, brokering some of their suggestions, revising and discarding others. The director found Oguni rarely in agreement with him but he nonetheless valued the discord between them as creative. Kurosawa credits Oguni with the best ideas for the film, even though this collaborator was not actually writing.

The development of a script for *Stray Dog* exemplifies another kind of intertextuality. Kurosawa first drafted its story and characters in the form of a novel in which he deliberately adopted the style of Georges Simenon, the French master of the police detection genre. In trying to transpose his novelistic treatment into a screenplay, Kurosawa encountered great difficulties, particularly in trying to convey psychological portraits of characters without recourse to the kinds of narration common in a novel. These difficulties in working at the textual boundaries between the two media ultimately enhanced his filmmaking: "Thanks to the unexpected travail of adapting the descriptions of the novel form to a screenplay, I attained a new awareness of what screenplays and films consist of. At the same time, I was able to incorporate many peculiarly novelistic modes of expression into the script" (*Autobiography*, 173).

Generally, Kurosawa has considered his own perspective limited and inadequate to an understanding of the human matters that motivate his artistic interests. Intertextual film-making has provided the voices of differing experience and truth. Describing his participation in an ongoing dialogue with his material and with members of the production ensemble, Kurosawa has explained that construction of a film story does not begin with a concept of the whole but rather with an initial scene in which character, situation, and dramatic potential are visualized. Storyline and character conflict are shaped through continuous discussion among the writers, starting with the momentum inherent in the initial scene but trying to avoid premature closure to the story.

A Life and Its Intertexts

In 1981 Akira Kurosawa completed a volume of autobiography that he titled ironically *Something Like an Autobiography* because to his mind the record of his personal life apart from filmmaking is of negligible importance: "take 'myself,' subtract 'movies' and the result is 'zero'" (*Autobiography,* xi). The data of Akira Kurosawa's family history, education, and career is readily summarized in a chronological account, but the meaning of these biographical facts is often instead figurative and paradoxical in structure. In interviews over the years Kurosawa has insisted that his films are autobiographical only in terms of emotions, ideas, and their understanding of humanity, not in terms of incidents. His 1990 release *Dreams,* the first self-referential film in a forty-eight-year career that has produced twenty-nine features, is no exception in its exclusion of actual outward events and its concentration on the director's imaginative truths.

Something Like an Autobiography describes his experience as writer, director, and editor with each film as the adoption of surrogate identities and the completion of a lifespan for the duration of the production process from inception to release. In closing the autobiography with events of 1951, after *Rashomon* won international recognition, Kurosawa advises:

> I think that to learn what became of me after *Rashomon* the most reasonable procedure would be to look for me in the characters in the films I made after *Rashomon*. Although human beings are incapable of talking about themselves with total honesty, it is much harder to avoid the truth while pretending to be other people. (*Autobiography,* 188–89)

The truth to be found by such a method is that Kurosawa as a filmmaker remains in a tireless, reversible search for truth. When the search is compelling, as it often is in his cinema, truth is not be be found within a single character but rather among characters engaged in dynamic, mutable conflict.

An aspiring painter before his film apprenticeship, Kurosawa was so receptive to artists he admired like Cézanne and Van Gogh that he was unable to develop his own style. His impressionable, imitative traits led him to abandon any hope of success as a painter, but he credits these same traits for his progress as a filmmaker, freeing him to imagine greater reaches of human experience. On the evidence of Kurosawa's self-assessment at age seventy-one, he cannot be accounted an auteur in the original sense of the term: "I did not—and still don't—have a completely personal, distinctive, way of looking at things" (*Autobiography*, 88).

Kurosawa summarizes his affinities as a narrative, dramatic, and visual artist as follows: "I like unformed characters. This may be because, no matter how old I get, I am still unformed myself" (*Autobiography*, 129–30). Following the book's own directives, *Something Like an Autobiography* is to be understood as a minor text among the major texts of his films. To be sure, the book acknowledges influences of experience on the films, but the filiation of life to filmmaking is often not chronological or causal. At the point where Kurosawa writes the autobiography, the film texts have inscribed the life before filmmaking, marking in it what warrants recounting and giving the life a form in personal narrative.

In the autobiography, early scenes from childhood are evoked through processes of visualization affiliated with cinema, such as composition through a camera viewfinder and an alternation of focal perspective from wide angle to telephoto. Motion pictures seem to be the only adequate means to convey, for example, the effect of being carried everywhere on a nursemaid's back, creating for the infant's eyes continuous variations in the field of view, as in a sequence shot. Describing his training in martial arts during childhood, Kurosawa depicts images of his kendo outfit and high wooden clogs and through them recognizes an unconscious source for visual motifs in his first film, *Sanshiro Sugata* (*Sugata Sanshiro*, 1943). Similarly, in later chancing on a bar where he once encountered a fascinating yet repulsive stranger, Kurosawa for the first time recalls an unsuspected model for the corrupt, maudlin lawyer in *Scandal* (*Shubun*, 1950).

Having suggested that "perhaps it is the power of memory that gives rise to the power of imagination," Kurosawa is led by such examples to treat imagination equally as a stimulant to memory (*Autobiography*, 30). As a result, the autobiography is more an inquiry into the director's repertory of ideas and images than a full personal history. In basing earlier memory in the film works themselves, the autobiography presents subjectivity as a function of textuality.

Jacques Derrida has identified biography as a dynamic, shifting border region between life and work from which texts are produced. Derrida thus cautions the analyst or critic against the use of an author's name to stand for a fixed style or firm ideas. The name of the author should be used rather to indicate an ongoing problem or complex for interpretation.[1] Adopting a similar approach, Barthes terms the family history, incidents, personalities, influences, and encounters of a writer's life *biographemes*. These are the textual articulations where writer and life intersect and inscribe one another.[2]

The best introduction to Kurosawa's life and films is through an examination of the principal biographemes that mark *Something Like an Autobiography:* the paradoxes of family life, the shadow-self experienced through his older brother Heigo, the cataclysm of the Kanto earthquake in 1923, the formative role of storytelling, the shape of his professional life, and the perception of Kurosawa as a "Western" artist.

Family Life

On March 23, 1910, Akira Kurosawa became the last of seven children born to Yutaka Kurosawa, who traced his descent in an unbroken lineage to a legendary eleventh-century warrior, and his wife, who came from an Osaka merchant family. Yutaka Kurosawa graduated from the Imperial Army academy, as an officer was the teacher of future army generals, and, by the time of Akira's birth, worked as a physical education instructor in Tokyo. He maintained in the household a strict samurai ethos even though his social standing did not remotely approach the former prominence of this class, the instrument of political rule for nearly a millennium. With the abolition of the shogunate and the resumption of imperial power in the Meiji Restoration of 1868, a modern national army replaced the samurai class, which was entirely divested of its legal status and privileges in the 1870s.

Yutaka Kurosawa did not share in the ultranationalism or military fanaticism of the day and did not serve as a career officer. The material decline of the family was measured by moves to successively smaller and less fashionable quarters within Tokyo. In taking a position in a gymnastics academy, he developed facilities for Japanese martial arts like judo and swordfighting, but he was also a pioneer in the introduction of Western sports like swimming and baseball. Akira's first two years of primary education were spent at a school where European customs and style of dress were the norm, then he was transferred to a school structured according to purely Japanese traditions.

Kurosawa remembers his mother as a gentle soul, "impossibly heroic" in her sacrifices for the welfare of her husband and sons (*Autobiography*, 21). During her marriage she remained unschooled in the exacting samurai customs observed by her husband. In serving fish on a tray at the table, for example, she by chance positioned it in the manner prescribed for the meal that precedes a samurai's ritual suicide. Each infraction, though unintended, was met with his angry outbursts. In spite of the samurai mystique of masculinity, for Akira his mother was a model of stoic perseverance in the face of adversity, including the loss of a son and a daughter in their childhoods. Looking back, he esteems her as a realist and his father as a sentimentalist, thus inverting conventionalized gender traits that are deeply encoded in Japan. Such inversions are found as well in his film characterizations of marriage pairs and of individual male and female psychology, making his treatment of gender issues more extensive and complex than critics have commonly perceived.

Despite the martial spirit of the household, Akira was an indulged, sensitive boy whose childhood nicknames were "Crybaby" and "Gumdrop." When he was age eight, his nearest older brother Heigo (then age twelve) failed the school entrance exams that would have ultimately assured admission to Tokyo Imperial University. After this turn of events, the father treated the youngest son more strictly and, with the family's expectations for success now placed on him, Akira began training in martial arts and fine arts. As an adolescent he was sent to his father's family in Akita prefecture in order to lead a "mountain samurai" existence for the summer. There he became fully conscious of his samurai heritage when a relative showed him their genealogy, stored in a compartment just under the "god shelf" of the household Shinto shrine. Irrespective of his heritage, Akira failed compulsory military instruction in middle school.

Yutaka Kurosawa was an enthusiast about foreign movies in spite of the prejudices of professional Japanese educators against them as disreputable entertainments. Liberal in regard to culture, he often took the entire family to the American and European motion pictures exhibited in Tokyo. In the face of growing reactionary attitudes toward foreign influences, he asserted the educational value of such recreations. A great admirer of calligraphy, Yutaka sent his sons to a master for training, but he also supplied the necessary oil paints once Akira developed an interest in Western landscape painting. Whatever his initial expectations for Akira had been, he encouraged his son's passion for art. Nor was he disappointed, given the political climate, when Akira was exempted from military service after his conscription physical.

In *Something Like an Autobiography* Kurosawa confronts

an inescapable contradiction between the family's reputation and his own experience of family life: "People have often
praised us as sensitive and generous, but we appear to me
to have a measure of sentimentality and absurdity in our
blood" (*Autobiography*, 5). What emerges most forcefully
from his account is a structure of paradox initiated in early
life through the family but that he has come to attribute to
the Japanese personality collectively, as in the population's
reaction at the end of World War II. Prepared by propaganda
for the "Honorable Death of the Hundred Million" should
Japan be defeated, the populace awaited the Emperor's announcement on August 15, 1945 in near hysteria. As Kurosawa observed on the streets of Tokyo, the tension and panic
in anticipation of the call to mass suicide quickly changed to
joy and festivity once citizens were freed from their patriotic
obligation. Though at the time he puzzled over whether this
social phenomenon was representative of "Japanese adapta-
bility or Japanese imbecility," Kurosawa finally claims the
paradox itself to be typical of both the national character and
his own personality (*Autobiography*, 145). The paradox is reiterated through the director's author-function in his frequent
reverse-typecasting of the lead actors Takashi Shimura and
Toshiro Mifune. From one film to another, Kurosawa might
shift a leading player from an active role to a passive one, or
from a heroic exemplar to a case study in instability.

   The first impression that Kurosawa gives of his brother
Heigo in *Something Like an Autobiography* is rooted in pain
and a violent fate. Having explained that his clarity of memory is in direct proportion to the degree of shock experienced, Kurosawa recalls as a small child seeing his brother
near death from open wounds suffered in a gymnastics accident caused when a sudden wind blew him off a balance
beam. His brother's condition, the circumstances of the accident, and his own trauma stand at the outset of the autobiography as configurations of their intense, intimate frater-
nity. With a mixture of fascination, fear, and compassion,
Kurosawa secretly shared in his brother's later suffering,

alienation, and moral outrage. Heigo's affinities for European literature of social protest—particularly Russian fiction and nihilist thought—established an unauthorized curriculum for Akira's education. The autobiography treats their relationship as the prefiguration of an intense curiosity over destructive personalities and psychological doubles, restimulated by the fiction of Feodor Dostoevsky, Nikolai Gogol, Edgar Allan Poe, and Ryunosuke Akutagawa.

For the period they were in primary school together, Heigo was a harsh but protective mentor, assailing Akira with insults yet defending him on the schoolyard from the taunts of other children. Once, on a swimming excursion in the Arakawa River, Heigo led him into deeper water and watched with fascination as Akira flailed and panicked before pulling him to the surface. On their way home Heigo bought sweets and consoled him with the observation that drowning people indeed seem to face death with a smile on their faces. Though furious over his brother's betrayal and flippancy, Akira had to agree that a strangely peaceful sensation overcame him as he sank. The family crybaby discovered a cynical alter ego in Heigo.

Heigo's failure on the advanced entrance examination was entirely unexpected, since he had previously ranked first among all Tokyo primary students. Its impact led to growing conflict and finally estrangement between Heigo and his father. Four years later, as valedictorian of the primary school, Akira was provided with a graduation day speech by his teacher. Appalled by this hypocrisy, Heigo prepared a substitute statement that denounced the school's conservatism and repressive methods. Though a spirit of rebellion had enticed Akira into rehearsing the ghost-written protest and carrying a copy inside his formal kimono, once at the podium he dutifully read the school's scripted remarks. Unsuspecting of both the teacher's deception and the temptation laid by Heigo, the father praised Akira for his mature, respectful remarks, leaving the twelve-year-old feeling ashamed and cowardly.

At midday on September 1, 1923, a devastating earthquake hit the Kanto region, taking an estimated 70,000 lives in Tokyo alone. Separated from the rest of his family long enough to think them all dead, Akira was shocked to find them unharmed and seemingly unperturbed. The morning of the earthquake, a wind rose with such suddenness and violence as to register indelibly in Kurosawa's consciousness. In the narrative structure given to experience in *Something Like an Autobiography,* wind figures as a premonitory force. It is established at the outset within the circumstances of his brother's childhood accident. Narration of the death at age sixteen of his beloved sister Momoyo is preceded by recollection of a childhood incident when they were momentarily lifted by strong gusts. The reversals of Heigo's fortunes in adolescence and early manhood are likened to a whirlwind sweeping the family apart. Consistently in the film narratives, wind is an acoustic and a visual signal of impending conflict or denouement. The effect is inaugurated in his directorial career with great rhetorical flourish for the climactic battle in *Sanshiro Sugata,* set on reed-covered slopes buffeted by storm gales. According to the autobiography, the film's production was stalled on location until a *kamikaze* — a "divine wind" — brought the desired effect.

A Brother's Legacy

With a total loss of electricity after the earthquake, Tokyo was plunged that night into darkness broken only by fires that began to rage in some quarters. In the social chaos that followed, long-held superstition and racism toward Korean immigrants escalated into a massacre. Once the fires burned out, Heigo led his brother on a tour of the city's ruined neighborhoods. These areas were now populated by unburied corpses and Heigo regarded the various postures of death with a clinical and at times perversely appreciative attitude that Akira, in spite of his horror, shared.

In Kurosawa's estimation, Heigo was "addicted" to foreign literature and movies (*Autobiography,* 72). Together on fam-

ily outings they had viewed the imported action serials, slap-
stick comedies, and adventure features of the day. Their father
also took them frequently to the storyteller halls where masters of impersonation and pantomime like Kosan performed.
Such influences led Heigo, after drifting from the family, to
write commentary for film programs and to become a silent
film narrator or *benshi*. Heigo was already a devotee of foreign films as a teenager, recommending the latest releases to
his younger brother, who conscientiously saw as many as he
could. For a ten-year period starting at age nine, the autobiography lists about one hundred foreign films Kurosawa saw for
the first time. These showings, which would have been accompanied by benshi, included the work of directors like
Griffith, DeMille, Stroheim, Chaplin, Ford, Renoir, Buñuel,
Murnau, Lang, Lubitsch, von Sternberg, Eisenstein, and Pudovkin. As a professional benshi specializing in foreign cinema himself, Heigo developed a reputation for commentary
that offered refined psychological exposition.

After introduction of the new technology in 1897, the benshi soon became a regular component of film exhibition,
explicating for first audiences not only the visual images but
the mechanics of film projection itself.[3] The benshi was a
prominent figure during the film exhibition, seated on a
raised platform near the screen. In the period of their greatest popularity (the 1920s), the benshi was often the featured
performer in urban movie houses, more important to audiences than the films booked. With broad license for improvisation and vocal interpretation beyond the intertitles
screened, benshi impersonated dialogue roles, made sound
effects, and provided continuous commentary. The functions
of the benshi contributed to early experimentation within
the Japanese film industry with the long take and a sparing
use of dialogue and story titles. Kurosawa likens the benshi's
role to that of speakers in the Bunraku puppet theater, who
alone deliver the play's language, from scripts placed on lec-
terns and visible to the audience. The Bunraku text is half-
spoken and half-sung by the speakers and is accompanied by

musicians placed next to them.[4] The dialogue is displaced from the puppet characters through this method of delivery and it is further denatured through vocal stylizations. Bunraku theater offers its audience spectacle and abstraction rather than representation or simulation.

The institution of the benshi, which persisted in Japanese movie houses up to 1937 in spite of the development of sound films, is for the theorist Noel Burch a distinguishing structural feature of this national cinema, indicative of its presentational modes and its acknowledged instrumentality. Through the benshi's practices speech is applied to the images as an adjunct and supplement and the film story is received by spectators not as transparently representative in meaning but as subject to interpolation and interpretation.[5] While reflexivity in Kurosawa's cinema is most often anchored in its representative codes, the functions of the benshi and traditional storyteller are traceable in the ambiguous presence of an external narrative voice in *Stray Dog* and *Ikiru* and to the multiple narrative interventions in *Rashomon*, *Ikiru*, and *Red Beard*.

Like others in Japan's young and unemployed urban intelligentsia at the time, Kurosawa was receptive to the communist promise and joined the Proletarian Artists' League in 1928. Initially sympathetic with the League's social vision and artistic goals, Kurosawa soon discovered that he had no avocation for Marxist theory or ideological debate. Though he had been inclined toward the populist rhetoric of its art, he gradually lost the passion for painting altogether. In his four years of membership his activism progressed from poster art to assisting the political underground movement. A prolonged illness led to his voluntary separation from the League in 1932. Looking back on this period forty years later, Kurosawa admits to a persistence of "Marxist ideas somewhere in me" and to an equal disinclination for doctrinal thought.[6]

Without plans for the future, Kurosawa moved to a tenement in Kagurazaka where his brother Heigo lived. This urban district had retained its working-class identity since the

Edo era. The *Autobiography* associates the district with *uki-yo*, the "floating world" of common everyday life that was a favorite genre subject for woodblock prints, song lyrics, and popular stories from the seventeenth through the nineteenth centuries. The neighborhood was home to men who held menial jobs in the city's storyteller halls and movie houses. For a minor sum Kurosawa would use their courtesy passes to see all the popular entertainments of Tokyo—the *yose* or variety halls, the *kodan* or historical tales, the *rakugo* or parody skits and comic monologues, and the first foreign talkies to be exhibited in Japan.

The recreation of this social milieu in *Something Like an Autobiography* is inflected by Kurosawa's later creation on film of Japanese "lower depths" in *Drunken Angel*, his adaptation of the Gorky play *The Lower Depths* (*Donzoko*, 1957), and *Dodeskaden*. Neighborhood life centered around a common well in the alleyway. Among its inhabitants, Heigo was regarded with the same awe accorded *ronin* ("wave men," a masterless samurai) in the war romances of the feudal period and reinvented by Kurosawa in *Seven Samurai* (*Shichinin no Samurai*, 1954), *Yojimbo* and *Sanjuro* (*Tsubaki Sanjuro*, 1962). During his stay there, Kurosawa slowly awakened to a paradox that would persist in his imagination: "the bright, cheerful humor of tenement life I enjoyed so much harbored in its shadows a dark reality" (*Autobiography*, 82). The social masks of its inhabitants often concealed the brutal secrets of their private lives, as in the case of a respectable-looking woman who bound and beat her stepchild. After seeing for himself the helpless victim of this abuse, Kurosawa tried to free the bound girl once the mother had left her rooms, but the victim fiercely ordered him to stop in the certainty that she would receive a harsher beating if the mother returned to find her untied. This encounter confronted Kurosawa with the dilemma that sympathy can compound suffering, another basis for his profound interest in Dostoevsky.

With the conversion to sound among Japanese studios, theaters prepared to terminate all the benshi, who had formed one of the strongest unions in the movie business. Before the theaters initiated their plans, Heigo headed the benshi in a prolonged walkout. Now unemployed and facing the inevitable failure of this labor action, Heigo sank into despair and made a failed suicide attempt. In the aftermath, Akira attempted to reconcile his brother and father. He persuaded the family to accept marriage between Heigo and the woman he had been living with for years in his tenement rooms, but Heigo was uninterested in formalizing their relationship. Kurosawa failed to recognize the gravity of his inconsolable and hopeless condition and within a few months Heigo succeeded in his second suicide attempt.

The autobiography vividly recounts Kurosawa's state of lucid shock once he reached the scene, where he was unable to detach his gaze from the body, covered in a sheet bloody from Heigo's blade wounds. Brought back to his senses, he aided his father in the preparation and transport of the body for cremation. The events are described without any reference to Kurosawa's own suicide attempt, made by the same means, on December 22, 1971. At the time, the director was suffering from an undiagnosed gallstone condition (later relieved through surgery) and he faced the prospect of lifelong financial difficulties if he continued filmmaking. In interviews a year after, Kurosawa judged the attempt a foolish and thoughtless act committed in an untypically dark frame of mind.

Silence on this subject in *Something Like an Autobiography* reflects perhaps a sense of suicide already experienced with the death of Heigo, "who had had the same blood as I flowing in his veins [and] who had made that blood flow out" (*Autobiography*, 86). Kurosawa does remark that he has no knowledge on *seppuku*, or the samurai's ritual disembowelment by short sword, because he has never scripted such a scene. The acts of suicide depicted or reported in his film stories are not restrained or ceremonial but are instead sudden and impassioned.

In memorializing Heigo, Kurosawa speculates that his brother could have had a brilliant career as a filmmaker. With his talents, experience, and many associates in the film industry, Heigo had the opportunity to enter the profession had he wanted to. But Kurosawa brings such speculation short with an admission that, given Heigo's pessimism and inflexible nature, his course of action was irreversible. To conclude his recollections of Heigo, the director measures his own sanguine, unformed personality and his professional identity as qualities opposed to yet interdependent with Heigo's personality: "I prefer to think of my brother as a negative strip of film that led to my own development as a positive image" (*Autobiography*, 87).

Once separated from the Proletarian Artists' League and its tenets of socialist realism, Kurosawa embarked on a search for an entirely personal style as a painter. He consciously aspired to achieve the "intensity of realism" he admired in Courbet and the independence of vision in Cézanne and Van Gogh (*Autobiography*, 77). To pay for painting supplies he free-lanced as a commercial artist, turning out magazine illustrations and cartoons. With the death of their oldest brother shortly before Heigo's suicide, Akira was now his father's only surviving son. Though acutely conscious of social obligations to the family, Kurosawa drifted without career goals for over two years. His father remained patient and confident about Akira's future and counseled him with advice, common in Zen thought, to wait calmly until his true path in life opened.

A Career in Film

In 1935, Kurosawa chanced upon a classified advertisement for assistant-director trainees at P.C.L. (Photo Chemical Laboratory), a young company formed to produce sound films that would soon evolve into the major studio Toho. P.C.L. had rapidly expanded by hiring proven film directors like Mikio Naruse and Kajiro Yamamoto. It established a share of the film market primarily in the genres of comedy, musical, and *shomin-geki* or lower-middle-class drama. Disregarding the rising nationalism and militarism of the time, the company adopted entertainment formulas from Hollywood and favored carefree, lyrical stories.

Unaware that out of more than 500 applicants only five would be hired, Kurosawa completed the first phase in the application process—an essay evaluating the quality of Japanese cinema—in a half-mocking tone written from his perspective as an enthusiast of foreign films. To his amazement he advanced to the second phase, which entailed creation of a script from a story idea P.C.L. provided, in this case a working-class romantic situation. Without any idea of a script's conventions but following his instincts as a painter, Kurosawa depicted the love affair in a colorful and contrastive manner. In spite of an outburst at an officious studio executive during final interviews, Kurosawa was hired and began work in 1936. The first months were unrewarding and he considered resigning until he was assigned to Yamamoto's production unit.

The first mentor figure honored in *Something Like an Autobiography* for his influence in Kurosawa's education as an artist is his primary school arts and crafts teacher Seiji Tachikawa, who pioneered policies of free expression for children. The second is director Kajiro Yamamoto, who is cherished as open-minded, generous with his knowledge, nurturing of talent, and as a subtle and patient teacher. Highlighting personality traits that are just the opposite, Kurosawa characterizes himself in those years as obstinate, undiplomatic, short-tempered, and demonstrative. While Yamamoto may not have served as a model in the formation of Kurosawa's professional manner, he did in the establishment of artistic standards. Yamamoto's dedication to the integrity and totality of the film's imagined world inspired his assistants to make extraordinary efforts.

Even in the comic and musical genres, the Yamamoto unit did not consider itself engaged in churning out an entertainment product. The director instilled the importance of knowledge and craft for each script under production. Such commitment to a film's authenticity—not necessarily in relation to historical or everyday reality but within its own terms as an artistic construct — has reached legendary proportions in Kurosawa's own work. In the cases of both the carefully documented historical setting for *Red Beard* and the fantastic, entirely artificial setting for *Dodeskaden*, his production team designed and constructed full-scale locales with attention to minute details like the stains in old teacups, made for *Red Beard* by repeated pouring and draining of tea into replicas of period ceramics. Yet many of these details would remain, by intention, unphotographed.

The assignment as an assistant director in the Yamamoto unit was extensively collaborative. Over the next six years Kurosawa served virtual apprenticeships in crafts like stage construction, technical areas like film development, business concerns like location accounting, and the creative responsibilities of script, rehearsal, camera, lighting, direction, and editing. In these years, Kurosawa worked as an assistant on a few occasions for the other P.C.L.-Toho directors Eisuke Takizawa, Shu Fushimizu, and Mikio Naruse. Kurosawa has expressed great esteem for Naruse's ability to create seamless, invisible continuity in sequences constructed of many brief shots.

Perhaps the most fundamental lesson Yamamoto imparted is that filmmaking begins with scriptwriting. To encourage writing as a habitual activity, Yamamoto would set a friendly competition between himself and assistants to write treatments based on a simple word association. Through his own example and in commenting on their efforts, he gave instruction in finding visual solutions to problems in exposition and narration. These habits were ingrained early in Kurosawa, who has described the script as taproot to the finished film.

His apprenticeship also introduced Kurosawa to the range of dramatic effects possible through the combination of soundtrack elements with images. He traces to the dubbing experiments of Yamamoto the inception of his own ideas on sound and image as "mutual multipliers," which have much in common with Soviet director Sergei Eisenstein's theory of audiovisual montage (*Autobiography*, 108). As assistant directors progressed in their training, Yamamoto delegated greater responsibilities to them. Kurosawa's final tribute to Yamamoto as his mentor is that the master did not produce an imitative disciple.

On his last assignment with the Yamamoto unit, *Horse* (*Uma*, 1941), Kurosawa co-wrote the script, directed the principal location scenes, and made the final cut. Set in farmlands in the north of Honshu, this contemporary story follows the family life of a teenage girl, whose love for a foal cannot prevent its sale at military auction once it has matured. Combining fiction and actuality, the film uses a documentary visual style in portraying the emotions of this loss in the setting of a real horse auction. An anxious tempo is produced by extensive intercutting that constantly shifts attention among a crowd of onlookers, the horses, the girl, and the bidding officers. After the auction the style shifts to a pastoral, lyrical mode as, on the family's walk home, a stream of horses slowly passes before them, an event rhapsodically prolonged through the editing.

Kurosawa completed at least ten scenarios before becoming a director, and he went on to write—most often in collaboration—all of the films he has made. Some of these early scenarios were blocked from production by wartime censors who found them too lightspirited to suit the national cause, others by executives who found them too large in scale and budget.[7] His chance for promotion to director hinged on being assigned to film one of his own scripts. The first opportunity came with *A German at the Daruma Temple* (*Daruma-dera no Doitsujin*), which had been published in a film magazine in 1941. Before production began, however, Japan began its Pacific war operations and the studio's priorities changed. Based in part on the life of Bruno Taut (1880–1938), a German architect and a founder of the Bauhaus movement who stayed in Japan in the years 1933–36 and who died in Turkey after being exiled by the Nazis, the script remolds him into the fic-

tional Ludrich Lange. Like Taut in being a connoisseur of
Japan's traditional arts, the character departs from its model
in exemplifying the political and militarist alliance between
Fascist Germany and Imperial Japan. The fictional architect
condemns as unsafe the American building methods used in
many of Japan's public schools.

Having discovered scriptwriter to be a more lucrative occupation than assistant director, Kurosawa became adept at tail-
oring stories to the required patriotic formulas. Typical of
such work is his action-adventure script for *A Triumph of
Wings* (*Tsubasa no Gaika*), directed by Satsuo Yamamoto in
1942, which chronicles the rise of the poor yet honorable son
of a widowed mother to become the test pilot for an experimental aircraft designed to defend the homeland. These scenarios conform to the war effort's promotion of a Zen spirit
in the voluntary restraint of fear, of critical attitudes, and of
individualism. Assessing such projects in the autobiography,
Kurosawa frankly confesses that he lacked the courage to re-
sist his country's militarism and expansionism and that he
ingratiated himself with authorities to avoid censure.

The start of Kurosawa's career as a director came with Toho's agreement to acquire rights to the new novel *Sanshiro Sugata*; writing the adaptation alone and in one sitting, he
began filming in 1942. A suitably patriotic theme, the film
story concerns the replacement of jujitsu by judo in the 1880s
as Japan's foremost martial art. On Sanshiro's first search for
a master he naively joins a band of jujitsu fighters that plots
a nighttime ambush on the judo expert Yano. More like thugs
than disciples, the band is devoid of the spiritual integrity
that would qualify their fighting technique as a martial art.
The ambush becomes a debacle for the jujitsu group. As Sanshiro watches Yano defend himself a new technique is revealed—deployment of the attackers' own force as a weapon
against them. After entering his novitiate in judo, Sanshiro
begins to learn that the physical paradox whereby defense and
offense are reversed has spiritual counterparts. Part of the
path to judo is understanding the consequences of defeat to

one's opponents, as with the eventual death of the honorable jujitsu expert Murai, who loses to Sanshiro in an exhibition match.

Kurosawa undertook his first project as director determined to produce a film distinct from the Japanese tradition of simplicity. Working from conventions of the action film wherein tension builds to an outburst of violence, he fashioned visual figures of eruption and excess to portray Sanshiro's spiritual development as well. One such moment comes at the end of a night the judo apprentice spends in a pond, into which he has leaped on a self-dramatizing impulse. Expressive of a newly gained perception of his master's teaching, a pond lily bursts into bloom with the morning's first light. Its innovative exuberance, original imagery, and intuitive approach places *Sanshiro* in the company of inspired debut films by such masters as Orson Welles, Sergei Eisenstein, and Luis Buñuel.

For the next film, *The Most Beautiful (Ichiban Utsukushiku,* 1944), Kurosawa experimented again with a documentary approach, this time in telling a contemporary story about young women working in an optics factory as part of the war effort. Separated from home and family for the first time, the women adjust to their new communal life and work responsibilities. The artifice and glamour of contract actresses had offended Kurosawa even at the time of his interviews for a position with P.C.L. studio. For the purpose of conveying the practicality and efficiency of factory work, he went to lengths to break habits of affectation and theatrical self-consciousness in the film acting. He organized the actresses into a sports and drill team, housed them in a factory dormitory, gave them training on the shop floor, scheduled their activities according to a work routine, and filmed many scenes on location with the production line in operation. Though the storyline serves patriotic themes, the visual treatment conveys the extent to which individuals, even in a period of national emergency, are passionately complex in their behavior.

In 1945, Akira Kurosawa married Kiyo Kato. Known pub-
licly by her stage name Yoko Yaguchi, she played the leading
role of work team leader in *The Most Beautiful*. She had also
been a representative for the actresses during production and
Kurosawa found her as argumentative as himself. In entering
marriage, she gave up her acting career. A son, Hisao, was
soon born to the couple and a daughter, Kazuko, was born in
1954. After a long illness, Kurosawa's wife died in January,
1985. Hisao has acted for television, worked in the business
operations of a sports team and, most recently, formed a company to produce his father's films, starting with *Dreams*.

After the success of his debut film, Toho studio assigned
Kurosawa to make a sequel to *Sanshiro Sugata* and Part Two
was released in 1945 (*Zoku Sugata Sanshiro*). It resumes the
account of judo at a point where Sanshiro is now an expert.
The sequel is more explicit in its chauvinism, with Amer-
icans represented by a hostile sailor, a brutal boxer, and
drunken, bloodthirsty spectators. Judo is demonstrated to be
superior to foreign spectacles like boxing and to other martial techniques like karate. Though Kurosawa's involvement
is sometimes visibly half-hearted, the film continues to investigate the paradox of loss that comes with victory. Witness to the humiliation of a jujitsu fighter in an exhibition
match with a boxer, Sanshiro is confronted with the consequences to other Japanese of judo's superiority. Ready to quit
judo, he receives a precept from the master Yano that is consistent with contemporary war aims: "Fighting is a way to
win unification."

Gennosuke, Sanshiro's adversary from the original film,
has accepted defeat to the superior martial art. But his two
brothers seek vengeance against Sanshiro. The brother Genzaburo—with long, stringy hair and a leafy branch in his
hand—is presented as the figure of "madness" from a Noh
play. The two brothers are practitioners of karate, which the
film depicts as a cultural aberration. Gennosuke has wished
for Sanshiro's victory over his own brothers and he has provided a treatise to the judo fighter on the secrets of karate. In

defeating the one brother who fights him, Sanshiro breaks the spirits of both of them. But defeat is ultimately curative. In a mountain hut, Sanshiro tends to the two, though the mad one is still determined on vengeance. Genzaburo takes the cleaver he has concealed and approaches the sleeping Sanshiro. At that moment, Sanshiro smiles in response to a dream. The smile completely disarms Genzaburo. By morning, he is purged of his madness. The two brothers become grateful for the loss to Sanshiro.

The character Genzaburo marks the first adaptation by Kurosawa of Noh conventions for the screen. Noh is a classical stage art whose refinement was complete by the fifteenth century and it has maintained its integrity into the present. Noh performance combines the dramatic text with narrative, dance, music, pantomime, and masks. Kurosawa's study of the traditional Japanese craft and art forms as a resource for his filmmaking began during the war years. To strengthen the spirit of nationalism, the militarist government promoted public display and appreciation of these forms, though Kurosawa believes that his attraction to them was in part "motivated by a desire to escape from the reality around me" (Autobiography, 147). He attended Noh theater for the first time in this period and the experience inaugurated a lifelong passion for its unique means of expression. Kurosawa attributes to Noh the capacity to represent the core of an experience: "In Noh, the emotion of sadness is not the expression of sadness but sadness itself, its philosophical essence."[8]

Kurosawa's next film, The Men Who Tread on the Tiger's Tail (Tora no O o Fumu Otokotachi, 1945), adapts an episode from feudal history represented in the Noh play Ataka and most familiar to Japanese through the Kabuki classic Kanjincho. The historical incident entails the escape of the famous lord Yoshitsune with his generals across a heavily guarded border. The generals are disguised as priests on a pilgrimage to collect donations for their temple, while the lord himself impersonates their porter. On the verge of being detected by border soldiers, the loyal general Benkei berates and beats the porter. In Kurosawa's interpretation, the border officer Togashi still suspects deception, but this extraordinary violation of the samurai code to protect Yoshitsune gains Togashi's compassion and he allows the party to pass.

In writing the scenario Kurosawa created a role for a genuine commoner as a second porter, a character not contained in the austere Noh version or the popularized Kabuki spectacle. The idea for such a role is drawn from *kyogen*, or "wild words," the interludes or skits that often accompany a Noh program and in which comical, lowborn characters engage in earthy and ludicrous activities. Cast as the commoner in *The Men Who Tread on the Tiger's Tail* is the famous screen comedian Enoken (Kenichi Enomoto), with whom Kurosawa had worked on Yamamoto productions. His improvisatory, farcical manner is utilized for contrast to the aristocratic formality of the original theater characters. The film's lord is nondescript in comparison to the personable commoner. Kurosawa undertook the production with the feeling that Japan had already lost the war. The parodic nature of the commoner's reactions to the noble's world is one sign of skepticism. In the film adaptation, when the loyal retainer Benkei strikes the disguised lord it is a symptom of breakdown in samurai ideals. While the film's production was in progress, Japan was defeated and American occupation forces landed. At the time of completion, however, the Imperial censors still had control over the film industry and they banned Kurosawa's feature on grounds that it profaned Japan's feudal heritage. Under the occupation administration the ban remained in effect, but on the grounds now that the film promoted militarist and feudal values. *The Men Who Tread on the Tiger's Tail* did not receive general release until 1952.

With his next film, *No Regrets for Our Youth* (*Waga Seishun ni Kuinashi*, 1946), Kurosawa addressed political matters that would have been impossible to consider under the industry's "home front" policies during the war. The fictional events and characters in the film contain many parallels to the government's suppression in 1933 of a liberal intellectual on the faculty of Kyoto University and the execution for espionage ten years later of his protégé, an antiwar activist. The film's storyline advances up to the present (1946) with the restoration of the law professor's university position after Japan's defeat.

In the film there is greater dramatic concern with the future of the professor's daughter, Yukie, than with ideological matters. Full of undirected passion, she pursues beauty and innocent pleasure through the flattering attentions of two of her father's students, Itokawa and Noge. With the dismissal of university professors and the arrest of student activists, Yukie grows restless to experience life on her own terms and she leaves Kyoto for Tokyo. After some years there, she encounters her two former suitors. Itokawa is now married and holds a government position as prosecutor, while Noge has been publishing material critical of Japan's colonial and war policies. Though her maturation at this point is defined through a decision to marry, her union with Noge is an act of defiance. With her husband's subsequent death in prison, she leaves Tokyo to assist his peasant parents, who condemn their son's memory and are themselves condemned by other villagers. Defying these condemnations, Yukie moves in with Noge's parents and begins to work their fields. Eventually, she establishes a life for herself in the village.

There are many startling visual moments in the film, making evident Kurosawa's open experimentation with the medium. In conveying the freedom of youth before the rise of fascism, he links a succession of traveling and pan shots of Yukie and the university students running through a woods. This configuration of movement will be elaborated in action sequences for his later period films. Yukie's anxiety before meeting her two suitors is visualized in brief, intense images of her behind a locked door; the montage paralyzes her appearance in a variety of postures and symptoms of panic. The reversal in fate for Yukie after the arrest of her husband is marked by another set of still images—a frontal and two profile poses of her made for police records. These elliptical vis-

uals, lasting only a few seconds, form a dramatic bridge between the arrival of police at her apartment and her interrogation at headquarters; all intervening events of the arrest
and processing are eliminated. Yukie's long months of ex-
hausting but meaningful labor in the fields are conveyed
through dynamic montage in the heroic manner of Soviet silent cinema, particularly that of Eisenstein and Alexander
Dovzhenko.

By the conclusion, beauty has become redefined for Yukie as a matter of ethics rather than aesthetics. Her discovery
of a personal code of action, independent of society's dictates,
met with misapprehension and disapproval by Japanese critics. Female self-definition appeared perverse in a social context structured to guarantee male interests. Kurosawa admits
to creating such "strange," individuated women in films like
Rashomon, The Idiot, Throne of Blood, and *Ran.* He has attributed his lack of further attention to women's issues to
priorities at Toho studio, his principal producer for two decades, where that segment in the film market was assigned
to Naruse.

In collaborating with Keinosuke Uekusa on the original
screenplay to *One Wonderful Sunday (Subarashiki Nichi-
yobi,* 1947), Kurosawa was reunited with the school companion with whom he had shared his first artistic ambitions. As
boys Uekusa adopted the literary persona of Murasaki and
Kurosawa that of Shonagon Sei, the two female masters of
Heian literature. In recollecting their boyhood friendship,
the *Autobiography* emphasizes their distinctive but comple-
mentary styles of fantasy and play. Their scenario for *One
Wonderful Sunday* chronicles the grinding frustrations and
small pleasures of a young, engaged couple who can meet
only once a week in Tokyo. Between them, Yuzo and Masako
have thirty-five yen, which does not buy much in the postwar economy. As they share a meal brought from home, a
ragged beggar boy approaches and offers them ten yen in exchange for a riceball. Masako refuses the money but gives
him the riceball. Their generosity and compassionate inter-

est is met with the boy's resentment and his taunts that they are no better than he. This perverse response to their humane action is, paradoxically, an expression of the boy's own integrity and humanity.

Masako is determined to maintain her love of life in the face of Yuzo's increasing resignation to the corruption and malaise of the times. Their urban world is in constant, restless movement, much as one finds in Italian neorealist cinema of this period. Through techniques similar to neorealism, Kurosawa uses a hidden camera at street level for shots of his fictional couple among actual city crowds. The film's metaphor for the condition of their romance is Franz Schubert's *Unfinished Symphony*. To make an affirmative ending Kurosawa experiments with a reflexive device. The couple concludes their outing at the park. Unable to attend a concert of Schubert earlier because blackmarketeers had bought the inexpensive tickets for resale at a much higher price, Masako encourages Yuzo to conduct an imaginary orchestra in the park's empty outdoor bandshell. His pantomime is met by desolate gusts of wind. With this initial setback, Masako makes a direct appeal to film spectators to applaud on behalf of romantic hope. On the presumption of actual applause in the movie theater, Schubert's music rises on the soundtrack in tempo to Yuzo's outstretched arms. Kurosawa reports that, in fact, the sequence fails to evoke any participation from Japanese audiences.

One Wonderful Sunday inaugurated a series of contemporary story films set in "defeated Japan," in his phrase, made over the next three years: *Drunken Angel, The Quiet Duel* (*Shizukanaru Ketto*, 1949), *Stray Dog*, and *Scandal*. He has compared his motivation in making them to the purposes of journalism—not for topical or sensational effect, but rather to investigate in depth the truths underlying contemporary life. These film stories are structured by narrative lines such as a medical examination, a police manhunt, and a legal action in their examination of the postwar psychological and social conditions of the Japanese. The production of *Drunken*

Angel constitutes the filmmaking experience that, after five years of directing, gave Kurosawa "liberation from something resembling a spiritual prison" and he gained full artistic confidence with the medium (*Autobiography*, 163).

Since *Drunken Angel* and many of the subsequent films receive thematic and visual analysis in chapters that follow, I will conclude the discussion of Kurosawa's career here with an account of his evolving position in the Japanese film industry. Under the occupation administration the formation of Japanese trade unions was promoted and the Motion Picture and Drama Employees Union quickly became a powerful force at Toho studios. Two strikes in 1946 resulted in extensive union participation in the studio's operations and, as a reaction to this change, in formation of a faction headed by ten major Toho film stars. With technicians, writers, assistant directors, and other actors, this faction consolidated into Shintoho ("New Toho"), financed initially by the parent company and then becoming independent. Kurosawa remained at Toho and was generally supportive of the struggle against management despite the union Review Committee's requirement of script revisions to *No Regrets for Our Youth*. During a third strike in 1948, which began the same month *Drunken Angel* was released, he joined the union ranks in occupying the studio facilities. When the strike ended after six months with the intransigent company management still in power, Kurosawa left Toho to work at a succession of other studios until his return in 1952.

Kurosawa gained international recognition with the honors given to *Rashomon* at the 1951 Venice Film Festival and the American Academy Awards. The news of its success abroad came at a time of profound disappointment over the release that year of *The Idiot*, an adaptation of the Dostoevsky novel that held great personal meaning. Shochiku studios distributed the film in prints that excised, against Kurosawa's objections, more than ninety minutes of footage from the original release he had prepared. As a result of unanimously scathing reviews of *The Idiot* in the Japanese press, he was unable to secure a production contract for further projects. The account of his life and career in *Something Like an Autobiography* concludes with the reversal in professional fortunes that *Rashomon* brought. A succession of masterworks follows in his career, but Kurosawa ends on a note of self-irony with the assessment that both he and his autobiography are, like the characters in *Rashomon*, "incapable of talking about themselves with total honesty" (*Autobiography*, 189).

Kurosawa renewed his connections with Toho to write and direct *Ikiru*, a penetrating analysis of the meaning of life for a career bureaucrat in the civil service. From this *gendai-mono*, or drama of modern life, he turned to the genre of *jidai-geki*, or period drama, in making *Seven Samurai*. Well over a year in production, much of it on location, and ultimately the most expensive Japanese release made to 1954, this film severely tested Toho's commitment to Kurosawa. Though distributed domestically in its first run at full length, *Seven Samurai* in foreign release was shortened by some forty minutes until its re-release in recent years at its original length.

Over the next ten years his projects at Toho alternated between serious dramatic material, engaging issues of human ambitions and suffering, and material in the popular mold of cinema's action and adventure conventions, in which he also takes genuine artistic interest. In the first category can be placed the *gendai-mono Record of a Living Being* (*Ikimono no Kiroku*, 1955), *The Bad Sleep Well* (*Warui Yatsu Hodo Yoku Nemuru*, 1960), and *High and Low* and the *jidai-geki Throne of Blood, The Lower Depths*, and *Red Beard*. Into the second category fall *The Hidden Fortress* (*Kakushi Toride no San-Akunin*, 1958), *Yojimbo*, and *Sanjuro*, all *jidai-geki* action-comedies. By 1960 Kurosawa had formed an independent production unit that maintained an exclusive agreement with Toho for distribution. With Kurosawa's concern for historical accuracy and precise visual effects, which some film executives and journalists characterized as obsessive, work on the set of *Red Beard* extended over two years.

Intercultural Prominence

After release of *Red Beard*, the distribution deal with Toho dissolved. Kurosawa told the press that he considered the studio system in Japan to have declined from a means for creation to a media factory for cheap, formulaic production. He also aired the belief that any film critical of contemporary society is subject to a studio's inhibitions and censorship far more extensively than with historical or mythical material. Commenting on *The Bad Sleep Well* he admitted to "cowardly compromises" with Toho producers in limiting the exposure of social corruption, stopping short of high government circles. Reflecting in 1980 over the previous twenty-five years of his career, Kurosawa regretted that greater emphasis on historical settings over contemporary ones has made him appear reactionary.

In 1966, with a decline in domestic movie attendance by a factor of 60 percent over the previous five years, Kurosawa could not attract new Japanese producers and he signed a contract with 20th Century–Fox. The American studio executives encouraged him to consider their development script on General Custer, with the possibility of Toshiro Mifune in the role of an Indian warrior, but Kurosawa rejected the proposal as absurd. He offered as a counterproposal his new script *Runaway Train*, an American story that he wanted to shoot in upstate New York during winter. In the script, the climactic action aboard the locomotive matches completely the duration of events with the time they take onscreen, a span of nearly thirty minutes. It was to be his first color film, though by intention the winter light would greatly mute the color range. With weather delays on location, however, Fox terminated the project. Kurosawa is credited with the story idea for the 1985 American feature under the same title, directed by Andrei Konchalovsky.

Fox brought Kurosawa into plans for the war epic *Tora!*

Tora! Tora! and with two long-time collaborators he prepared an account of Japanese political and military events leading to the attack on Pearl Harbor. Having entered into the project with the expectation that he would retain complete control over the Japanese story material, Kurosawa adamantly resisted directives from his American producers and their contract was voided. (The Japanese portion of the production was completed by Toshio Masuda and Kinji Fukasaku and incorporated into the 1970 American release directed by Richard Fleischer.)

After the failure of his American ventures, Kurosawa joined with fellow directors Keisuke Kinoshita, Kon Ichikawa, and Masaki Kobayashi in founding the production company *Yonki no Kai* ("The Four Musketeers of Cinema") with the intention of financing one film by each director in a joint effort to revive the quality of Japanese cinema. The only release that resulted from their association was *Dodeskaden*, Kurosawa's first film in color. At the time of its production, he spoke of a desire to attain professionally *yuzumuge*, the state of transcendental awareness in Zen. The negative reception for *Dodeskaden* and his ill health ruined his hopes. At this low point in his professional life, Kurosawa attempted suicide.

During recovery, Kurosawa was approached by the Soviet state company Mosfilm with an offer to finance a co-production. As subject he chose the memoirs of the Russian soldier and explorer Vladimir Arseniev, who recounts his association in Siberia with an aging native hunter. The export release of *Dersu Uzala* (*Dersu Uzala*, 1975) contained cuts and a new music track unauthorized by Kurosawa. After protests over the premiere of this version in Italy, the director's intended release print was restored.

For several years Kurosawa tried unsuccessfully to interest Japanese studios in one of several new projects, which included an adaptation of Poe's "Masque of the Red Death" and a script for *Ran*. But the home industry had grown even more commercially cautious and conventional in the face of steadily declining movie attendance, which had dropped another

50 percent by 1975. With guarantees secured by George Lucas and Francis Ford Coppola with 20th Century–Fox in exchange for foreign rights, Toho agreed to sponsor his period drama *Kagemusha*. Though the film became the most expensive production to that time by Japanese standards, which are modest compared to those typical of Hollywood, the first-run world revenues in 1980 amounted to practically twice its costs.

His longheld intention to film *Ran* was finally realized through a French-Japanese coproduction whose European executive head was Serge Silberman, producer of Buñuel's later films. The costumes, armor, and sets for the sixteenth century story required over two years of preparation. Kurosawa began to plan his next film, *Dreams*, after receiving initial support from Steven Spielberg and making distribution agreements with Warner Brothers. The budget for *Dreams* was raised entirely outside Japan and it was managed through the American subsidiary of Kurosawa Productions. A departure in subject matter and visual treatment for the eighty-year old director, *Dreams* features special effects created by the George Lucas laboratory Industrial Light and Magic.

Within two months of the 1990 premiere of *Dreams* in Tokyo, Kurosawa was already engaged in work on his next release *Rhapsody in August* (*Hachigatsu no Kyoshikyoku*, 1991), produced by Shochiku studios. For the first time in twenty years a Japanese company fully financed the production costs of a Kurosawa film. Based on his adaptation of the novel *Nabe no Naka* ("In the Cauldron") by Kyoko Muraka, the story portrays the relations among three generations of a family. The husband of grandmother Kane died when the atomic bomb was dropped on Nagasaki. She survived because she was at their rural home, separated from the city by a mountain. Kane's own children retain an embarrassed silence about these events, while her grandchildren are respectfully curious. When Kane is visited by another bomb survivor, the two women share tea in complete silence. But the quality of this silence differs from that of the middle generation. To her grandchildren Kane explains the woman's behavior with the observation, "There are some people who are quiet even while they are talking." The film uses such expressive silence to convey a reflective mode of experience. Kurosawa's subject here is the processes of memory and commemoration at both personal and social levels.

In January 1992 Kurosawa announced production plans for his next film, to be released through Daiei Company, the studio for which the director filmed *Rashomon*. The new project is entitled *Mada Da Yo* ("Not Ready Yet"), an exclamation used in the children's game of hide and seek that is also meant to suggest Kurosawa's own perseverance as an artist at an age when most men are retired and inactive. The film story concerns the closing phase of a writer's life (based on the experiences of the Japanese essayist and scholar Hyakken Uchida) and his relationship with former students. Set in the period immediately following World War II, which destroyed the writer's Tokyo home, the story depicts the survival of his wit and dignity and the strength of his ideas and values in the face of personal loss.

Akira Kurosawa has experienced a double-bind in his identity as a Japanese filmmaker from the outset of his directorial career. For the nation's wartime censors in 1942, *Sanshiro Sugata* was "British-American" in its dramatic manner and emotional content. After Ozu's enthusiasm over the film, these censors approved it, though they required significant excisions before its release the following year. For Allied occupation censors the film was so traditionally Japanese in its views of loyalty and militancy as to be deemed reactionary and it was withheld from exhibition until 1952. The double-bind intensified after winning the awards in Venice and Hollywood for *Rashomon*. Such success was met with widespread skepticism in Japan since, according to an insular and purist logic, truly Japanese culture is unintelligible to foreigners and is thus untranslatable. The home press accounted for the film's foreign acclaim as Western curiosity in Oriental intrigue and exoticism. Not wanting to reinforce such preconceptions, Kurosawa regretted that a *jidai-geki* rather than one of his contemporary story films had received such recognition.

Submission of *Rashomon* to the Venice festival resulted from the initiative of an Italian distribution agent working in Japan, not from the studio Daiei, whose chief executive had found the film nearly incomprehensible. Its huge success abroad created the mindset among Japanese producers that Kurosawa was best suited for Western audiences. In a period of many Kurosawa masterworks, Toho entered in competition at Asian film festivals not one of his films but instead romantic and comic features like *Holiday in Tokyo* (*Tokyo no Kyujitsu*, 1958) and *Three Dolls in College* (*Daigaku no One-ichan*, 1959), while it sent *Seven Samurai* and *Throne of Blood* to European and Commonwealth festivals. In 1985, Japan's five major production companies passed over *Ran* in selecting an entry for the Academy's Best Foreign Film award. Though a definitively Japanese work, *Ran* was not considered by Japan's major studios to be representative of their national cinema since the film was financed principally by a production company based in Paris.

Since Kurosawa pays homage to Van Gogh in one segment of *Dreams*, it is worth considering further this specific intercultural context. Van Gogh's first opportunity to view a range of works by Japan's woodblock masters came in 1885. Inspired by this contact, the painter soon spoke of the South of France—with its diverse colors, open landscapes, and intense light—as "a new Japan." The woodblock prints appealed to him in their direct, simplified technique, which gave a reassuringly familiar look to their subjects: "I envy the Japanese the extreme clearness which everything has in their work. It is never wearisome, and never seems to be done too hurriedly. Their work is as simple as breathing, and they do a figure in a few sure strokes."[9] The young Japanese painter in *Dreams*, for his turn, takes inspiration from Van Gogh to pursue the truth of his vision with spiritual passion. In the sixth decade of his career in cinema, Kurosawa remains passionately engaged in the creative challenges of screenwriting and directing.

2

Russian Intertexts

Critical understanding of intertextuality is deeply indebted to analysis of the novel by Soviet literary theorist Mikhail Bakhtin, who has given an account of "the dialogic imagination" in a rich tradition that includes Rabelais, Cervantes, Dickens, and Dostoevsky.[1] In this tradition the novel's literary language is not a consistent, unified field nor the writer's private province but rather a dialogue among mixed and opposing ideologies, voices of authority, genres, and social idioms. Such a dialogic text, or intertext, uniquely represents images of language styles. The novelist is a point of contact for their interpenetration. The intertext thus functions as a field of linguistic and semantic interaction that is not finalized or end-stopped, even though the storyline may be. Contending within this field is a polyglot of discourses—from the popular languages of the man on the street and the daily press to the specialized discourses of science, theology, philosophy—and cultural traditions such as the tragic, epic, comic, speculative, and lyrical literary modes.

The special appeal of the Russian writer Dostoevsky for Bakhtin is in the plurality of unmerged voices and consciousnesses registered in his novels. Dostoevsky's greatness results from a vast receptiveness to different uses of language and thus to different evaluations of reality. The Dostoevsky novel is a hybrid textual construction that incorporates an array of genres and a diversity of speech types. Its typical hero is characterized in terms of the perceptions and consciousness directed toward the self and toward the world. A double momentum underlying the narrative—which is at once reflective and reflexive—directs the plot action toward encounters between the hero's subjectivity and a range of conscious-

ness and self-consciousness among other characters who are
not subordinate to either the hero's language or the narrator's
rhetoric.

Kurosawa's formative experience of reading Dostoevsky is
a biographeme with strong overtones to the relationship with
his brother Heigo. The sense of his shared yet opposed experience with Heigo in *Something Like an Autobiography*, and
of their bond as "negative and positive" variants of one image,
can be accurately termed intertextual (*Autobiography*, 87).
The distinctly discursive potential within cinema that Kurosawa has pursued over his career can also be termed dialogic
and intertextual. Kurosawa has explained that the category
"action film" in his own filmmaking commonly includes adventures less physical and more social, moral, or spiritual in
kind. Quite often he constructs the narrative as a means of
inquiry into social division, into the nature of power and powerlessness, or into other conditions of the human spirit. This
narrative construct can be literally investigative, as in the police procedures of *Stray Dog* and *High and Low* and the court
procedures of *Record of a Living Being*, or metaphorically investigative, as in the medical case histories of *Drunken Angel*, *The Quiet Duel*, *Ikiru*, and *Red Beard*.

Of all the literary intertexts that have occupied his artistic
attention, Kurosawa reserves the highest praise for the novels of Dostoevsky:

> He is the one who . . . writes most honestly about human
> existence. There is certainly no other author who is so at-
> tractive to me, so—well, gentle. When I say gentle, I mean
> the kind of gentleness that makes you want to avert your
> eyes when you see something really dreadful, really tragic.
> He has this power of compassion. And then he refuses to
> turn his eyes away; he, too, looks; he, too, suffers. There is
> something which is more than human, better than human,
> about him.[2]

Film criticism has examined parallels between Kurosawa
and Dostoevsky primarily in terms of a compassionate scru-

tiny into suffering, an ultimate moral reaffirmation of humanity, and a shared fascination with masochistic, single-
minded personalities.[3]

Kurosawa's affiliation with Dostoevsky is both more extensive and more deeply structured than has been generally acknowledged.[4] Throughout the Russian writer's fiction are to
be found scenes brought to the absolute limits of a psychological state, a social view, or a dramatic conflict, quite often
through the experience of an eccentric or antisocial protagonist. Kurosawa has described his own sensibility as oriented
toward situations extreme in their conditions and affect.
Within the medium, he frequently experiments with formal
limits, whether through heavy fragmentation of a continuous action, such as the woodcutter's excursion into the grove
in *Rashomon*, or through the prolonged duration of an action-
less situation, such as the halt by mountain climbers in "The
Blizzard" episode of *Dreams*.

The reader regularly encounters in Dostoevsky a psychological process of doubling. Manifest in the intimacy between contrasting personalities, as in the case of Raskolni-
kov and Inspector Petrovich of *Crime and Punishment*, the
process is equally evident in the internal split of a personality into diametric traits, as in the case of the Underground
Man. Among Dostoevsky's protagonists there is a common
compulsion to reflect and confess in response to the voice —
sometimes external and real, sometimes internal and imagined — of an adversary. The psychology of an individual character is thus often double-voiced, affirming one moment,
gainsaying the next. That individual's language conveys, simultaneously, both a direct purpose and a refracted one.

Psychological doubling is one manifestation of the paradoxes that structure much of Dostoevsky's writing. As a figure of speech, *paradox* reveals, through a surprising turn of
meaning, the measure of truth in a seemingly contradictory
or absurd statement. As a textual function, paradox links
qualities and assertions that are normatively defined through
opposition in binary pairs like tragedy/comedy, spiritual-

ity/materialism, compassion/dread, and life/death, examples which are of foremost concern to Dostoevsky. Placed in static antithesis like this, the dividing line in a pair would suggest that the quality and value of each term is inevitably and irreducibly contradistinctive. In fact, within Dostoevsky's narratives paradox ceaselessly operates as a crossing-over, a transgression, a breach into the "other" of the novel's central values and truths. It is the interpenetration of opposing values and voices that is dialogic, intertextual. The composite that results from the intrusion of one truth into another is a temporarily full breach; the composite is not bound to hold together. Fission in the brief, new-found truth and catastrophe in delicately balanced personal bonds are the usual result. Paradox is another mode of the extremism in his fiction. It is a subversive action against the era's *doxa*, the common opinions and received truths that govern its perceptions, practical wisdom, and reality principle. Paradox disputes and confronts *orthodoxy*, beliefs hardened into social authority.

Kurosawa's affiliation with these traits in Dostoevsky of extremism, psychological doubling, and paradox did not become explicit in his cinema until after the war. They are evident in *No Regrets for Our Youth*, when Yukie tirelessly persists in aiding her in-laws in the face of their silence and animosity. With *One Wonderful Sunday* they are disclosed in Yuzo and Masako's fluctuations between defeat and hope. A specific instance occurs in the scene concerning an army comrade who was a misfit unable even to salute properly but who now in peacetime owns a private cabaret in the Ginza. In waiting to meet him at the cabaret, Yuzo is sent to a service pantry where he encounters a drunk who wolfs down leftovers from customers' plates and a hostess sick from the drinks she has coaxed from men. Yuzo, who struggles throughout the film to maintain his dignity, is at first mistaken by the drunk as a fellow sponger. He is finally refused a meeting with the former comrade, who remains an unseen character. Yuzo exits through the club's lobby, where stares from elegantly dressed patrons cause him to examine in a full-length mirror

his own shabby appearance. As with such contact between social extremes in a Dostoevsky novel, he is made to take his
own psychological measure.

Kurosawa identifies *Drunken Angel* as the first film in
which his affiliation with Dostoevsky fully emerges. In the
original draft for the screenplay, an idealistic young doctor
was created as the complete antithesis to a tubercular *yakuza*, or gangster, challenged by others for control of the blackmarket district where the doctor has just set up practice. This
perfect humanitarian, however, established static, schematic
contrasts that left the story lifeless. When Uekusa and Kurosawa remembered an alcoholic gynecologist they had met in
a Yokohama bar, they broke through their impasse and con-
verted the character into an older, drunken cynic with a hatred for disease and a passion for curing humanity.

While Dr. Sanada views the yakuza Matsunaga with contempt, through their individual pathologies they form a vital
bond. The doctor, like the gangster, dissembles his compassionate concern, but they remain emotionally vulnerable to
one another. As incorrigible and temperamental in behavior
as his patient, Sanada is a physician who has not healed himself. In a typically refractory manner, he articulates his emotional paradox: a doctor needs patients to make a living but he
is devoted to curing them and thus losing his livelihood.
When his condition worsens, Matsunaga lapses into uncon-
sciousness and hallucinates a scene in which he frees his own
corpse from a coffin. Once raised, the body menaces its savior.
Matsunaga experiences this psychological division and confrontation with the doctor at his side.

Central to the setting of *Drunken Angel* is a stagnant drainage pool and dump around which blackmarket activities and
the yakuza proliferate. A similar urban swamp, infested with
vermin and mosquitoes, provokes social conflict in *Ikiru*. A
district that has risen amidst uncleared wartime rubble, with
its back alleys inhabited by drug addicts, is explored in *High
and Low*. In *The Bad Sleep Well*, the denouement to a story
of corruption in the *zaibatsu*, or business conglomerates,

takes place in the ruins of Tokyo's bombed factory district. The social ills Kurosawa represents, however, are frequently not at their most malignant in these pockets of urban devastation and crime but rather in the boardrooms and bureaucracies of executive power.

Drunken Angel marks the debut in Kurosawa's cinema of Toshiro Mifune, who played leading roles in all but one of the director's next fifteen films. Their collaboration was severed after the 1965 release of *Red Beard*, whose lengthy production extensions caused Mifune to break commitments to other projects. It became evident to Kurosawa from the initial audition at Toho in 1946 that Mifune possessed a uniquely uninhibited and elemental energy. In his first two films, made by other Toho directors, Mifune exhibited a range of behavior from unpredictable violence to detached indifference. Under his own direction, Kurosawa found Mifune unique in the economy and directness of his expression and in the rapidity of his emotional shifts. Mifune has praised Kurosawa in turn as a great teacher who innovated new methods in Japanese film acting and for whom he has done the only work he values in the first twenty years of his career.

Even though script revisions to *Drunken Angel* turn Dr. Sanada into a more credible and involving character, Mifune's unrestrained performance makes Matsunaga's personality dominant. Attracted by his raw power, Kurosawa was not inclined to curb Mifune on the set, even though a dramatic imbalance between the doctor and the gangster resulted. Kurosawa acknowledges that this result is consistent with his inherent attraction, as both writer and director, to villains. His dangerous, often nihilistic characters usually avoid the clichés of evil to emerge as antagonists or, more accurately, agonists in the narrative's ongoing dialogue about human nature. They become recognizable as inevitable and necessary counterparts to the heroic potential that develops within his protagonists over the course of a narrative.

Cast as Dr. Sanada is Takashi Shimura, who appeared as the honorable jujitsu master in *Sanshiro Sugata* and who played roles in all but three of Kurosawa's films through 1965. His persona in leading roles is often endowed with shrewd insight borne of wide experience in the world and it is possessed with focused restraint and inwardness. In roles opposite a belligerent and posturing Mifune, this persona is typically impassive. Kurosawa has admitted to giving Mifune license to improvise and self-dramatize in these situations. Shimura's deliberate, sparse technique places in relief the affinities and the mutual comprehension that are, paradoxically, based in their characters' differences.

Kurosawa switched Mifune from the role of a resentful, incurable patient to that of a stoic, self-sacrificing physician with his next film, *The Quiet Duel*. Infected during a surgery performed on a wounded soldier later found to have syphilis, the doctor returns to civilian practice but breaks off his marriage engagement without any explanation. The closest he comes to confiding in his former fiancée is by posing to her a riddle in which a pure man, a virgin, becomes sick with venereal disease. The film story develops a solution to the riddle through the recognition, by the audience, that corruption is a legacy of war for all Japanese survivors, corrupt and pure alike.

Inquiry into postwar disorders in the social fabric and the national psyche continues with *Stray Dog*. Kurosawa has explained that this film story originated as an unpublished novel he wrote in the manner of Georges Simenon. The parallel extends, however, no further than an interest in the social ramifications of crime and in the details of police procedures employed to solve it. Simenon's master detective Maigret understands criminals insofar as they are professionals who share some of the same hardships as police in surviving city life. The expertise of Maigret lies in his ability to simulate criminal logic and behavior. He professes that his knowledge of the urban underworld is technical, not philosophical. Maigret does not pretend to understand or even to take interest in any "deep human mystery" pertaining to criminals.[5] In fact, he consistently dismisses such notions as romantic fantasy.

In *Stray Dog* Shimura and Mifune are paired as the veteran police investigator Sato and the young, returned soldier Murakami, newly recruited into the force. Sato displays some of Maigret's professionalism and wisdom, but the film's protagonist is the new recruit. When his service revolver is stolen by a pickpocket on a crowded bus, Murakami becomes single-minded in his efforts to recover it. In the course of his manhunt, Murakami adopts the dress and manner of a penniless, desperate veteran in order to move freely in the blackmarket and underworld districts. Through this assumed identity he begins to empathize with fellow soldiers who have resorted to crime after the horrors of war and in the social chaos of defeat. The detective Sato, who remained in the civilian police during wartime, attributes this misdirected empathy to a legacy of war that separates their generations. In conversation with Murakami, Sato attempts to use a popular European phrase he only half-remembers: *"après guerre"* ("after war"), adopted into Japanese to identify a new social syndrome. In this overtly dialogic scene, the young officer repeats the full phrase twice in an attempt to imprint it in the mind of the older detective.

After the two police officers trace the gun to a holdup man living with his sister in a burned-out area of Tokyo, they search through his meager belongings in a shed he occupied. A crumpled journal entry, in which is recorded his mood of worthlessness and slaughterous rage, fascinates Murakami. The camera gradually scans inked characters written in the criminal's hand. Moments later we watch Murakami pore over the page, his face pressed so close that his eyes consume each character. This textual evidence of a criminal's passionate despair is juxtaposed with the commendations for police work Murakami later admires in Sato's home. The official documents are framed and hang in a place of pride on the wall; Murakami regards them from a respectful distance. Murakami's psychological position is thus again dramatized as intertextual, as at a crossroads traversed by polar values and discourses. During the savage confusion of Murakami's climactic struggle with the gunman over the police revolver, they become indistinguishable from one another. Even after making the arrest and recovering his pistol, the young detective remains preoccupied with his criminal adversary, while Sato counsels him that further police experience will resolve his entangled sympathies.

In the course of writing *Drunken Angel*, Kurosawa's collaborator Keinosuke Uekusa made contacts with the blackmarket underworld in Tokyo. Uekusa became inclined to exonerate the yakuza system as a social outcome determined by postwar conditions. Kurosawa vigorously counterargued determinism with principles based on individual moral responsibility. Disagreement over the issue was so strong that it brought an end to their collaboration. In re-engaging the debate, however, *Stray Dog* places the protagonist closer to Uekusa's position than to Kurosawa's own. Both the perspective on crime and the rationale explaining its causes shift with each subsequent film on the subject. In *The Bad Sleep Well*, criminality reaches into business and political circles at the highest levels of Japanese society. The *jidai-geki Yojimbo*, in which rival factions bring destruction upon an entire town, indicates through satire that corruption within Japanese society is deep-rooted historically.

Scandal extends the idea of criminality to include the "verbal gangsterism" of gossip in the popular press, now free from wartime censorship (*Autobiography*, 178). There is a reflexive dimension to the visuals, and to their organization into narrative sequences, early in the film story. A fully dramatized scene during which a journalist takes a candid photograph of two celebrities, a young singer and a recognized painter brought together entirely by chance at a mountain resort, is followed without transition by the image of a darkroom. In a basin, cinematically enlarged through closeup, a photographic enlargement of the man and woman paired in the same image emerges. After some discussion among editors and staff over the gossip value—and thus commercial value—of the image, the film story advances through a montage of the photograph's dissemination in advertisements, posters, and finally on magazine covers at newsstands. In reassuring his editors and writer that the magazine is not likely to be sued, the publisher boasts that the general public "idolizes photographic proof." The mobility and exchange of images in consumer society is conveyed through a rapid succession of wipe cuts that synopsize the round of interviews and public statements made by the celebrities and the editor after the magazine's publication.

With *Drunken Angel, Stray Dog,* and many of the later films, Kurosawa is far closer to Dostoevsky than to Simenon in his outlook on crime and sociopathic behavior. In his era, Dostoevsky freely adapted the genre of urban action-adventure melodrama popularized by the French novelists Victor Hugo, Honoré de Balzac, and Eugène Sue. As imagined by Dostoevsky, the criminal, the underground man, and the idiot stand at a threshold where none of society's institutional powers or orthodox truths are secure. This threshold opens onto a realm of possibility for humanity beyond the spiritless prescriptions and dictates that govern everyday experience.

The Idiot

The scene of murder and madness Dostoevsky wrote as a conclusion to *The Idiot* is in Kurosawa's judgment "the most beautiful, the most agonizing, the richest, and finally the most haunting in the history of literature."[6] The events leading to that catastrophic conclusion entail immense reversals in fate over the short span of eight months. At the outset of the novel, the destiny of Dostoevsky's characters is suggested by the course of their monetary fortunes. With his father's death, Parfyon Rogozhin returns to Saint Petersburg to claim the family inheritance. He has been without money and in exile from the family for several weeks after a violent argument with his father. Rogozhin shares a third-class compartment on the train with Prince Lyov Myshkin, whose worldly possessions all fit into the small bundle he carries. The prince is returning to Russia after years of treatment in a Swiss sanatorium for nervous disorders. Without a coat adequate for the winter weather or the means to secure lodging for the night, Myshkin seeks out his distant relations in Petersburg, the Epanchins. Some hours later, Myshkin learns that he is the sole beneficiary in a will left by a wealthy, and even more distant, relative.

At the home of General Ivan Epanchin the prince is ensnared, within minutes, in the romantic confusion between the youngest daughter Aglaia and the general's personal secretary Gavril Ivolgin. Despite his infatuation with Aglaia, Gavril is on the verge of contracting marriage to Nastasya Filippovna, the former mistress of a wealthy patron now interested in a courtship with the oldest Epanchin daughter. Gavril is lured by a large cash settlement the patron has offered in exchange for Nastasya's betrothal, which is to be announced at her birthday party that same evening. Though uninvited, Rogozhin arrives at the party with a huge sum of rubles to outbid the patron and win Nastasya from Gavril. Five weeks earlier, Rogozhin had been nearly disowned by his father for squandering family savings on diamonds for Nastasya.

Confronted with this situation at the birthday party, Nastasya leaves the decision of her future to the prince, whom she has known for only a few hours. Deeply sympathetic to her emotional turmoil, Myshkin makes his own declaration of love and offers to marry her. To the further astonishment of the birthday guests, he discloses the news of his inheritance. When Rogozhin presses his own offer again, Nastasya protests that she is not to be bartered over and she tosses his bundle of banknotes into the fireplace. At the sight of burning money some guests instinctively make the sign of the cross. One observer compares her action to hara-kiri, Japanese ritual suicide.

Though he entered Petersburg unprotected and alone, by nightfall Myshkin acquires the fortune of a prince and in pure innocence embarks on a doomed romantic quest. With Part Two, the novel's action resumes after six months have

passed. In the interim Rogozhin, Myshkin, and Nastasya
have traveled to Moscow, where her ambivalence over the
two men becomes more intense. From the point of their return to Petersburg, the narrative follows events to a catastrophic end four weeks later. Once back in Petersburg, Rogozhin and Myshkin swear brotherhood by exchanging personal crosses. The cross from Rogozhin is gold, as befits a
member of the merchant class. The cross Myshkin gives is
tin, though he charitably bought it from a blasphemous drunk
who claimed it was solid silver. Their symbolic pledge does
not remove, however, the dreadful uncertainty between them.
Later in the same day Rogozhin lunges at Myshkin with a
knife, but at that very moment the prince is stricken with an
epileptic seizure. The seizure is providential: it spares Myshkin from murder; Rogozhin flees in terror at the sight. For an
instant that will persist lucidly in memory, Myshkin senses
his soul opening to an intense flood of inner light before the
seizure obliterates consciousness.

   Though completely inexperienced in matters of the heart,
the prince becomes further confounded in them with Aglaia.
Myshkin steadfastly maintains that he has no new intention
of marriage until, in an awkward moment caused by Aglaia's
naive and direct questions, he suddenly proposes to her. While
Aglaia is too puzzled herself to accept the proposal uncondi-
tionally, Nastasya becomes jealously enraged and is determined to ruin the innocents' relationship. When all four
meet in Rogozhin's house, Nastasya binds Myshkin to her by
appealing to his compulsive empathy, which causes him to
comfort Nastasya in her hysteria and to disregard Aglaia in
her anguish.

   At the hour of the wedding planned for Myshkin and Nastasya, she flees with Rogozhin. A short time afterward, crazed
passion drives Rogozhin to murder Nastasya as a means of
completely possessing her. Rogozhin brings Myshkin into his
family's deserted Petersburg home to hold vigil over Nastasya's corpse. She has not escaped her destiny as a prized object,
to be exchanged among men. In the night hours Rogozhin

goes temporarily insane and Myshkin relapses into idiocy.

Each of these characters contains a psychological and spiritual complex that knits him or her to the complexes contained within the others. At issue in the narrative is the question of which drives determine a character's action: passion, acquisitiveness, compassion, hate, spirituality, nihilism? The dialogic interrelation of characters on matters such as materialism, faith, and anarchism incorporates polemics current in Russia and Europe during the 1860s. Prominent intertexts in *The Idiot* derive from the principles and discourse of Eastern Orthodoxy, rational utopianism, the nihilists, Slavophilism, and Russian Westernism. Further at issue is the question of what bonds characterize shared humanity: romantic passion or passionate hate, brotherly love or fratricide? Ultimately at issue is the spiritual position of a mortal: with Christ through belief and faith, or godlessly with the antichrist through materialism and nihilism?

The empathy Nastasya inspires in Myshkin is a powerful example of ties in the novel that knit a character with the complex that divides another character's personality. In regarding her portrait photograph before he has met Nastasya in person, Myshkin responds to signs of emotional torment and vindictive rage that he senses beyond the surface of her beauty and elegance. In that instant he predicts that Rogozhin will likely kill her within a week should she marry him. Myshkin attributes to Nastasya a legacy of innocent virtue that endures in spite of her victimization as a mistress, but he also cannot ignore the symptoms of ruthlessness and madness that will lead her on emotional rampages. In conveying Myshkin's complicated reaction to Nastasya, the novel states that her face "stabbed his heart, for ever."[7]

Myshkin's compassion intensifies rather than tempers the complexes that conflict each personality. Often he acts as peacemaker, deflecting moral judgment away from the failings of others and onto himself, but the ultimate effect of this psychological charity is to torment its recipients with shame. Myshkin's good will is incongruous among the nor-

mal hypocrisies of social life and its consequences are antithetical to his intentions. His compassion more often arouses
hatred or ridicule than understanding. The spirituality of
Dostoevsky's peaceful and meek prince proves reckless. Given
the soulless condition of Russian life as Dostoevsky perceives
it, compassion proves crueler than brutality.

The most disturbing of *The Idiot*'s paradoxes lies in the recognition that matters of goodness are equally matters of destructiveness and evil. The day of Rogozhin's attack on him,
Myshkin reflects that "compassion was the chief and perhaps
only law of all human existence" even while he admits that
"in his own soul there was darkness, since he could imagine
such horrors" as preoccupy Rogozhin (*Idiot*, 218). The exchange of their personal crosses comes just after Myshkin
tells Rogozhin the story of a man who murdered his dearest
friend, praying for Christ's forgiveness as he slit the friend's
throat. In the course of their long conversation that day Myshkin twice, and without any thought to his actions, seizes a
large knife from a desk while listening to Rogozhin confess
his murderous passion for Nastasya. Once Nastasya is killed,
Myshkin exhibits a morbid fixation on the crime's violent details and on the murder weapon, which is the same knife he
absentmindedly handled. In the company of her dead body,
Rogozhin and Myshkin fulfill a murderous brotherhood.

Kurosawa's film story retains all of the major events summarized here, with the exception of Nastasya's flight with Rogozhin at the hour of her wedding. The exchange of crosses is
modified to an exchange of talismans. The film does not contain prominent scenes involving secondary characters in the
novel, many of whom serve Dostoevsky's intertextual purposes. Involved in the affairs of Myshkin and Rogozhin from
the moment they meet aboard the train is a petty official
named Lukyan Lebedyev, who claims to be an intimate in
matters of Petersburg high society. Though Lebedyev is heavily caricatured, Dostoevsky develops major themes through
his voice. Lebedyev attempts to relieve Nastasya from her
emotional turmoil by reading from the Book of Revelation

and offering as comfort the promise of apocalyptic ruin that will come with the antichrist. Dostoevsky thus entrusts to this character's idiosyncratic perceptions a fundamental paradox: the revelation of Providence through a reign of evil and through destruction of the world order.

The novel includes a number of other caricaturable yet consequential personalities, such as the consumptive teenager Ippolit, whose failed suicide is met with ridicule by his nihilist associates, and the unruly Burdovsky, who makes a patently false claim to Myshkin's inheritance. A few like Lebedyev have undeveloped minor roles in the film, others are merely glimpsed. This reduction in the cast of characters results from the film's substantial abridgment at the hands of the Shochiku studio. The finished film that Kurosawa submitted had a running time of 265 minutes, which his producers reduced to 166 minutes. The director's original version has not been preserved.

In explanation of his enduring interest in Dostoevsky, Kurosawa has said that the novelist's era, with social oppression and the destruction of truth under the tsars, is a direct analogy to the epoch of Japan's imperial expansion in Asia and the Pacific, during which he matured as an individual and an artist. He finds in Dostoevsky a sensibility that is at once empathic in response to a great range of human experiences and objective in its methods of representing those experiences:

> Dostoevsky's novels are, well, like subjecting the human spirit to a scientific experiment. The people are put into an extreme situation, a pure situation, and then he watches what happens to them. . . . If I do say so myself I think that after making this picture my own powers increased considerably.[8]

Kurosawa acknowledges a forced, strained quality to his adaptation that he accepts as the consequence of trying to render Myshkin's compassion. In his estimation the film lacks equilibrium, but that is a sign of its gravitation toward the perspective of Myshkin.

In scripting the film with Eijiro Hisaita, Kurosawa made

the crucial decision to treat their literary source as the basis for a contemporary Japanese story. In doing so they maintain the intertextual function of voicing multiple and often contentious perspectives on worldly and spiritual experience. At its intended length, the film compounded a greater variety of such voices into its structure. Ideas and emotions originally conveyed in early dialogue scenes are now synopsized by long title inserts. As released, the narrative is segmented into two parts, "Love and Suffering" and "Love and Hate." These three primary affects characterize the psychological interrelation of the central characters Kinji Kameda (Myshkin), Denkichi Akama (Rogozhin), Taeko Nasu (Nastasya), Ayako Ono (Aglaia), and Mutsuo Kayama (Gavril). Provided in a section at the back of this book is a complete list of film characters and of their original names in the novel.

With *The Idiot*, Kurosawa applies Dostoevsky as an intertext to his explorations of "defeated Japan." This intertext affords him a perspective in depth on the mental burdens and moral lessons of defeat and on the implications of new individual wealth and regained social power. The film story opens on a steamship bound for Hokkaido, Japan's largest northern island, whose proximity to Russia has brought widespread importation of European styles of dress, furniture, and architecture in this century. The camera descends from an outer deck swept by a winter storm, down to the steerage section below, and it surveys a mass of sleeping humanity. Many sleepers are aroused by the sudden screams of Kameda, who is tormented by a recurrent nightmare. The narrative is thus inaugurated and the first character identified through this agonized outburst. Kameda explains to the man who chances to be closest to him, Akama, that the nightmare carries through events that in reality stopped just short of his execution. When his death sentence was lifted at the last minute, Kameda disintegrated into nervous fits. He is traveling north from Okinawa, where he had been confined in an American prisoner of war camp. In listening fixedly to Kameda's account, Akama burns his fingers with the match he had struck to relight a cigar. Their first encounter entails mutual pain; Kameda's is distinctly mental, Akama's physical.

A strong intertextual correlation between the film and the novel is apparent in this scene. A unique attribute of Myshkin as a protagonist is his heroic function simply as a storyteller. Setting and narrative movement within the novel become a matter of where and how Myshkin and other characters (some of otherwise minor importance) place their stories. A similar advancement in the film narrative by Kurosawa to a point, and for the purpose, of a character's delivery of a story or an account is apparent in *Rashomon* and several subsequent films. Kurosawa's plans to adapt *The Idiot* were formulated before he began filming *Rashomon*. In addition to these two films, this narrative function is a fundamental structural feature of *Ikiru*, *Red Beard*, and *Dodeskaden*. The wipe cut, in which a frame line sweeps across the visual field, displacing one image with a new one, is an editing figure expressive of this narrative impetus, and it will be discussed in the chapter on *Rashomon*.

Dostoevsky's novel is narrated by an unnamed authorial voice, but events and ideas are frequently advanced through the stories Myshkin relates to other characters. Within the first hours of his acquaintance with the Epanchins, Myshkin recounts three stories. Though they are not retold again, their situations and possible meaning are developed over the full extent of the novel through processes of reconfiguration and recontextualization. The first story is Myshkin's eyewitness account of an execution by guillotine. With a seriousness vastly inappropriate to his audience and the occasion, Myshkin imagines the spiritual agony of awaiting an appointed hour of death. The second story recounts the experience of a fellow patient at the sanatorium who was spared execution by firing squad by a margin of only three minutes. Myshkin encourages his listeners to imagine what it might mean to live "counting each moment" on the threshold of certain death (*Idiot*, 56). The last story concerns a young village recluse Marie, a consumptive abandoned by her seducer and

abused by all her neighbors, including the children. Through
the example of his own charity, Myshkin converts the village
children to an understanding of her suffering.

The film script distills the focus on dread, existential awareness, and compassion within Myshkin's three stories into
Kameda's account of his own near death. At Taeko's birthday
celebration Kameda recounts his experience of awaiting execution. The event is intensified with the added explanation
that the others condemned that day were shot and that his
life alone was spared. Kameda places this retelling as a clarification of the emotions he recognizes in Taeko's eyes. He recalls the exact expression on the face of one victim: "His eyes
seemed to scream asking us why he had to be put through
this. He must have been in great pain."

Kurosawa selected this event and transposed it to represent his protagonist's own experience because it closely ap-
proximates the mock firing squad Dostoevsky faced in 1849,
at age twenty-eight. As have many biographers and critics,
Kurosawa locates in these minutes of mortal terror the well-
spring for Dostoevsky's powers of imagination and spirituality. In Myshkin's account, the prisoner first experiences utter
powerlessness and uncertainty, but he regains his spirit in the
face of the unknown by promising that should he be spared he
will treasure each moment of life. Yet soon afterwards, the survivor admitted to Myshkin, the vow was all but forgotten. In
the case of Myshkin himself as in that of Kameda, however,
life is subsequently measured with more acute awareness and
compassion.

A challenge for Kurosawa in adapting *The Idiot* was that
Dostoevsky is far more psychological than visual as a novelist. The key to its adaptation lay in the fact that Dostoevsky,
while inventing subjective complications in each character,
maintains a narrative method that discloses the naked human paradoxes linking characters together. Kameda's identification with the condemned man who is executed is indicative of the film's concern to convey profound emotional
recognition. Often Kurosawa places greater dramatic atten-

tion on the perception or recognition of suffering, corruption, and spirituality than on the raw experiences themselves. Of course, the dramatic codes of character reactions were already highly developed in the silent cinema of masters like Griffith, Lang, Dreyer, and Eisenstein that Kurosawa admired in the 1920s. Japanese culture is already deeply structured by indirect communication, or *haragei*. Encoded in traditional performance and visual arts, *haragei* refers there to a mutual understanding reached through nonverbal signs such as facial expression and posture, the unspoken disposition of a person.

A dramaturgy of exchanged regards gives visual structure and psychological texture to each scene. The resulting imagery of perception and recognition constitutes a great part of the film narrative. Once the two arrive in Sapporo by train, Akama leads Kameda through a blizzard to a shop window where a large photograph portrait of Taeko Nasu is displayed. In a shot composition that introduces a psychological complex of interrelationships, her photograph is centered and framed by their faces reflected by the shop window. Within this composition no one of the three is represented in person; it contains only a photographic replica of Taeko under the regard of the mirrored reflections of Akama and Kameda. She is manifestly the object of a masculine attention that has a disembodied quality. This quality is suggestive of the extent to which their identities are reflected in hers. During this shot Kameda does not take his eyes away from the photograph, while Akama divides his attention between it and Kameda in explaining that Taeko is the beautiful woman he had spoken of earlier. Kameda intuitively responds with tears to an image that in itself conveys no pain or sorrow. Such dramaturgy captures not only the regard of one character (here, Kameda) for another (Taeko), but also—for a third character (Akama)—the image of the regard in which the first character holds the second.

An early episode at the family home of Kayama, taken from the novel, indicates the extent to which the process of

perception is imbricated and multiple. With the unexpected
arrival of Taeko, she asks Kayama to introduce her to his family. Kayama first presents her to his sister Takako, who moments before had protested their marriage arrangements.
The sequence that depicts their introduction is only forty
seconds in duration, but it involves fourteen changes in composition and over twenty shifts in the look characters direct
toward one another. The shots it contains are all of a single
character in closeup except for one composition that groups
the three characters.

Compositional relations within this sequence can be indicated through the use of a few symbols: a character onscreen
is identified by the *italicized name*; ( ) bracket the character
off-screen who is being regarded; ← and → mean "in the direction of"; and the placement of → (the character off-screen) is
consistent with screen directionality from the audience's position. The sequence is constructed as follows:

1. (Taeko) ← *Takako*
2. *Taeko* → (Takako)
3. *Kayama* → (Takako), then → (Taeko) as she moves →
   (Takako); the camera pivots with *Kayama* as he
   moves between them, making a continuous transition
   to the next composition.
4. *Taeko, Kayama,* and *Takako* grouped together, as Kayama makes the curt introduction "My sister, Miss
   Nasu."
   Taeko → ← *Takako*, both seen in profile; in the middle, *Kayama* alternates his regard between ← and →
   as he is positioned frontally.
5. (Taeko) ← *Takako*
6. *Kayama* → (Takako), then (Taeko) ←
7. *Taeko* → (Takako)
8. (Taeko) ← *Kayama*, then → (Takako)
9. (Taeko) ← *Takako*
10. *Kayama* → (Takako), then (Taeko) ←
11. *Taeko* → (Takako)

12. (Taeko) ← *Takako*
13. *Taeko* → (Takako)
14. *Kayama* → (Takako), then (Taeko) ← and back → (Takako), finally he moves off-screen → his mother, standing behind Takako.

In their last exchange of regards (11, 12, 13) Taeko forms a smile; Takako responds with a fixed and blank expression; then Taeko's smile fades into a hard stare. A frown forms on Kayama's face as he looks back and forth at the two (14) until he attempts to break the tension by bringing his mother over to greet Taeko. Kayama is here principally a third party to the looks exchanged between Taeko and Takako and his face registers the shifts in judgment with which they regard one another. Kameda is present in the room through the duration of the sequence. While the exchange in regards is not anchored in Kameda's perspective in this case (he is glimpsed *behind* Kayama as the camera pivots in shot 3), the exchange circulates back to him by the dramatic climax to the scene in the Kayama household. The sequence's dramaturgy is not dependent on a single, internal narrative authority for the images. Rather, it is constructed along principles of intertextual dynamics, with each look a text to be read by the characters exchanging regards and read into the main characters who are on the scene but not within the exchange.

Kayama's introduction of Taeko to his mother does nothing to defuse tensions. Conflict in the household reaches its highest pitch with the arrival of Akama, who reasserts his romantic claim on Taeko. Finally, Kayama strikes Kameda, who has tried to stop the brother's attack on Takako. A montage of closeups articulates a spectrum of human response without a word being spoken: Kameda in emotional shock, Akama in rising anger, Taeko in stunned sympathy, Kayama's father Jyunpei drunkenly sentimental, and Kayama's younger brother Kaoru in tearful outrage. In the course of the scene at Kayama's, camera movement within the shot varies the purely visual dialogic response to a character's speech or behavior by regrouping the scene's ensemble of characters, by rearranging the geometry of their regards, or by reorienting the viewer's perspective on them.

Under the camera's prolonged gaze, a single face will often register multiple reactions. In response to Kameda's assurances to Taeko that at heart she is pure, a smile forces itself onto her face but within moments it retreats from the anguish that remains there. At Kurosawa's directions, some actors were encouraged to display unrehearsed emotions so that the camera could register a fresh reaction from another actor in the scene. This method was used to articulate reactions on Masayuki Mori's face in the role of Kameda. To another assurance Kameda makes in a later scene, Taeko responds with an outburst of laughter that brings to Kameda's face an expression by degrees surprised, puzzled, and gratified. In other contexts, closeups of Kameda show him visibly widen his glance as he attempts to penetrate compassionately into a person's inner spirit.

Akama's eyes often disclose an impassioned spirit divided between devotion and murderous hate. The scene of their exchange of personal charms concludes when Akama reenters his family home through an outer door, leaving Kameda on the street in the gathering darkness. After Kameda turns back in the direction of the house, there are four progressively closer views of Akama's eyes, taken along the same perpendicular axis at eye-level and in direct line with his gaze. Akama stares through a viewing slot in the door, commonly known in the West as a judas window. In the final shot his penetrating eyes alone are seen, in extreme closeup; the frame of the window is no longer visible. In a lap dissolve making the transition to the next sequence—of Kameda walking the city streets just prior to the attack by Akama— the image of these eyes remains for a moment superimposed over the first traveling shot of Kameda.

Kurosawa has categorized his adaptation of *The Idiot* as "a new kind of melodrama."[9] In the original, generic sense of a dramatic action put to music, the street scene comprises the film's most innovative and powerful audiovisual montage. It is representative of the collaboration with Fumio Hayasaka in relating sound to image as "mutual multipliers," well beyond the conventional illustrative uses of soundtrack effects (*Autobiography*, 108). Immediately prior to the opening of the street scene there is respite from the turmoil of Akama's alternations between love and hate. The attention of Akama and Kameda is directed toward Akama's mother by the prayer bell that has chimed steadily during their exchange of charms. They join her in the family's Buddhist chapel, where she serves tea and rice cakes as a traditional Japanese melody plays on a music box. When the men separate in front of the home the same theme is heard, rendered now through light organ music. Their brief tranquility is broken at the moment when Akama, overcome by intense anxiety, pledges Taeko to Kameda in guarding against his own violent impulses. The music has stopped by the point Akama speaks; after his pledge, dark chords by strings and brass rise on the soundtrack.

The extreme closeup on Akama's eyes marks the transition to a montage sequence that lasts over five minutes and is without any dialogue. The only words it contains are three brief sentences from Kameda's inner monologue, delivered in voice-over. The sequence's music starts with a steady, nervous drone of strings over which is heard the increasing harsh sound of bell chimes from draft horses on the streets. This ambient sound is replaced by a repetitive theme for muted brass. As Kameda's movements become harried, the music accelerates in tempo and other ambient noises come briefly into focus: a passing train, automobile traffic, a rail trolley, the confusion of voices in a marketplace, a city bus, a noisy car motor, the scrape of a snowplow across the roadway.

Kameda stops in a coffee shop to recover his senses, but his trembling hands make the cup chatter in its saucer, as an insistent tango or mambo tune plays in the shop. After resuming his aimless movement, Kameda stops on a pedestrian overpass when he senses danger and turns to see an unidentified figure at the other end. From a distance the figure resembles Akama in dress and posture but it is quickly obscured by bursts of vapor when a steam locomotive passes underneath, its whistle screaming. As Kameda's flight through the city continues, the initial musical theme is wound tighter in tempo and tone. At the point where the theme momentarily gives way to sharp, piercing notes on a piccolo, Kameda abruptly stops on the sidewalk and asks himself, "What was it? What did I see? What was it that shone?" He turns back a few paces to a shop window where cutlery is displayed, every blade on the shelves of knives pointed at him. The music track shifts to falling strings and piccolo notes. This image of an innocent shortly before a knife attack on his life ironically recalls and reverses a similar moment in Fritz Lang's *M* (1931), when the psychopath and child murderer stops in fascination before the knife display in a shop window.

Kameda's terrified flight takes him past the fantastic night-time shapes of giant ice sculptures for winter carnival and it finally returns him to the Kayama house. He enters the outer gate, panting in animal exhaustion, then the gate door slams behind him to reveal Akama standing in wait, a knife in hand. With an outburst of anguished cries Kameda falls into a seizure at the instant Akama begins to attack. Now Akama is terrified and in turning to flee he lunges into a gatepost, causing snow to crash down from the roof. With Akama's flight into the dark the film's first part, "Love and Suffering," concludes.

Another original dramatization through music comes in Kameda's account of the execution he faced. Without any visualization of the past, a sound flashback evokes the scene through the cadence of marching boots, a drumroll, and a trumpet signal. A night scene of the ice carnival is composed visually as a fantasia set to a soundtrack score from Mussorgsky's *A Night on Bald Mountain*. Many other uses of melodrama in *The Idiot*, however, are highly conventional by the standards of the film genre in the West at the time. Specific musical cues accompany the appearance of Kameda and

In *The Idiot*, the innocent Kameda pauses before a shop window, where his anxiety is reflected.

Akama, and the music baldly announces changes in emotional key. Violin strings and an airy vocal chorus provide the typical musical coloring to Kameda's emotions. The moment of his seizure is signaled by an otherworldly sound effect. With Akama the musical accompaniment often turns to deep, brooding, or menacing chords.

The film's characterizations entail as well visual analogies conventional in melodrama. Taeko is linked with fire in a number of scenes, and for Akama the visual analogy is to ice, frost, and driving snow. In conclusion to the scene in which Ono and his wife agree that Akama is capable of murder, there is a transitional cut to an exterior roof, from which piled snow suddenly slides and crashes to the ground. The next scene opens with Kameda's arrival outside the gate to Akama's house. To reach Akama's rooms, they walk through high embankments of snow and dark interior passageways that have nearly become ice caves in the cold. Taeko and Akama are associated with dark purposes in the emphasis on their black clothing and on nighttime settings or shadowed interiors, while Ayako and Kameda are associated with daylight and spacious, open environments.

In melodrama, personality is rendered along lines of extreme behavior and of situations that threaten total disaster or promise complete success. Its plots rely on accident, coincidence, and fortuitous or fatal chance to create spectacular and horrible events. Without question, some of these melodramatic qualities are evident in Dostoevsky's fiction. The Russian writer adapted genres of urban adventure, melodrama, and mystery fiction as a starting point for an exploration into the depths of human emotion and spiritual possibility. Plots in these genres involve extensive instability in the structures of personality, family, and society and thus further free the novelist from orthodox rationales.

The Kurosawa film in its abridged form is often reduced to broad melodramatic devices that bring simplification to character psychology and an intensification of affect. In such instances, the novel's paradoxes are reduced to one-dimensional antitheses. An introductory title flatly summarizes the film's thematic direction: "Dostoevsky, the author, wished to portray a truly good man. Ironically, he chose an idiot for his hero. But a truly good man may seem like an idiot to others. This is the tragic record of the ruin of a pure and simple man." But the alternatives of strength or weakness and purity or corruption, which in tragedy interpenetrate one another frequently, become static and isolated in the film.

The novel's chronology and narrative arrangement—Part One covers one day in late November, Parts Two through Four encompass about four weeks in the period of June and July the following summer—are compressed by the film into a continuous action covering some weeks in the winter months. This compression and the deletion of secondary events lessens the intertextual complex that links the fate of tragic characters like Myshkin with that of farcical ones like Ippolit.

The exchange of personal crosses symbolizes for Myshkin each individual's fundamental relation to Christ. In the Buddhist context of the film's adaptation of the scene, Kameda admits to Akama that he is not truly a religious man. Though his life is spared in the process, Kameda's seizure does not convey the sense of divine intervention that Myshkin attributes to it. In those moments of agony, Myshkin experiences an instantaneous *inner* light. They contain a higher synthesis of life for the sufferer and a horrifying spectacle for the witness, in direct analogy to the painting of Christ being lowered from the cross described elsewhere in the novel. The meaning of such seizures remains paradoxical for Myshkin, as it did for Dostoevsky: physical agony awakens the spirit.

The film regains the impact of Dostoevsky in rendering the final episodes in the emotional struggles of its four main characters. A prolonged silence, punctuated only by howling winds outside, greets Kameda and Ayako when they arrive at Akama's rooms, where Taeko has been staying for some time. Ayako has come with the intention to understand Taeko with the same compassion that Kameda holds for her. In anticipation of the meeting, Taeko has confessed to Akama that she imagines Ayako to possess an ideal female self.

Events in the room quickly devolve, however, into an outcome that reverses the expectations of the two women. To break the strained silence, Ayako addresses Taeko in a conciliatory manner. But Taeko holds Ayako in a measured, penetrating regard that deflects Ayako's initial intentions. Ayako's resentment surfaces and she accuses Taeko of selfishness and of cruel indifference to Kameda's well-being. When Ayako demands that Taeko should stop interfering in Kameda's life, Taeko reacts with sharp laughter, but her face is off-screen. Once her face is disclosed, no sign of laughter remains; instead there is hysteria. Taeko claims that where Kameda is concerned, pity and love are equivalent. She demonstrates this claim by first appealing to his compassion, while advising him to leave with Ayako. The next moment, Taeko reverses herself and she acts to coerce Kameda into a declaration of love. Terrified by his confusion of emotions, Ayako flees the room.

After Taeko has been murdered, Kameda returns to Aka-

The climactic meeting of Akama, Taeko, Kameda, and Ayako in
The Idiot.

ma's house for the last time. Curtains, freestanding screens, and lacework cast a patchwork of shadows around Akama when Kameda enters the room. No melodramatic accompaniment to the scene is provided on the soundtrack. Only the distant, ironic chime of the mother's prayer bell is heard. The camera tracks closer in on the two men, huddled together in a vigil for the slain Taeko. In the cold, candles are their only source of heat or light. Finally, the last candle flickers and gutters out. The individual of passionate brutality and the one of compassionate humanity are both driven mad.

For its concluding chapter, the novel gives a summary account of events in the months after the murder of Nastasya. Rogozhin recovers from temporary insanity to stand trial for the crime and he is sentenced to fifteen years penal servitude in Siberia. For information on Myshkin, the narrative is dependent on a report from Switzerland by Yevgeny Radomsky, an unsuccessful suitor to Aglaia. Early in the novel Radomsky is characterized as modern, intellectual, very wealthy, and European rather than Russian in his inclinations. In the end, Radomsky has left Russia in the belief that he is a "superfluous man" as far as his native land is concerned. His interest in Myshkin and the events of the novel are essentially intellectual rather than emotional or spiritual. By bringing an end to the story of Myshkin through such a distanced perspective, the novel persists in its dialogic examination of Russian beliefs.

The film provides a compassionate witness to Kameda's suffering through the words of Ayako, who recognizes a lost romantic and spiritual possibility with the loss of Kameda to madness: "If we could only live our lives just loving people like he did instead of hating all the time. . . . I must have really been crazy. I think I'm the one that is an idiot." The emotional identification and exemplary lesson provided through this conclusion function as the film's melodramatic coda. The novel, in contrast, leaves the reader with a disturbing recognition that the moral measure of humanity is contained in Myshkin's victimized innocence, which proves to be socially chaotic and psychologically destructive.

Kurosawa continued to develop intertexts that are affiliated with Dostoevsky's work long after the adaptation of *The Idiot*. In *Record of a Living Being* there is a paradoxical inversion in the standards of sanity and madness. A volunteer mediator in family court, a dentist by profession, becomes compassionately involved in the case of a foundry owner whose family tries to have him found legally incompetent. The industrialist is convinced that Japan faces imminent catastrophe from nuclear radiation and he has initiated measures to relocate his family, mistresses, and children to South America. The film story dramatizes the reactions among Japanese to nuclear testing in the Pacific conducted by Western powers in the postwar years. In the context of the industrialist's fears, common environmental features such as the roar of military jets or the gathering of dust clouds become menacing. The mediator starts to doubt the rationality of his own complacency as he gradually recognizes the dangers of weapon testing. The industrialist loses his sanity, however, after the family succeeds through the courts in declaring him incompetent.

In *High and Low* there is a troubled psychological affinity between a successful businessman and a murderer that has many counterparts in Dostoevsky. The medical drama *Red Beard* represents through scenes set in the outpatient waiting room and the wards of the clinic the same density, the same human *richness* of suffering and need to be found in the earlier films *Stray Dog, Drunken Angel, The Idiot, Ikiru,* and *The Lower Depths.* In adapting a Japanese novel for *Red Beard,* Kurosawa created the new character Otoyo, an adolescent girl rescued from a brothel by the public clinic's director. The character is deliberately modeled on the young victim Nellie, similarly spared from complete degradation in Dostoevsky's novel *The Insulted and the Injured* (1861). In both personalities an animal mistrust of humanity and a fierce independence have developed. The process of their rehabilitation is consequently slow and arduous, impeded by compulsive behavior and habits of self-torment. Both characters exhibit the egoism of suffering that fascinates their artistic creators. In the 1970s Kurosawa stated on several occasions his interest in an adaptation of *The House of the Dead,* Dostoevsky's account of convict life in a Siberian penal camp, but he could not attract producers with the project.

The Lower Depths

The Lower Depths by Maxim Gorky, first produced in 1902 by Constantin Stanislavsky's famous Moscow Art Theater, became one of the most prominent foreign plays in the repertory of Japan's *shingeki,* or "new drama" movement.[10] *Shingeki* was established by 1909, with the opening of the Free Theater (Jiyugekijo) in Tokyo. In effect, it served as a principal intertextual medium for the introduction of European realism and naturalism into Japanese drama and film. Japanese intellectuals during the Meiji period (1868–1912) of westernization and modernization were receptive to nineteenth-century utilitarian and determinist thought, and there was translation and broad discussion of John Stuart Mill, Charles Darwin, Herbert Spencer, and other materialists and positivists. But over the first decades of the Meiji era the dominant form of Japanese theater remained *kabuki*. In its highly stylized and codified conventions, kabuki presents theatricalization of emotion and an often illogical movement from climax to climax rather than psychological development. An attempt to bring historical accuracy and psychological realism to kabuki in the 1870s met with failure.

Shimpa, or "new style" drama, which had its greatest popularity in the years 1888–1905, arose from a need to stage drama in contemporary settings. Formulaic in manner, *shimpa* favored sensationalistic material and sentimental, romantic, and gothic styles. This movement brought women onstage for the first time in Japan, but the same production would often continue the traditional use of impersonators, or *onnagata*, in other female roles. At the turn of the century, Japanese literary critics began to promote the drama of Henrik Ibsen, and under his example several writers in Japan began to examine contemporary social issues in a realist and naturalist vein.

Director Kaoru Osanai, the most influential figure in the *shingeki* movement, staged Ibsen's *John Gabriel Borkman* in Tokyo, though with *onnagata*. Until its closure in 1919, Osanai's Free Theater introduced new Japanese plays and featured the work of European writers like Leo Tolstoy, Anton Chekhov, Maurice Maeterlinck, Gerhart Hauptmann, and Gorky. Osanai traveled through Western Europe and Russia in 1913, attending performances in the major cities, including those by the Moscow Art Theater. He staged Japanese productions of *The Lower Depths* in 1910 and again in late 1913, using his own detailed notes on the Stanislavsky production he had seen that year. This play's focused concern for the pathos of common humanity, familiar in Western theater since the Renaissance, was a novelty in Japanese theater.

In the 1920s Osanai enlarged his repertory and his acting

company, for which the Tsukiji Little Theater (Tsukiji Sho-
gekijo), seating an audience of 500, was built in Tokyo in
1924. The Little Theater in its first two seasons staged *The
Lower Depths*, Chekhov's *The Cherry Orchard* and *Three Sisters*, George Bernard Shaw's *Saint Joan*, and Georg Kaiser's
From Morn till Midnight in addition to plays by Romain Rol-
land, Ibsen, Arthur Schnitzler, and Maeterlinck. The Little
Theater gave new independence to the stage director and its
productions often featured innovations adapted from the
ideas of Gordon Craig, Vsevolod Meyerhold, and Max Rein-
hardt, directors who had transformed European theater.

Kurosawa frequented Osanai's theater in the 1920s and he
reports that "it was with the greatest wonder in my eyes that
I watched the performances" (*Autobiography*, 72). The innovations of *shingeki* would have lasting influence on Kurosawa's dramaturgy, design, and visual sensibility. Photographic
evidence of the Tsukiji Little Theater production of *The
Lower Depths* bears striking resemblance to the Kurosawa
film.[11] A short play written by Osanai, *The Trap Cellar* (*Na-
raku*, 1926) was also staged at the Little Theater. A drama of
the men who work in a theater below stage in a cramped and
darkened space, its action depicts a brotherhood characterized by labor, gambling, quarrels, and fights. The dramatic
situation reflects a further influence on Osanai from the
Gorky play.

Of all Japanese literary arts up to this point, *shingeki* went
the furthest in adopting western influences and discarding
national traditions. Effects of the *shingeki* movement were
quickly apparent in early Japanese cinema. The 1914 release
Katusha is based on a *shingeki* adaptation of Tolstoy's *Resur-
rection*, though female impersonators took the film roles. Another Tolstoy adaptation appeared in 1917 titled *The Living
Corpse* (*Ikeru Shikabane*) and directed by Eizo Tanaka, a
former student of Osanai. Traces of plays by Hauptmann and
Gorky are to be found in Japanese film stories of lower-class
life in the early 1920s.

In 1921 Osanai produced the film *Souls on the Road* (*Rojo no Reikon*), directed by Minoru Murata. One of the film's two storylines—the experience of two convicts wandering the countryside in search of shelter—is developed from an incident recounted by the pilgrim Luka in *The Lower Depths*. The film is episodic and plotless in structure, with most of its fictional events recorded in actual locales. From such origins, the Japanese film genre *shomin-geki* developed stories of lower-middle-class life with an emphasis on simple incidents and everyday atmosphere. The genre's conventions stress an economy of emotional means and a simplicity of situation instead of a theatrical acting style or elaborate plot mechanisms. Starting from the silent period, Mizoguchi, Ozu, and Naruse made *shomin-geki* with regularity. Mizoguchi was instrumental in developing the genre's capacity for detailed, photographic realism.

The Gorky play *The Lower Depths* is set in a Volga town at the end of the nineteenth century, with Russia under the tsar's rule. In transposing the action and characters to a Japanese context, Kurosawa changed the setting to late in the Edo era (1603–1868, named after the capital city Edo, which is present-day Tokyo). In explanation of the recontextualization, Kurosawa has stated: "Gorky's setting was Imperial Russia but I changed it to Japan, the Edo period. . . . During this period the Shogunate was falling to pieces and thousands were living almost unendurable lives. Their resentment we can still feel in the *senryu* and *rakushu* of the period. I wanted to reveal and show this atmosphere."[12] *Senryu* and *rakushu* are satirical poems and entertainments. Their techniques of wry observation and witty commentary contribute to the film's acid social observations.

In several respects Gorky created *The Lower Depths* as a countertext to Dostoevsky's *The House of the Dead*. Gorky condemned what he considered a false spiritualization of suffering and an ethics of meekness in the Dostoevsky canon. In Gorky's experience, pain and defeat are the outcome of mean lives, not a path toward redemption. When the Moscow Art Theater performed stage adaptations of the Dostoevsky novels *The Brothers Karamozov* and *The Devils* in the 1913 season, Gorky made public his outrage over the choice of material. Gorky's next plays, *The Zykovs* (1914) and *The Old Man* (1915), made more explicit the polemic against Dostoevsky and against the belief that pacifism is a form of godliness. Up to the time of his death in 1936, Gorky opposed the elevation of Dostoevsky to the status of a Russian master and denounced him for sentimental humanism, acquiescence in injustice, nonresistance to evil, masochism, and acceptance of Orthodoxy and tsarism.

For the plot of *The Lower Depths*, Gorky lays down an inexorable series of defeats, humiliations, losses, and deaths. The stage setting is a cheap lodging quarters, a basement room that contains a common living area and many plank beds. Its heavy vaulted ceiling is blackened by years of smoke from an old stove. In the opening act, the basement echoes with sounds of the lodgers' coughing, their complaints, oaths and bickering, and the locksmith Klestch's rasping files. With its dimness, dirt, and clamor, the place is like contemporary Russian society's primal cave or infernal underworld. Sickness, brutality, and death are inescapable in this environment. Anna, wife to Klestch, has coughing fits in the terminal stages of her illness. Some boarders expect the old landlord Kostylyov to die of natural causes in a short while, but they still encourage the thief Peppel to murder him.

The gambler Satin awakens bruised from the beating he took the night before, and the Actor rises convinced that he is in the final stages of alcohol poisoning. The Baron, who claims an aristocratic past, prepares to go to market with the dumpling peddler Kvashnya, who is thankful for the death of her husband and the end to years of his abuse. The landlord's wife Vassilissa regularly beats her younger sister Natasha. Peppel vows to die as a testament of his love for Natasha, but she rejects the pledge as a hollow pose. A refrain that runs through all of this is a comment that the capmaker Bubnov reiterates, "This thread is rotten."[13] In context, the remark is a cynical variant on the mythic analogy of the thread of life.

The theme of death is also comically registered. The drunken cobbler Alyoshka wants to play a funeral march on his accordion. The prostitute Nastya is enthralled by the story in her penny novel *Fatal Love*, while the Actor boasts of playing the role of gravedigger in *Hamlet*.

Luka, an old pilgrim, arrives at the lodging house and greets its inmates as "honest people" (*Lower Depths*, 15). To their snickers, Luka explains that all mankind is one and thus even the lowest person can deserve respect. The Baron, Vassilissa, and the policeman Medvedev challenge Luka to prove he is an honest citizen, but he has no official documents to verify his legal standing. In the face of the place's prevailing nihilism, Luka asserts the value of compassion. In the tenement there are small acts of kindness and moments of sympathy among the regular lodgers, though their effect proves transitory. Kvashnya gives a hot dumpling to Anna, who also receives a few words of sympathy from her husband. More often, however, Kvashnya and Klestch are impatient and harsh in their attitude toward her. To Anna, who is grateful for his kind attention, Luka explains that he is soft because life has put him through the wringer. It is this character note that led Kurosawa to comment: "To me, Luka is not really a good, honest person. I detect a dark side, probably something that happened to him in his past."[14]

Luka acts as a peacemaker among the quarrelsome lodgers and dispenses a form of hope in the assurance that "Whatever you believe in exists" (*Lower Depths*, 33). For Anna, he instills the hope that death will come soon and transport her to a realm free of suffering. When she dies shortly afterward, Bubnov is grateful that they are free of her incessant coughing. Even Vassilissa, who appears to have no soul, has needed the hope that Peppel will free her from her miserable marriage to Kostylyov. But Peppel's hopes, encouraged by Luka, are that he can live as an honest man in marriage to Natasha. A timely interruption by Luka prevents Peppel from harming Kostylyov once, but not a second time. To the Actor, hope comes in the form of finding a clinic to cure his alcoholism.

To the prostitute Nastya, it comes in Luka's willingness to believe her story of a great lost love.

Occupants of the lodging house cannot detect a selfish
motive in Luka's kindness and thus are at a loss to explain it.
Luka's account of two escaped convicts clarifies his humanitarian motives. Driven by hunger, the men are capable of
murder. Fed, they prove to be kind and trustworthy. Invoking
the example of Christ, Luka believes in the power of individual acts of goodness in the reformation of mankind. But the
effect of Luka's teaching is tenuous, temporary, and finally
paradoxical. In another account, a parable really, Luka tells
of a poor man's search for "the true and just land" (*Lower
Depths*, 48). Belief in the existence of such a land was the
only comfort in his life. When told by a scholar that the land
cannot be located in the known world, the poor man knocked
the scholar down, returned to his quarters, and hung himself.

Two alternatives to existence at the lower depths are posed
by Luka: persistence in the search for a belief that will relieve
human suffering, or hopelessness. Luka tells the others that
he is ready to resume his wandering, now in the direction of
the Ukraine, where a new faith is reported to have taken root.
Given the sequence of events in the plot, as an embodiment
of hope Luka leads a fugitive and illicit existence. Under his
coaxing, Peppel and Natasha agree to leave and make a new
life together. But then Vassilissa makes a vicious attack on
Natasha in the landlord's house. In the chaos that ensues,
Peppel strikes Kostylyov and the landlord dies. Natasha turns
against Peppel, accusing him of conspiring with Vassilissa in
murder. Afraid that authorities will call him as a witness,
Luka slips away at the first sign of serious trouble.

In the last act, characters report that Natasha has disap-
peared and that Vassilissa and Peppel will stand trial for
murder, with the probable result that the wife will go free
and the thief will be sentenced for manslaughter and sent to
Siberia. The lodgers' conversation touches as well on the
power of religious law, whether it be Muslim or Christian,
and it raises for the theater audience the question of the exis-

tence of any universal human laws or values. For the gambler Satin, the hope Luka promoted is a falsehood designed for weak people. After indulging in a drunken impersonation of Luka's wisdom, Satin offers in its place the pragmatic axiom "Everything in man, everything for man" (*Lower Depths*, 68). Events quickly demonstrate that his axiom is not humanitarian in spirit.

Alcohol and squabbles continue to divert lodgers from their individual miseries. Klestch has sold his tools to pay for Anna's burial and has exchanged his pride as a craftsman for idleness and alcohol. Kvashnya has assumed the duties of landlord and has taken as her companion Medvedev, who has lost his official position and now fraternizes with these social outcasts. In the course of the night's drinking party, the Actor asks a Muslim working man to pray for him, then departs into the cold darkness. Minutes later, just as lodgers begin to sing, the Baron arrives to announce that the Actor has hung himself in the vacant lot outside. Satin's deadpan response "Ah, spoiled the song—the fool!" stands as the play's curtain line (*Lower Depths*, 73).

The play presents a dialogic set of responses to the problems of suffering and evil and to the issue of whether the problems themselves are social or spiritual in origin. Through Peppel and Klestch are voiced the view that well-being is a privilege and conscience is a luxury of the owning classes. Though Luka prays to Christ and is a religious pilgrim, his teaching is more secular than spiritual in its intentions. It proposes an ethic of common sense and mutual kindness in relieving the burdens of existence for the poor. The true and just land is only to be found within a person's heart, and even then it is no guarantee of truth or justice for others or for oneself over a lifetime. The power of belief and hope is itself a truth, but one that does not assure any material transformation in the conditions of human life. In the case of the Actor, the grain of hope that a charity hospital will cure him of alcoholism proves lethal once he suspects that no such hospital exists.

Luka's piety and oaths to Christ are primarily social data.

By comparison, Dostoevsky offers a testament of faith in *The House of the Dead*. The Christmas holiday portrayed in the novel spiritually revives even the most hardened prisoners in the penal camp. Their awe and respect for the season's religious significance bring peace and dignity into their lives, if only for a few hours. Though other prisoners return to their indifferent and cruel ways, Dostoevsky's narrator regains faith in the potential for mankind's moral transformation.

The Lower Depths leads to a contrary conclusion, that the final measure of truth is social. Even if it is spoken by the defeatist Satin in an episode of drunken bravado, the principle that "Only man exists, the rest is the work of his hands and his brain" underpins debate in the play about human fate as an inclusive, material, and historically determined truth (*Lower Depths*, 68). This early play defers the message of social revolution found in many of Gorky's other works.

In the decision to film *The Lower Depths*, Kurosawa readdresses issues of goodness and spirituality pursued in his adaptation of *The Idiot* and issues of a socially unimportant individual's responsibilities and potential explored in *Ikiru*. The return to these issues is reflective of his intertextual filmmaking, and the 1957 film marks shifts in dramatic conception, visual treatment, and ideological position on these matters. The film production of *The Lower Depths* began with rehearsal in full costume and makeup on a complete set for a period of forty days before any footage was taken. Director, assistants, and crew worked steadily on lighting, composition, and the camera's movements during the cast's preparation on the same set. Once the cameras began shooting, Kurosawa applied a directorial method based in a precept of the fifteenth-century Noh master Zeami, that of "watching with a detached gaze." Kurosawa has interpreted the precept as follows: "Watching something does not mean fixing your gaze on it, but being aware of it in a natural way" (*Autobiography*, 195). As practiced in the direction and editing of *The Lower Depths*, this principle differs greatly from the dramaturgy of exchanged regards that structures *The Idiot* and from the funeral debate in *Ikiru* over the meaning of Watanabe's last active months of life.

Visual compositions under the film's opening credits give an initial perspective *from* the lower depths. From the bottom of a ravine, the perspective is up toward its slopes and rim as the camera pans gradually and nearly completes a full circle. Looking up and out at the respectable, free world for the only sustained interval in the film story, even this perspective is narrow and brief. Glimpsed is a solid wall and ornamental roofs suggestive of a temple; the resonating gong from a heavy cast-metal bell is heard. Two workers above dump trash into the ravine while commenting that the place below is no different from a junkyard. Transition to a lower perspective shows this trash landing on the roof of a lodging house. This ramshackle tenement is similar to the *nagaya* or "long house" of the period, a narrow and low structure partitioned into many small living spaces under the same roof. Residents of a *nagaya* were commonly described as "leaning upon one another's shoulders" in their cramped environment. The communal spirit in the film's environment, however, is incidental and transitory.

In the course of the characters' conversations, the lodging house is referred to as hell, as a grave, and as a world inhabited by vipers, vermin, devils, and demons. Departure from this underworld is possible in only three forms. In the case of the thief Sutekichi, his fate will be imprisonment. (A full cast of characters from the play and the film is provided in the Film Characters section at the back of this book.) Disappearance is the means of escape for the wanderer Kahei and and the landlady's sister Okayo. Death brings the departure of the tinker's wife Asa and the landlord Rokubei. With her husband's death, the landlady Osugi is freed from a bitter marriage and, the lodgers predict, she will be shortly released by the authorities who detain her. Suicide is the Actor's means of departure. Temporary escape *within* the environment comes through drink, ridicule, and cynical laughter.

Inside their quarters, broken screens, partitions, and cur-

The gambler Yoshisaburo in *The Lower Depths* at his sleeping
berth while the Actor, above him, remains behind a curtain.

tains barely separate people from one another and from the
harsh elements. When the thief listens unwillingly to Osugi,
who is encouraging him to kill her husband, they are spied
upon by Rokubei through the tattered paper covering of a sliding door. Walls to the flophouse are reinforced by heavy exterior beams, while the walls to the landlord's quarters only a
few feet away are freestanding. Coughs, gasps, scraping metal, and the clatter of sliding doors and windows incessantly
punctuate the tenants' world.

Events in the lodging house follow the same order and division into four "acts" as in the play. The film's act divisions
are marked by a gradual fade out to black and fade into the
next sequence of events. The act divisions are the only occasions in which this optical process is used. For the rest of the
film, editing devices are distilled down to the simple cut and
the reframing that results from camera movement. Physical
properties of the setting—sliding doors and windows, cur-

tains, bedding—serve as a kind of editing device for the disclosure and concealment of characters within the film's dramatic space.

The method of "watching with a detached gaze" is conveyed in dialogue scenes by the indirect regards among characters. The quality of detachment is compounded by oblique camera perspectives on the characters in conversation, who are often positioned with their backs to the camera, and by conspicuous alterations in the camera's position during dialogue scenes. In the course of early sequences, for example, Tomekichi is seen from the front, one side, the back, and the other side.

An exchange between the thief and the tinker on the subject of work exemplifies the film's qualities of detachment. Using the directional symbols already explained, with the addition of vertical directional signals, the sequence can be summarized as follows, with the understanding that all of the frequent and subtle shifts in regard cannot be tabulated in this schematic form. The first composition indicated is the concluding half of a complex sequence shot that contains previous dialogue and character movement:

1. *Sutekichi* ← *the Actor* ← *Yoshisaburo,* all seated in background

$$\downarrow$$

   seated in foreground: ← *Tomekichi*
   —As the thief gives some coins to the actor and the gambler, ← *Sutekichi* ← *the Actor* ← *Yoshisaburo:* "We can't do without thieves."

$$\uparrow$$

   Tomekichi
   —In the course of the complaint by Tomekichi, "They make money, but they don't work for it," ← *Tomekichi* and he resumes scraping a metal pot.
   —With Yoshisaburo's reply, "If sweat and toil would help, I'd willingly work," the regards shift again:

Sutekichi   *the Actor*   *Yoshisaburo*
               (looking downwards)

↓   ↓

← *Tomekichi*

— As Yoshisaburo's reply continues, "But I know differently," ← *Yoshisaburo* and he begins to stand up. His
next remark, "Actor. Let's have a drink" is met with
the *Actor* →, and the two get up. In leaving, the Actor
responds in a comically mannered voice, "A drink is
always welcome."

— With the departure of Yoshisaburo and the Actor, the
composition has changed to:

   Sutekichi, looking down and stirring the small fire
in the floor hearth

← *Tomekichi*, scraping louder on the pot

— *Sutekichi* looks up to ask, "How is your wife?" and as
Tomekichi grunts in response but without looking
over at him, *Sutekichi* turns his body ninety degrees
to his left, to lean his back against a support and face
a wall.

2. Close shot of *Sutekichi* with his back to the camera;
he turns his head slightly in several directions without focusing his regard. No dialogue.

3. Close shot of *Tomekichi* seen directly from the front;
he is bent intently over the pot on which he works.
No dialogue.

4. From same camera position as 2, close shot of *Sutekichi* → (Tomekichi): "You persevere. But I don't think
you'll get anywhere." His head turns back to face the
wall as he ends this statement.

5. From same camera position as 3, close shot of *Tomekichi*, who continues to look down: "What should I
do then?"

6. From same camera position as 2, close shot of *Sutekichi*: "Nothing."

7. From same camera position as 3, close shot of *Tome-*

kichi, looking down as he reaches for another scraper: "Then I'd starve."

8. From same camera position as 2, close shot from the back, *Sutekichi:* "No one is starving here." Flames in the floor hearth are visible.

9. From same camera position as 3, close shot of *Tome-kichi,* looking down: "I'm [a] craftsman. I'm not like those idlers." As he finishes this statement (Suteki-chi) ← *Tomekichi.*

10. From same camera position as 2, close shot of *Suteki-chi* → (Tomekichi). No dialogue.

11. From same camera position as 3, close shot of (Sute-kichi) ← *Tomekichi,* putting down the pot for the first time: "Do you think I'll ever get out of this dump?" Leaning further (Sutekichi) ← and turning his body to face the thief more fully, he continues: "I'll get out . . . even if I have to crawl." *Tomekichi* returns to his frontal position and takes up the pot again as he says, "Wait till my wife dies . . ." His head bends down to resume the mending, then abruptly he looks around the flophouse as he muses, "I've only been here six months, but it seems like six years." He spits in disgust →.

12. From same camera position as 2, close shot of *Suteki-chi* → (Tomekichi); he pivots his body to face → fully: "You talk as if you were better than me. Well, you're not!"

13. From same camera position as 3, close shot of (Sute-kichi) ← *Tomekichi,* then he turns his attention downward to resume work.

14. From same camera position as 2, close shot of *Suteki-chi* → (Tomekichi), his body still facing in that direction. His attention is next directed slightly toward the front by the gentle sound of a bell.

Shot 14 makes a transition to new dramatic action with the arrival of Kahei, brought into the lodging quarters by Okayo. Kahei appears to be a pilgrim or an itinerant priest.

For the duration of the interaction between Tomekichi and other lodgers just detailed, responses are deflected and attention is displaced with great frequency. Sutekichi's kindhearted inquiry into the condition of Asa is met with a brusque sign of disregard from Tomekichi. As a consequence, the only direct exchange of regards between the two men comes in their assertions of self-importance and hostility. It is evident from the routines of starting their day in the opening scene that bickering and mockery are vital elements in the social bond among tenants. A later instance is revealed by the expectation of cheating as a regular part of their card games.

In the film as in the Gorky original, the ensemble effect in characterization and composition is thorough. That is to say, there is no protagonist: in the dramatic action no single character remains either the motivating cause or emotional center of events. The film's dramaturgy consists in a succession of brief interactions and visual correlations between characters. Toshiro Mifune, in the role of Sutekichi, was a major Japanese film star by this point in his career, but his character is not given dramatic priority nor is the visual treatment reoriented because of his casting. In many scenes Mifune delivers lines with his back toward the camera, as in an impersonation of a subservient man testifying before a court judge, a marvelously vivid segment of acting that the film viewer can only partially glimpse.

Within the film's complete ensemble effect, characters are often an audience and witness to one another's dramas. As audience, they alternate between interest and indifference. During a conversation, additional characters may suddenly emerge from behind doors, sleeping curtains, or quilts to listen or speak and, as suddenly, retreat behind them again. Silent characters frame speaking ones and constitute a human architecture to dramatic events. This effect is universalized in one brief sequence when a number of tenants are seen filing through the passage between the landlord's quarters and the flophouse. These anonymous individuals do not enter the dramatic action, but their brief presence indicates a greater human scope to the events dramatized.

The film consistently provides a larger human context for each individual's experience, though humanity will not finally shield the individual from pain and defeat. In the foreground of one shot within an early sequence of the second act, the police agent Shimazo is playing checkers with the bucket-maker Tatsu. In the course of their game Tatsu half-turns to listen to Kahei in the background talk with Asa, who is just out of view in the shot composition. A subsequent shot shows a reverse field of this composition, with Kahei now prominent in the foreground as he comforts Asa with the promise that death will end her suffering. Shimazo turns for a moment to focus on the pilgrim's words. In the course of the two shots, at the moment one player becomes attentive to this conversation, the other player gains the advantage in their game.

Often there is a dichotomy between the visuals and the dialogue heard on the soundtrack. In one instance, while we see Tatsu and Sutekichi, a loud, crude chant suddenly begins from somewhere immediately off-screen. The next shot cuts to a point of view further back, revealing Kahei in the lower right foreground of the new composition. In another example, the bucket-maker and the gambler are seen onscreen, and the Actor has just drawn his sleeping curtain, while over the noise of scraping metal the film audience hears Asa tell Tomekichi to eat the sweet given her by the peddler. In continuation of this shot the camera tracks back and pivots to recompose the image, now centered on Tomekichi and Asa. For a moment the tinker is reassuring to his wife, then he leaves to consume the sweet alone. From a high angle just outside the flophouse, the camera follows his movement to a corner of the ravine's walls. With a shot change, the camera is at ground level and at some distance from Tomekichi as he slowly eats in the stony, barren surroundings. The only sound is the hard crunch of his teeth on the confection; the expression on his face is animal and vacant.

In the course of the first act, the camera and editing register the inconsequential and often absurd efforts of characters. Minutes after her husband Tomekichi ignores Asa's choking plea for fresh air, the Actor leads her outside with the hope that despite the cold they will find a spot of sunshine for her. Some time later, Tomekichi is told to bring his wife inside. He answers that Okayo has taken her into the kitchen, where it is warm. In doing so, Okayo risks the anger of Osugi and Rokubei. Next, Okayo advises Tomekichi to retrieve Asa from the kitchen, but he ignores the warning. Kahei eventually brings her back to the common quarters, having found her outside alone. When he advises Asa not to go out into the cold unattended, she complains that she was callously "thrown out" (a comment not made in the play).

In the initial action of this absurd circle of exits and entrances, the Actor gestures and sings as if on the kabuki stage when he takes Asa out for fresh air. His theatrical manner suggests the stylizations of the *shinju* (love suicide), a favorite subject on Bunraku and kabuki stages. In leaving the lodging house, the Actor and Asa encounter the landlord Rokubei, who comments sourly, "You make a fine couple . . . a pair of love birds." The Actor tells Rokubei to stand aside and announces, "This is a grand exit before the final curtain." As he escorts Asa away, the Actor assumes a theatrical posture and delivers a stage melody. The irony of the reference to *shinju* is that each of these three characters will die in the film drama — the Actor a suicide, Asa by natural causes, and Rokubei by manslaughter. This brief scene is the only moment all three are brought directly together. Theirs are the only deaths within the film and not one of them will be granted a grand exit.

As Kahei helps make Asa comfortable in her spot on the floor, she explains the fight between Osugi and Okayo that can be heard outside by saying, "It's just [that] they are too healthy. They always get enough to eat." In reply to her grat-

itude for his kindness, Kahei describes himself as a humble
man, "like a pebble in the river washed down from the mountain and polished smooth all over." (The change from Luka's
self-description in the play at this moment suggests an intertext with the pebble Kameda grasps after he has been spared
execution in the film *The Idiot*.) The landlady Osugi takes
Kahei's prayer bell as security during his stay in the lodging
house. The members of the "respectable" class and their
agent—the landlord, the landlady, and the policeman—immediately suspect Kahei of a criminal past.

In the second act, Osugi enters the flophouse and orders
Kahei out so that she can be alone with Sutekichi, but Kahei
remains inside, undetected. Only Asa is knowingly left inside, and she may be dead by this point since her coughing is
no longer heard. Asa is, at any rate, already considered nonex-
istent by many of the others, including Osugi. In the course
of Osugi's attempts to lure Sutekichi into a murder plot
against her husband, their physical movements and the editing combine to shape a series of reversals. From the initial position (again, schematically)

Osugi   Sutekichi, she pulls him around:
Sutekichi   Osugi, then he moves nervously back to the
other side of her.

This figure of Osugi's efforts to ensnare Sutekichi and of his
withdrawal is reiterated two more times in the sequence.

The film's detachment and mobility in visual perspective
creates an effect of emotionally distancing the viewer from
each character and, in pronounced instances, of paradoxically
negating a character's presence. Off-screen noises and words
and the sudden emergence or disappearance of characters
create a dimension of absent space in the film. In other cases,
the visual field can become empty of animate expression. In
the second act, Tomekichi starts to leave for relief from the
noises and sight of his wife's suffering. As he faces the door,
his motionless back fills a shot composition prolonged beyond the natural duration of such a pause in his movement.

**The landlady Osugi attempts to entangle the thief Sutekichi in
The Lower Depths.**

After Kahei intervenes and prevents Sutekichi from reck-
lessly attacking the landlord, the two discover that Asa has
died. The only fear that the thief is shown to experience
comes with her death. They leave the quarters and the camera, aimed in the direction of the doorway, dwells on the
empty room for many seconds. The only sounds heard are
made by a violent wind, which groans and whips through tattered screens and broken boards, and by an unidentified voice
from afar. The shot is literally a quietus; it captures a palpa-
ble absence from the living. Then the Actor returns from a
binge. Having finally remembered the lines from a kabuki
monologue, he drunkenly recites them. Though he thinks
Kahei is somewhere in the room, unknowingly his only audience is the dead, until Okayo arrives. After her discovery of
the body, other lodgers return. Tatsu's only reaction is to comment, "We won't have to hear that coughing anymore," before he falls asleep.

The third act is set outside the flophouse, but even there

the inhabitants are hemmed in by buildings, retaining walls, timber supports, and the ravine's cobbled slopes. In a remarkable opening shot, which continues unbroken for over six and a half minutes, Osen's fictionalized confession of lost love is met with sympathy from Kahei and Okayo, with amused disbelief by Tatsu and the Samurai, and with silence from Tomekichi, who is nearly concealed in background shadows. Osen's sentimental tale and a set of responses ranging from compassion to insults unfold seamlessly in this sequence shot. In the brief silences, a chant from the temple above is distinctly heard. The spatial relations among characters remain static and unchanged for over the first three minutes in the shot. Its compositional balance is broken when Osen rushes at the Samurai, incensed over his ridicule, and the camera pivots to capture the sudden disturbance.

With the priest's steady encouragement, Sutekichi pleads with Okayo to leave and make a new life with him. The sequence is developed through a visual figure of *impediment* to their love. When his plea starts, both Sutekichi and Okayo are seen to one side of a heavy supporting timber that cuts diagonally across the composition. From this initial figure — or, schematically, \\ Sutekichi   Okayo — the principal variations that follow after she makes her first objection are:

Sutekichi \\ Okayo
Okayo \\ Sutekichi
Okayo \\ [empty]

When Okayo finally agrees, the two embrace, but their joined bodies are half-blocked from view by the beam in front of them. This shot is thus an incomplete and ambiguous resolution to the visual figure of impediment and separation. Their embrace is short-lived as well. It is broken when they hear the bitter laughter of Osugi, who has eavesdropped on them.

Events that take place just outside the flophouse lead to a sudden, chaotic conclusion with the death of Rokubei. An omen of his end appears when the landlord is alone for a moment, after talking with the pilgrim. Above him a crow

Sutekichi's efforts to persuade Okayo to leave with him are obstructed by the environment in *The Lower Depths.*

caws in its flight, and around him dead leaves are stirred by
a sudden wind. Soon after, tenants enter the landlord's house
in trying to protect Okayo from another beating. They destroy some of his property and attack him. Sutekichi arrives
to find Okayo scalded on the leg. In going to her aid, he
pushes Rokubei roughly aside, an act far less violent than the
one the thief commits in the play. In fact, Rokubei's death
occurs as a fatal accident that kills as well all hope of love
between Sutekichi and Okayo. When Osugi announces that
her husband is dead, she accuses Sutekichi of murder. Okayo
becomes hysterical and makes accusations of conspiracy
against her sister and the thief. The third act closes with her
terrified screams and her outcry, "Arrest them. . . . Arrest
me, too!"

The fourth act opens with general agreement among the
tenants present that the old man Kahei had been kind, clever, and decent. But the cynicism, ridicule, and arguments
among them persist. To the Samurai's dissenting opinion

that Kahei was a fraud, the gambler explains, "His lies were to encourage those who cannot be cured." The gambler continues with an impersonation of the old man's chants and one of his teachings on the need for acceptance of fellow humans. The teaching is immediately violated by a heated argument between the Samurai and Osen that ends with the prostitute screaming "I'll kill myself" as she runs out into a rainstorm. In the background, the Actor can be seen staring blankly ahead as she departs.

The gambler has a bitter laugh over his own temporary lapse into kindness, which the Samurai attributes to *sake*. The Actor, in a disturbed state of mind, drinks deeply from the *sake* bottle and leaves. As in the play, the peddler has married the police agent Shimazo thinking she would profit from his official power. Though she has gained control over the flophouse and lives in the landlord's quarters, her new husband has lost his position and has taken to drink. She arrives to retrieve Shimazo, who is wearing her coat. To the tenants' general amusement, she defends herself against the gossip young Unokichi has spread. Her situation and behavior reiterate, though in a good-humored tone, that of the landlady Osugi in the first act.

In their drunkenness the tenants inside are in animated spirits. They begin a satiric song about a poor man's prayers for money. A similar song had been taken up by the gamblers at the start of the second act but it soon stopped with the bitterness of one player over his losses and an argument about cheating. Now, four tenants join in a grotesquely comic dance as the song continues. They are interrupted by the entrance of the Samurai, who starkly announces that the Actor has killed himself outside. In the speechless room, only the sound of heavy rain is heard. The brief diversion has done nothing to alter their dispirited environment. After a moment's reflection, the gambler summarizes bluntly: "He died . . . to spoil the fun. Fool."

Indeed, the drunken song has been a rare sustained experience of mutual pleasure in the film, even while the celebrants' joy seems somewhat forced. The gambler's face contains a disheartened, deadened expression. His words and his facial expression invite a range of readings, one of which points to the futility both of the Actor's self-destruction and of their own temporary escape from misery. At the instant the gambler's terse remark is completed, dramatic action is cut off by the Japanese character for "The End," displayed in white against a black screen. The end title is held only a few seconds. One stroke from the wood clapper traditional in kabuki marks a complete termination; there are no closing credits.

Thematic interpretation of the Gorky play typically attempts to resolve a debate between acceptance of life in all its cruelty and without illusion or acceptance of hope, however illusory, to alleviate life's cruelty. The play does not function, however, as a moral debate. Luka is the voice of a radical humanitarian ethic: "If a man hasn't done somebody good, he's done him ill" (*Lower Depths*, 32). Explicitly, Luka's inspiration is in the social teaching of Christ, particularly the messages of *caritas* and hope for the least of humanity. Luka is not so much a True Believer or a believer in truth as he is one who believes in the human need for belief. The possibilities for belief are infinite. For a person like Anna, it may be the comfort of death itself, independent of all matters of salvation. For one like the Actor, it is the possibility of a cure for his alcoholism. For the thief, it is a future with Natasha, free of criminality. Satin's drunken assertion that a strong man can live without faith or illusions is his form of belief and an illusion of strength. The failure of many hopes within events of the play may not disprove the need for hope, but it demonstrates that hope alone does not change conditions in the lowliest lives.

The Japanese characters prominent on the back of Kahei's robe refer to the "sacred ground Sakamoto" and identify him as the follower of a religious sect. Kahei's principles bear some resemblance to beliefs in the Jodo Shinshu ("True Pure Land") sect, which has had followers since the twelfth century. This Buddhist sect is distinctive in its tolerance toward worldliness and its emphasis on the primary power of faith rather than social prominence or good works. Sincere devotion itself can empower a follower to reach paradise, even in the case of a wicked past. With a doctrine of transcendence outward to Buddha's Western Paradise, which gives hope to the common people, the sect has for centuries had great popular appeal at the bottom strata of Japanese society. But in the film there is finally less of a spiritual context for the pilgrim's beliefs than in the play. While Luka leaves the flophouse in search of another school of faith, Kahei leaves simply in search of "a better place."

Though the film retains the statement of the pilgrim's humanitarian ethics, it does not retain the social and psychological clarification of his principles provided in the play through stories like that of the two convicts or of "the true and just land." With less explanation of the social roots of crime, or of the power of lost hope to destroy humanity, destructive events in the film seem more inexplicable and meaningless. In place of the play's indirect indictment of a class-divided society, the film confronts its audience with an *absurd* world, in an existential sense. From this perspective, existence — no matter how brutal — is the sole manifestation of human essence, without any guarantee of transcendence beyond the conditions of existence.

Along with the *shingeki* movement and the Gorky play, another direct intertext to Kurosawa's *The Lower Depths* is the Sadao Yamanaka film *Humanity and Paper Balloons* (*Ninjo Kamifusen*, 1937). Yamanaka was a director with P.C.L. studio when Kurosawa began his apprenticeship there. He was killed in 1938, at age twenty-nine, while serving with the Japanese army in China. In his autobiography, Kurosawa places Yamanaka among directors "I revere as teachers" (*Autobiography*, 56). *Humanity and Paper Balloons* is a work of genius remarkable in its views on samurai culture, in narrative method, and in its screen geometry. In each regard, Kurosawa learned a great deal from this master film text and the lessons are apparent in many Kurosawa films.

A *jidai-geki, Humanity and Paper Balloons* is based loosely
on a play by the kabuki dramatist Mokuami Kawatake, who
was immensely successful in the Meiji period. Though Yamanaka and his scenarist Shintaro Mimura worked with material common to the spectacle and action genres on stage and
in film, they avoided predictable generic conventions. With
the material, Yamanaka and Mimura pursued instead their
own contemporary psychological and social interests. In place
of the nostalgia typical with such subject matter, their film
offers a modern, critical view of the past.

Humanity and Paper Balloons is set in the late Edo period
in a tenement block within a poor working-class section of
the city. An open sewer is the first feature of this setting depicted onscreen. The suicide, by hanging, of a local *ronin* is
reported in the first scene. The *ronin* had been unable to commit suicide the honorable way, through disembowelment,
because in the desperation caused by poverty he had sold his
swords for rice. In gathering to commemorate the dead *ronin,*
the tenement dwellers turn the occasion into revelry and
join in drunken music, song, and dance. The same irrever-
ence toward death is expressed with frequency in Kurosawa's
The Lower Depths.

Another *ronin* lives in the tenement block with his wife,
who earns a meager income by assembling paper balloons.
Though the *ronin* bears the customary short and long swords,
their blades are never drawn. The reported incident from the
film's first scene leaves a clear implication that this impoverished *ronin* has sold his metal sword blades and that his
sword handles are now attached to bamboo shafts. If this situation were exposed, it would be a mark of profound shame.
Throughout the film story he remains a samurai in name
and appearance only for he is unable, after persistent and hu-
miliating attempts, to secure a position with a *daimyo* (lord).
In pursuing a potential patron, the *ronin* behaves in a servile
manner.

The setting and dramatic circumstances are devoid of the
sentimental, cultured charm traditionally associated with

the Edo period in Japanese society. The tenement's other inhabitants are vendors, tradesmen, and artisans. The alleyway that runs through the tenement quarters is a stage for their otherwise anonymous dramas. In narrative structure the Yamanaka film shares with Kurosawa's *The Lower Depths* a decentered, ensemble effect. In both film texts, no single protagonist organizes the narrative action, whose trajectory is more circular than linear.

Another tenement dweller, an immediate neighbor to the *ronin*, runs a gambling operation that puts him in trouble with the men who control such activities in the district. This man kidnaps the daughter of a pawnbroker, then enlists the aid of the *ronin* in hiding her. Rather than necessary or destined, the *ronin*'s connection with these events is chance and circumstantial. The connection proves fatal nonetheless. After the kidnapping plot unravels, the neighbor is hunted down by his enemies. In the face of further loss to his dignity as a samurai, the *ronin*'s wife kills him in his drunken sleep and then commits suicide. These events bring the film story full circle and its concluding image depicts one of her paper balloons, now floating on the surface of the tenement's open sewer.

The film's scenic geometry and connection of shots is inventive. The tenement quarter is depicted from two distinct perspectives. One perspective is external, from a public street onto which a few shops and a *sake* bar face. The other is from within a crowded tenement alley where the living spaces are located. Unseen from the street, the alley is reached by a short passageway that leads there. At points the film links the two perspectives by depicting a continuous action that passes from alleyway to street, or vice versa. Within a given sequence, the film sustains great variety through clever and unexpected shot changes. It also explores visual resources in marking scene transitions. One gradual lap dissolve, for example, is patterned as a soft wipe cut leading from an open city setting in daytime to the cramped alley at night.

Tadao Sato values *Humanity and Paper Balloons* as a "tragic

masterpiece": "There is a rejection of heroism for a philosophy in which strength is juxtaposed with gentleness. This
was not an inherited artistic tradition."[15] Donald Richie
identifies Yamanaka as central to the development of a distinct Japanese film genre, "the serious period film in which
history is presented with complete realism and the present is
criticized in the context of the past."[16] Yamanaka's profound
interrogation and reinterpretation of Japan's Edo era, which
was conventionally the source of a picturesque and mythic
heroism, established a process of demystification and social
critique to be found also in period films directed by Mizoguchi and Kurosawa. The pathos and pessimism that merge in
Yamanaka's view of the past have strong affinities with the
perspectives on history in Kurosawa's *jidai-geki*.

3

Modernist Narrative and Intertextuality

Kurosawa identifies narrative as the essential principle in his filmmaking. He considers narrative his best means as a film artist to make an intervention into modern reality, while ethical or political perspectives, in themselves, would not have as effective an impact on mass audiences. A Kurosawa film often starts abruptly with a scene, or sometimes simply an image, that is an amalgam of the narrative to come. In explanation of this practice, he has stated: "The opening is 'dramatic,' it announces a story. I have a subject, I enrich it progressively, but I am bent on developing it in the form of a story. In sum, I enjoy storytelling. I am familiar with the general plot line, but the greatest difficulty is to find a point of departure."[1] In *Rashomon*, the opening scene at the gate is both the outer frame of reference for plots to come and the initial episode in its own plot, which unfolds over the duration of the film. In *Ikiru*, the opening is an image—the X-ray of the protagonist's cancerous stomach—that anticipates an event about to take place, once the plot commences. By the point in his career when Kurosawa worked on these two projects, narrative served purposes well beyond a one-dimensional "through line" for the film drama, as it had served in earlier works like *Sanshiro Sugata* and *One Wonderful Sunday*.

The uses of multiple perspectives on the same set of characters and events, with each perspective constrained by individual consciousness, is a modernist narrative practice associated with novelists like Dostoevsky, Joseph Conrad, James Joyce, Virginia Woolf, and William Faulkner. Such narratives are limited and relative in their degree of objectivity and truth. Techniques of multiple perspective in modernist theater are explored by playwrights like August Strindberg, Luigi

Pirandello, and Bertolt Brecht. Within world cinema there is an analogous visual and narrative tradition, with origins in the work of impressionists and expressionists during the 1920s like directors Abel Gance, Jean Epstein, Robert Weine, and Fritz Lang. Kurosawa had seen many films by these directors by the time he reached thirty. An early Japanese example is Teinosuke Kinugasa's *Page of Madness* (*Kurutta Ippeiji*, 1926).

The most influential instance of narrative modernism within American cinema is *Citizen Kane* (1941) by Orson Welles, who had intended to adapt Conrad's *Heart of Darkness* until studio disapproval led him to develop this masterwork. Modernist narrative flourished during the European New Wave movement of the 1950s and 1960s, in seminal films like the Marguerite Duras and Alain Resnais collaboration *Hiroshima Mon Amour*, Resnais's *Last Year at Marienbad* (1961), based on a text by novelist Alain Robbe-Grillet, and Michelangelo Antonioni's *Blow-up* (1966). In a study of European cinema of this period entitled *The Ambiguous Image*, Roy Armes places Welles and Kurosawa at the origins of much radical experimentation in film narrative:

> Modernism in the cinema may be said to begin with a re-examination of a structure based on flashbacks in order to bring out the ambiguity inherent in the construction of a narrative out of images derived from different points in time or from differing personal viewpoints. It is here that the originality of such films as *Citizen Kane* and *Rashomon* lies.[2]

A more recent example of such storytelling methods is the Barbet Schroeder film *Reversal of Fortune* (1990), which, despite great differences in setting and subject matter, bears striking resemblances to *Rashomon* in structure.

All these literary and film works reflect fragmentation and relativism in the very narrative syntax through which the usual components of a fiction—setting, character, description, plot, and dialogue—are conveyed. In them, story components are not fully known or governed by one manifest, controlling consciousness as would be common in nineteenth-century realist conventions. Their narratives are marked by dislocation and incompleteness in the chronological order and causal logic of events. To identify these modernist narrative properties, David Bordwell has usefully adopted the term "boundary situation."[3] A boundary situation is present in narrative when extreme circumstances or psychological crisis motivate *plot* structure in the retelling of *story* elements.

Story designates events in the "original" chronological order and spatial context of their occurrence. *Plot* designates the order in which story events and their constituent elements (such as setting, description, and characterization) are told, the context of that narration, and the causal relations that are constructed from events and story elements. In formulating the story/plot distinction, the Russian Formalist Yuri Tynyanov is one of the first critics to point out the paradoxical status of story as an "original" order. Writing in 1926 about narration in cinema, Tynyanov specifies the following differences:

> Story-line [is] the whole story-prospectus of the thing. Plot, then, is the general dynamics of the thing, which is put together from the *interaction* between the movement of the story-line and the movement, the rise and fall, of the stylistic masses. The story-line can only be guessed at, but is not a given. The spectator can only guess at it from the unfolding plot — and this riddle will be an even greater motive force for the plot than the story-line.[4]

"Stylistic masses" refers to a film's specific qualities of composition, dramaturgy, movement, and editing construction.

The properties of interaction and perplexity that Tynyanov notes are indicative of an intertextual relationship between story and plot. From the plot the spectator reconstitutes a hypothetical story. The plot motivates an audience to make inferences, to fashion circumstantial and causal relationships, and to draw conclusions among various story elements.

The sense of an ending to a narrative is a matter of the con-
clusiveness or inconclusiveness to the plot's construct of a
story for the spectator.

Furthermore, story components within a narrative plot can
themselves serve as manifest intertexts. In such cases incidents, descriptions, thoughts, images, and dialogue are subject to reiteration, recontextualization, or revision over the
course of narration. Narrative meaning is to be detected in
the network or grid of cross-references among such elements.
There is in modernist narrative continual, dynamic exchange
between the *contexts* in which a narrative is told and the *content* of what the narrative tells.

As mentioned in the Introduction, Seymour Chatman proposes a valuable supplement to our understanding of intertextuality through his examination of relationships among
principal text-types narrative, description, and argument.
possesses a unique "chrono-logic" or "doubly tem-
the duration of its time of presentation (plot)
and   of time represented (story). Narrative also
entails   causality and contingency. Description
conveys, a   "casual contiguity." Description can
also take mo   forms, such as juxtapositions or the
summary of ten   ral, causal processes, without becoming
narrative. Argument establishes through logic or rhetoric a
sense of consequentiality. While the thrust of argument may
be oriented in time (drawing conclusions from history, for example), its own structure is not temporal.[5]

Extending these definitions to the case of modernist narratives formulated in boundary situations, interactions between story and plot can be seen as an engine to intertextual
dynamics that bind narrative to argument. As the textual
analysis in this chapter intends to make clear, the conflicting
narrative motives in *Rashomon* derive from differing modes
and objectives of argumentation. In *Ikiru*, an interconnec-
tion between narrative and argument is made immediately
apparent as an unidentified narrator intrudes with a sum-

mary judgment on the story of the protagonist's life before
the film's plot even gets underway.

In his account of Japanese New Wave cinema, David Desser
divides film narrative in Japan into three primary paradigms:
classical, modern, and modernist. Ozu is a master in the classical mode, which conserves traditional values and exemplifies chronological, cyclical, mythic, and transcendental qualities. Kurosawa is representative of the modern mode, which
marks the emergence of bourgeois individualism in Japan, exemplifies chronological, causal, linear, historical qualities,
and advocates universal humanism. Nagisa Oshima has innovated the modernist mode, which asserts achronological,
arbitrarily episodic, dialectical, antimythic, and antipsycho-
logical properties.[6] By the measure of Desser's differentiation of narrative categories, Kurosawa's narratively innovative films fall, in my view, into a gap between the modern and
the modernist modes. Without abandoning or negating such
properties of the modern as linear continuity or a discernible
causality, Kurosawa problematizes them in pursuing interactive, enigmatic relations between story and plot and between
narrative and argument. Moreover, these Kurosawa film narratives typically place values of humanism into an inseparable,
paradoxical relationship with acts of inhumanity.

Rashomon

The film *Rashomon* evolved from a script by Shinobu Hashimoto that adapted material from the modern short story
writer Ryunosuke Akutagawa (1892–1927). Hashimoto's original screenplay, entitled "Male-Female," consisted of three
episodes drawn from the Akutagawa story "In a Grove," which
is cast in the form of testimony from seven individuals in a
criminal investigation. Finding the script too brief for a feature film, Kurosawa collaborated with Hashimoto to develop
more screen action by incorporating ideas and images drawn
from another Akutagawa story, "Rashomon."

The fiction of Akutagawa is rich in intertexts where a modern Japanese consciousness joins ancient Japanese sources with the grotesque vision and psychological extremism of foreign literary masters like Poe, Gogol, Guy de Maupassant, Charles Baudelaire, and Dostoevsky. In many ways, Akutagawa was representative of the Taisho or "Great Righteousness" era (1912–26), which promoted a modern sensibility in the Japanese arts and embraced Western culture. After the earthquake and fires of 1923, Akutagawa was also a witness to the devastation throughout Tokyo; in the family of one of his relations, nine of the ten members died in the destruction. As had the adolescent Kurosawa in the company of his brother Heigo, Akutagawa toured Tokyo to observe the corpses and ruins. In his autobiographical account *The Life of a Fool (Aru Aho no Isso)*, published a few months after his suicide in 1927, he describes with envy the dead, whose decaying flesh carries an odor of overripe fruit. Clearly, in his imagination Akutagawa has strong affinities with the boundary situations of modernist art.

Akutagawa's primary source for the stories "Rashomon" (1915) and "In a Grove" (1921) is the classic Japanese collection *Konjaku Monogatari* ("Tales of Times Now Past"), which was compiled at the end of the eleventh century and contains some one thousand tales. The section in *Konjaku* that contains the original material is headed "Evil Deeds."[7] (The traditional Noh repertory also includes a play entitled "Rashomon.") Akutagawa was chiefly responsible for stimulating twentieth-century interest in *Konjaku* as literature. He drew regularly from the collection in his writing and greatly admired its primitive beauty, raw power, and psychological realism. Akutagawa was most responsive to what he termed its "beauty of *brutality*, . . . remote from such things as elegance and grace."[8] In borrowing from *Konjaku*, however, Akutagawa disregards the moralizing typical of tales in the collection.

The original tales in *Konjaku* are brief and unambiguous. In one of the sources (book 29, story 18), a thief comes to the capital Kyoto and awaits darkness in the ceremonial Rasho gate. (At the start of the Heian period—794–1185—the magnificently ornamental Rasho gate was erected at the southern entrance to the city.) To avoid detection from passing crowds, the thief climbs to the upper level in the structure, where he glimpses in torchlight the macabre sight of an old woman plucking hair from the corpse of a young woman. Seized for a moment by a fear of demons, the thief then rushes with his sword drawn toward the old woman, who explains that she was servant to the dead woman and that she is taking the hair for a wig. Disregarding her pleas, the thief strips both women of their clothing, steals the hair, and leaves the gate. The story ends at this point with the comment that it was common in that period for unburied bodies to be deposited in the upper level of the Rasho gate and that the tale is handed down from the thief's own account.

The other main *Konjaku* source (book 29, story 23) opens with the description of a journey by husband and wife westward from the capital, with the wife on horseback and the husband keeping guard on foot. Out in the provinces a brawny young man bearing a finely crafted sword joins them. The stranger interests the husband in the sword and the samurai greedily exchanges his ordinary bow for it. As the journey continues, the stranger asks for two arrows from the husband's quiver. Once he has been obliged, the stranger coaxes the couple deep into a grove of trees. There he confronts the couple, coerces them further toward the mountains, forces the husband to turn over the sword and a knife, then ties him to a tree trunk. Now that the bandit looks closely at the woman, his desires are aroused. After ordering her to remove her clothing, he undresses and rapes her as the husband looks on. When he is finished, the bandit gathers the sword, the bow, and the quiver of arrows and takes flight on the horse. The final location and disposition of the knife is left unstated. The bandit has spared the husband's life and leaves clothing for the wife. After freeing her husband, the wife belittles him as a coward and an untrustworthy fool. The couple continue on their journey westward, but no further mention is made of the fate of these three individuals after the events in the grove. The story closes with commentary that the bandit demonstrated a degree of respect and shame in not stealing the woman's clothes and that the husband was stupid and worthless for handing over his bow and arrows to a suspicious stranger.

Akutagawa sets "Rashomon" at least a century later than the *Konjaku* tale, advancing the historical time to an era of social disorder when, in addition to the natural calamities of fire, famine, and earthquake, there was armed strife in the capital Kyoto among rival political factions of the imperial court. The story explains that times are so difficult that Buddhist icons are sold for firewood. Through dialogue that comments on human savagery in the capital and through visualization of the monumental city gate in a condition of ruin, the film *Rashomon* also conveys the decline in Japanese society at the end of the Heian era, a period of great cultural achievements.

In a significant departure from the *Konjaku* original, both "In a Grove" and the film specify the social identity of the husband as that of a samurai and add as the sign of this status the fact that he bears his own long sword. A well-known early history of Japan by the Buddhist priest Jien (1155–1225) links the Heian decline with the emergence in his lifetime of a new historical era, "the age of warriors." The social order enforced through the samurai class convinced Jien that he was living in the period of *mappo* ("latter days of Buddhist law"), a final, cataclysmic disintegration of moral and social values.

In Akutagawa's telling of "Rashomon," a servant, discharged that day by his samurai master, waits out a rainstorm in the dilapidated and deserted Rasho gate as he tries to determine his future. His choices have narrowed to the alternatives of remaining honest and starving or of resorting to thievery and thus living. The story comments ironically that while the second alternative is the only viable one, the servant "was still unable to muster enough courage to justify the conclusion that he must become a thief."[9] With nightfall, he decides to remain at the gate and climbs to the upper level for greater shelter from the rainstorm. There, in the faint glow of a fire, he can distinguish numerous corpses strewn on the floor, and the stench begins to overpower him. He detects a ghoulish form bent over the head of a corpse, plucking out its hair. The terrifying sight arouses his conscience to a hatred of evil and to make a decision, for the moment, to starve rather than resort to crime.

In reply to his demand for an explanation, the old woman identifies her robbery victim as a merchant woman, dead from plague, who cheated army guards by selling them snake meat under the pretense that it was dried fish. (Akutagawa derives this last detail from story 31 in the same book of *Konjaku*.) For the old woman, both the merchant's dishonesty and her own thievery are justified by the need to survive. That logic frees the servant from his moral dilemma and "a certain courage was born in his heart," enabling him to rob the old woman. He overpowers her, tears the clothing from her body, then flees into the night. The story's amoral, Darwinian imperative of the struggle for survival is reinforced by insistent animal imagery that draws comparisons to species of reptiles, predators, and scavengers.

In composing the story, Akutagawa visited a morgue in order to render convincingly the morbid scene set in the gate's upper level. His innovations with the *Konjaku* material provide a dramatized inner portrait of the protagonist's reactions and rationalizations. Evil accumulates over the series of events that lead to his decisive crime. The inexorable march of events points to the conclusion that predation is a universal law of life.

"In a Grove" marks a more radical departure by Akutagawa from his source in *Konjaku*. The story is presented in the form of seven first-person accounts: testimony by four different parties, two confessions, and a statement from a dead victim through a spirit-medium. The accounts concern the crimes committed after a traveling samurai and wife encounter a bandit in the forest. The samurai is lured off the public road and deep into the forest by the bandit's tale of buried treasure. Read as a composite of these varied sources, the narrative is uncentered, fragmentary, and relativistic in nature. The seven components do not even share the same narrative context. The testimony is given before a police commissioner, the wife's confession is made at the Shimizu temple, and the locales of the bandit's confession and the husband's statement are unspecified. Akutagawa's technique in this story contains parallels with two specific literary antecedents: the Ambrose Bierce story "The Moonlit Road" (1907), which contains three statements about a slaying, including one by the victim through a spiritualist, and Robert Browning's *The Ring and the Book* (1869), which through a cycle of dramatic monologues presents twelve versions of events leading to murder.

"In a Grove" leaves the reader with conflicting accounts of events and does not provide a developed moral, social, or historical milieu for a frame of reference. The designation of social roles gives the only indication of possible standards of behavior or value. But there is no accord or reconciliation among these standards. In his confession the bandit Tajomaru makes a rebellious indictment against respectable society for killing the spirit of people through money and power. The samurai's mercenary motives in following the bandit fundamentally violate the code and ideals of his class, though this transgression is not acknowledged in the statement by his spirit. The reader is left with the dominant impression of a human condition defined by rapacious selfishness and rivalry.

The *Rashomon* film script retains much of the story material from "In a Grove," but it develops plot lines that deeply implicate characters in each other's stories. The resulting film narrative is a shifting intertextual complex that maps the psychology of each main character as an indeterminate variable. In broad terms, *Rashomon* falls within the screen genre *jidai-geki*, but it is distinctive in its departures from generic norms. The film provides little in the way of action spectacle, costume drama, or historical re-creation. When such qualities are represented, the treatment is ironic. Kurosawa's only previous *jidai-geki* up to this point in his career is *The Men Who Tread on the Tiger's Tail*, based on a histor-

ical incident from the end of the Heian period that became a
classical legend. This film's unique addition of a commoner
to the storyline provides a modern and comic understanding
of the feudal order. The famous lord Yoshitsune is with-
drawn or disguised through much of the screen drama while
the common porter, who lives by his wits rather than by social codes, has great prominence.

Over his career, in making films that can be categorized as
jidai-geki Kurosawa has invariably developed a dimension of
modernity that makes manifest important connections to
contemporary reality. Kurosawa embraces the action and adventure often associated with *jidai-geki* as an essential dynamic, present from the beginnings of cinema in the chase,
suspense, and mystery genre formulas. But he also makes a
distinction: "For me . . . adventure is spectacle in the historical film, while in the modern film adventure is more often
metaphysical, moral, and social in nature."[10] While *Rashomon* is historical and classical in subject matter and setting,
the methods of narration are insistently modernist. Its spectacle is demythologized, sometimes through ironic contradictions among the versions of events, sometimes through
caricature and parody in the representation of events.

A major aspect of *Rashomon* is the act of narration itself
and this aspect greatly distinguishes the film from the story
sources in both *Konjaku* and Akutagawa. The first words
spoken in *Rashomon* are the woodcutter's remark to the
priest, "I can't understand it."[11] Between them, the woodcutter and priest reiterate this reaction six more times, until the
commoner prevails on the woodcutter to start recounting the
events that so perplex him. The commoner has just joined
them under the city's half-standing, monumental gate for
shelter from the torrents of rain. He is the single character added by the script and he brings the same popular voice of cynical skepticism heard in *The Lower Depths* and *Throne of
Blood*.

The motives that underlie storytelling vary among the
three men gathered at the gate. In an attempt to reach an

Rasho gate as a scene of narration: the priest, the commoner, and the woodcutter in *Rashomon*.

understanding through the responses of a complete outsider, the woodcutter begins to recount to the commoner the accounts of events in the forest told by the three participants—the samurai, his wife, and the bandit Tajomaru. In the woodcutter's own initial narrative, his association with these events is completely after the fact, with the discovery of some personal property and then a dead body. Both he and the priest have also been witness to the accounts given in the prison courtyard. The priest participates in the telling in an obvious effort to make some sense of the contradictory accounts from the perspective of his spirituality. The commoner is interested in any story, no matter how horrible or perplexing, in order to pass the time, but he has no patience for moralizing or sermons. Later the commoner makes the observation that a human cannot tell the full truth, even to oneself, and thus all personal accounts will contain lies. That a story contains deceit is of no concern to him; all that matters is that it retain his interest.

Rather than the macabre main action or the servant's inner moral dialogue in Akutagawa's "Rashomon," the film
principally adopts from this story an atmosphere of ruin, the
historical condition of social chaos, and an unfolding inquiry
into human behavior. The film reduces the story's grotesque
intensity to a mention by the commoner of corpses in the
gate's upper level. Ethical choice is not explicitly debated as
in the story. It remains implicit until the confrontation and
resolution among the characters at the gate in the film's closing scene.

The film includes accounts by six individuals who have
some relation to the forest events, including the police agent
and counting as one the samurai and his spirit-medium.
Among these accounts there is great multiplicity in the dis-
tances in time, in directness relative to events in the forest,
in emotional identification, and in the contexts from which
narration is conducted. From the dramatic present, set at
Rashomon during a heavy rainstorm, are measured three previous time frames for the core story in the forest. Earlier the
same day, statements are made by involved parties and witnesses in a prison courtyard. Two days earlier, the police
agent put the bandit under arrest after finding him incapaci-
tated by a riverbank. In the afternoon three days earlier, first
the priest and then the bandit encounter the traveling samurai couple at different points along a forest road. Subsequent to the second encounter, events occur in the forest involving the samurai, his wife, and the bandit. At the least,
the woodcutter is concerned as a witness on the scene in the
forest after the occurrence.

The multiple aspects of setting can be categorized according to two kinds of drama. The Rashomon and the prison
courtyard are locales defined by scenes of narration. The
road, the forest, the countryside, and the riverbank constitute scenes of action. The countryside is featured in only two
shots, which depict the bandit's explanation of how he became ill and how he dismounted the stolen horse. A single,
brief shot indicates the scene of another reported event, the

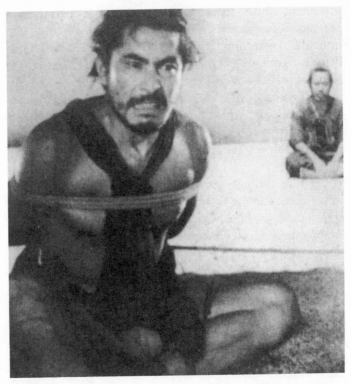

The prison courtyard as a scene of narration: the bandit and the woodcutter in *Rashomon*.

wife's attempted suicide by drowning in a pond, but the composition excludes characters or any signs of action.

Voice-over narration bridges the courtyard scene of narration with the major scene of action in the forest at least once for each of the three principal characters. A visual bridge between the two scenes of narration is an early shot from the prison courtyard of huge clouds gathering; they bring the rainstorm that continues in the dramatic present. In the course of the storm's conclusion during the film's last few minutes, the Rashomon scene of narration becomes a new scene of action.

A paradox of representation arises for the film viewer. For the most part, in each variant of events depicted in the forest the narrative mode is present and actual in appearance. In the accounts by the samurai, his wife, and the bandit, the effect of presence and objective reality is qualified, however, by cutaways to the prison courtyard scene three days later and, inversely, by voice-over narration carried from there into scenes in the forest. The refrain "I can't understand it" during the initial gate scene cautions the film viewer that events may remain unexplained even after narration is completed. On the basis of this context in the outer narrative frame, the mode of each forest event is to be recognized as subjunctive and conditional in nature.

Kurosawa describes the forest setting as a place "where the human heart loses its way" (*Autobiography*, 185). The common motive for narration among the three principals in the forest events, and for the woodcutter as well, is egoism. Each individual version promotes an understanding of events that reflects favorably on the self, either through heroic inflation or through claims of innocence, victimization, or uninvolvement. Elements within one version become intertexts to the other versions. That is, incidents and images associated with one version are revised, contradicted, or denied in the course of the other participants' retellings. In unique ways, *Rashomon* demonstrates in the context of the courtyard and gate locales (scenes of narration) how plots are made from story events set in the forest locales (scenes of action). The narrative process of interaction between plot and story and the hypothetical reconstruction of story through plot are forms of argumentation.

After the first plot construction in *Rashomon*, each subsequent plot reconstructs major story elements and implicitly deconstructs the other versions.[12] Thus the progression of plot constructions also traces implicit forms of rebuttal. The plotting of story events in each version can be more clearly followed from a summary of the core elements.

Story Components of Events in the Forest

A. The samurai and his wife travel along a road through the forest; the couple encounters first a priest, then the bandit.

B. The bandit entices the samurai deep into a grove with the tale of a treasure cache of swords and mirrors recovered from a tomb. Once there, the bandit binds the samurai with a rope.

C. The bandit leads the wife into the grove after reporting that her husband has been bitten by a snake.

D. In the presence of the bound husband, there is carnal union between the bandit and the wife.

E. The samurai dies.

F. The wife flees.

G. The bandit leaves with the samurai's bow, arrows, and sword; he also steals the horse, left outside the grove.

H. The wife's dagger is variously accounted for.

I. The samurai's body is found.

The sequence (A) through (I) reflects a rough chronology generally agreed upon among the versions told over the course of the film. The order of events (E) and (F), however, is in dispute. The priest's encounter with the couple extends only partway into event (A). The police agent's involvement occurs after event (I), but his capture of the bandit entails the outcome of event (G). The most important discrepancies among the versions entail the underlying *causes* of components (D), (E), (F), and (H), and here the functions of *plot* are most evident. The differences in plot causation reflect differing explanations of character motivation. Was the carnal union a rape or a seduction? Does the samurai die the victim of a duel, a murder, or a suicide, and what was the instrument of his death? Was the dagger stolen or left behind?

From these story components five distinctly different plots are woven, two by the woodcutter and one each by the bandit, the wife, and the samurai. The samurai's mercenary motives in event (B) remain undisputed among the varying accounts, a factor indicative of the pervasively corrupt circumstances. In his initial telling, the woodcutter comes upon a woman's reed hat, a samurai hat, pieces of cut rope, a small case, and finally a stiffened corpse, lying face up. This plot places the woodcutter on the scene after events (A) through (H), leaving him unimplicated. The impression of a concrete and unequivocal account is reinforced by an insistent rhythmic pattern in the musical accompaniment—derived from Ravel's *Bolero*—varied by sparse but emphatic coloration. When the same music accompanies a portion of the bandit's account, however, this impression is brought into question. A variation on this musical theme is also used in the wife's account. The "In a Grove" source has the woodcutter testify only once, in the story's initial segment, and that testimony is also limited to the discovery of personal effects and the samurai's corpse. The film's first version by the woodcutter reaches its climax when he reaches the corpse. For a moment, the woodcutter is glimpsed as he discovers the body. The perspective places in the foreground the rigid outstretched arms of the corpse, which *frame* the frontal medium shot that discloses the woodcutter's shocked reaction.

In contrast to the posture of a social rebel taken in "In a Grove," the film's bandit credits himself with a heroism that makes him the romantic equal of the samurai. This role is unlikely. From the perspective of others, he is a pest-ridden, half-naked roughneck. In his own account, the bandit is first seen as a natural creature, slumbering at the foot of a giant tree, brushing off insects that gather on his flesh. The bandit explains his motives as free of any base instincts of lust. Rather, the wife's angelic beauty and childlike vulnerability inspire his crimes.

The assault against the wife becomes a seduction after her efforts to defend herself with the dagger fail and he can embrace her. The sword duel with the samurai is motivated by the wife's pledge of loyalty to the victor. The bandit wins the duel fairly, but his superiority comes from ingenuity and strength, not from classical swordsmanship. In this, the film departs from conventions of *chambara*, or traditional sword-play, in the Japanese popular arts. Victory comes when he hurtles the sword as a spear into the exhausted samurai. His plot places the wife's flight (F) before the samurai's death (E). Though the bandit took the samurai's horse and sold the stolen sword for drink, he forgot to take her dagger, an over-sight he now finds comic.

At the outset of the bandit's account, an epic visual of him astride the stolen horse, galloping along the crest of a hill with a lowering sky as backdrop, is accompanied by heroic action music. These visual and melodic clichés of Hollywood action and adventure genres—an intentional cultural and historical anomaly in the context of a medieval Japanese set-ting—comically convey the self-inflated quality of his claims to prowess and bravery. In self-image, Tajomaru is romanti-cally impulsive and free-spirited. A chance breeze gives him a glimpse of the wife's ankle, then her face. This vision of beauty appears with music of an exotic, ethereal nature on the soundtrack. On the instant, he conceives a plan to abduct her. A crescendo of harp strings accompanies this moment.

His motive is thus not robbery but a grand passion. Senti-mental music plays on the soundtrack when, from his per-spective, the wife is shown waiting by a stream after the sam-urai has been led into the grove and bound. Tajomaru is antic and irrepressible in his behavior. In love, he is a madcap rene-gade. Suddenly jealous, he is gratified to have an opportunity to humiliate the bound samurai by bringing his wife into the grove. Tajomaru mocks the wife's desperate attempts to de-fend herself against rape.

In the bandit's version, his attack on the wife becomes a consensual seduction once he has her in an embrace. After their sexual union, the bandit starts to leave the scene, bear-ing the valuables he has stolen. He is stopped by the wife, who hurls herself at his feet in anguish over her disgrace. With her pledge of devotion to the man who wins in a sword duel, Tajomaru unbinds the samurai and honorably gives him a sword to make the fight even and fair.

The forest as a scene of action in the bandit's version: the bandit, the samurai, and the wife in *Rashomon*.

Within the prison courtyard the bandit reports, for the purpose of self-flattery, that the samurai was the first opponent ever to cross swords with him more than twenty times. At the point in the interrogation when the bandit responds to questions (though unheard *within* the film narrative) about the couple's valuable weapons, the shot composition shifts slightly to now include a view of the woodcutter in the background. But the woodcutter is only intermittently visible in this composition and he is positioned at such a distance that any facial reaction is undetectable.

The wife's account begins just as event (D) has concluded, starting with her statement that the carnal union resulted from rape. Event (G), the bandit's departure with the couple's valuables, is the first to be depicted visually. Over the course of her narration, a variation on the *Bolero* theme gradually rises in intensity on the soundtrack. With the bandit's departure, she is left alone to face her husband's shocked stare. His frozen expression, which she interprets as utter hatred, drives her hysterical. After cutting him free from the rope, she pleads to be killed by him but he remains immobile. Faced with his persistent stare she hypnotically moves toward him, only half-conscious of the dagger in her hand, until finally she seems to collapse in his direction, off-screen. At that moment she loses consciousness and visualization of these events ceases. From the prison courtyard she recounts how, after regaining her senses, she found her husband dead, a dagger in his chest. She makes this statement in a shot composition that directly aligns her with the woodcutter, who sits with the priest at the back of the courtyard. She reports that next she fled and that, finding herself by a pond, she tried to drown herself but failed.

The four essential elements in the wife's plot—the rape, her husband's death, the last location of her dagger, and her attempted drowning—are treated elliptically. At the climactic moment in each event, the narrative is exclusively verbal and, at that, it is highly abridged and undescriptive. The dramatic emphasis is placed on her double victimization, by the bandit and then by her husband's hatred, and on her present emotional agony. The wife's plot conveys initial compassion for her husband and subsequent terror over condemnation by him. But the account does not directly acknowledge that the duty of a samurai wife is to commit suicide in such circumstances. By custom she is armed with a dagger to defend against rape or, when that fails, to preserve the honor of her marriage through suicide. The wife's plot turns her plea for her husband to put her to death and her claimed attempts at self-destruction into acts of pathos. And it makes the stabbing of her husband an act of self-defense against his incriminating contempt.

In the Akutagawa story "In a Grove," the death of the samurai at the hands of his wife is a calculated act. She explains that in reaction to his silent stare she determines that they shall both die now that she is shamed. She interprets his paralyzed expression to signal consent and stabs him while he is still bound. After a fainting spell, she unties his corpse and attempts *jigaki*, the piercing of her own throat with a dagger thrust, a ritual method of suicide for samurai women. She only wounds her neck superficially, and soon after she fails in an attempt to drown herself. The wife despairs that her survival is proof of her dishonor.

The film's next version is given by the dead samurai through a spirit-medium. It is immediately preceded by an exchange among the three men under the Rasho gate, during which the commoner explains to the priest: "Look, everyone wants to forget unpleasant things, so they make up stories. It's easier that way." For the commoner, storytelling and the repression of truth are synonymous acts.

The medium's account also begins at the conclusion of event (D), which the samurai refers to as an attack against his wife. Tajomaru's seduction of the wife starts at this point, as he encourages her to abandon the husband and leave with him. Their dialogue is summarized by the samurai up to the point of the wife's fateful responses to the bandit: "Take me away with you" and "Kill him. As long as he is alive I cannot go with you." When the bandit honorably refuses to carry out her betrayal she flees and the bandit gives chase. Some hours later the bandit returns to free the samurai and then departs, though the details of his theft of weapons are not provided. Alone and in the torment of the betrayal committed by his wife, the samurai plunges her dagger into his chest. The sequence of events in this plot is thus (F), (G), (H)–(E).

The suicide is presented as a desperate act of passion, for the samurai ignores prescribed ritual in putting himself to death in this manner. The heroism in his version does not conform to the ideals of *bushido*. Instead, it derives from traditions of romantic agony. His emotional turmoil brings a dissociative state in which he hears "someone crying," who subsequently is identified as himself. Some time after the dagger has pierced his chest, "Someone seemed to approach me. . . . Then someone's hand grasped the dagger and drew it out." With its removal, the samurai dies. This statement alone does

not unequivocally implicate the woodcutter. Given his dissociative condition and his prior statement, the samurai con-
ceivably could have removed the dagger himself.

In the prison courtyard setting, the woodcutter is not prominent in the background during the medium's account until
the point where the concluding remarks about the dagger are
made. With that conclusion, however, the woodcutter is directly aligned with the medium and within the closest range
to the foreground among all of the shots in which the woodcutter overhears others testify during the courtyard scenes.
The woodcutter visibly quavers when this last information
is disclosed.

The medium's version of events conforms to that by the
samurai in "In a Grove." The film, however, greatly enlarges
the emotional scale through its additional representation of
the medium summoning the samurai's spirit from the dead.
This séance in the police courtyard begins with the rattle of
a hand chime and is accompanied with a hollow, droning
chant and a deep drum cadence. A whirlwind stirs the medium frenetically. The medium is an androgynous figure. It
is female in appearance, but the voice that echoes through it
is the samurai's. Portrayal of his self-slaughter is musically
colored by a melancholy theme, performed by strings and
woodwinds.

At the Rasho gate, the woodcutter reacts to the medium's
account by insisting that the samurai did not die from a dagger wound. In fact, in his insistence the woodcutter denies
altogether the presence of a dagger on the scene: "That's
not true. There wasn't any dagger there—he was killed by a
sword." This denial initiates his second ordering of story
events into a plot that at the same time is expressly an argument. But plot and argument quickly devolve into contradiction in this second version. In visualized form, his plot begins at the conclusion of event (D), the carnal union. The
woodcutter's plot now intervenes into the story at a significantly earlier point than in his first version.

The famous bandit Tajomaru humbles himself before the

raped wife in a plea of love, even vowing to become honest if
only she will marry him. To his threat of murder if she does
not consent, she replies that she cannot make such a decision, then she cuts her husband loose with the dagger. This
conspicuous use of the dagger as a story element flatly contradicts the plot claim the woodcutter has just made in opening
this second version. After depiction of initial events in the
forest, however, his plot elides the dagger as a story element.

Tajomaru understands her action to indicate that she will
accept the man who wins in battle, but her freed husband refuses to rescue her. This turn in events causes Tajomaru to
distrust the wife, but she ridicules and shames them into a
swordfight. In this plot, the wife witnesses the murder of her
husband but flees when the bandit approaches her. In pursuit, the bandit trips and lies exhausted for some moments.
Next he removes the second sword from the body of the slain
samurai, which remains offscreen and thus unseen, and the
bandit leaves the scene.

In preparing Machiko Kyo, Toshiro Mifune, and Masayuki
Mori for the forest scenes, Kurosawa instructed them to imi-
tate the animal behavior recorded in the jungle adventure
films they had watched during the preproduction of *Rashomon*. His instructions are most evident in the performances
of this last story section, which contains only one line of
dialogue during the fight scene. While there is absolutely no
guarantee of authenticity in the woodcutter's second version,
it has by comparison to the other versions a greater initial
appearance of objectivity in being unembellished by soundtrack music. As an argument, the woodcutter's second plot
discredits all of the participants through its contradictions
with previous accounts. Their motives are base and narcissis-
tic, their emotions grotesque and brutal.

The wife is revealed to have a dishonest, savage soul. Her
tears transform into scornful, demonic laughter. The bandit's
actions are crude, animalistic. The heroic music in his version is displaced here by the noise of his heavy panting. The
husband does not fulfill any of the masculine ideals of sam-

urai culture, ideals that are alluded to explicitly in this version. Unwilling to defend his own honor, he offers his wife to the bandit and ignobly pleads for his life during battle. The wife's ridicule initiates their sword battle. The battle is a clumsy and terrified affair, with each man doing his best to avoid the other at the outset. Once they cross swords, the two prove inept as they scramble across the forest floor. Their bodies quiver with fear and exhaustion.

The woodcutter's second version marks a significant departure in narrative form from the previous four accounts, including his first one. Previously, each narrator is featured centrally as the protagonist in his or her own account. The woodcutter does not appear at all in the forest scene of action, however, in his second version. His absence from the scene places him even further dramatically from involvement in the truth of events. The woodcutter's second plot thus serves the same underlying argument as his first in keeping him unimplicated by these events.

In discrediting the integrity of the others, he strives to preserve his own credibility and innocence. But his insistence that no dagger was involved becomes self-incriminating. This behavior reflects the familiar psychological paradox that denial is a veiled form of admission. His refrain of "lies" in reaction to the other stories, and the inconsistency between his two versions, leads the commoner to apply a variant of the liar's paradox to the woodcutter: "No one tells lies after he has said that he's going to tell one." That is, a human is truthful only when he or she *openly* pledges to tell a lie, a pledge not made in any of the accounts.

The contradictory plotlines and their attendant arguments cannot be reconciled. They do not yield even a shared chronology that might be accepted as the natural logic of story events. After all has been said, the commoner asks, "Which one of these stories do you believe?" Though the question is directed to the priest, the woodcutter replies that none of them makes sense, implicitly including his own two versions. The composite truth that emerges from the plots, then, goes entirely beyond the particulars of each story and argument. The conclusion to be drawn by the film spectator is that individuals can be depended upon to give dishonest and unreliable accounts of themselves.

At Rashomon as a scene of narration in relation to forest events, the woodcutter is in the role of eyewitness and possible participant, the priest is in that of intermediary, and the commoner is in that of audience. Visuals in the gate scenes constantly reinforce a triangular interrelationship among them. In addition to his own versions, the woodcutter provides the narrative bridge into the statements by the police agent and the priest and into the bandit's story. The priest provides the bridge into the accounts by the wife and the samurai-medium.

In the priest's only statement as a direct witness, simple Japanese music plays on the soundtrack, as befits his traditionally idealized social role. The priest also serves a role similar to the *waki no shite* ("side doer") in Noh theater. The *waki* reflects the thoughts, emotions, and motives of the main figure, or *shite*, though he typically remains a commentator rather than an agent in the play's action. The *waki*'s position in the play is literally peripheral. Seated to the side of the platform, often obscured from view, he emerges after introduction of the *shite* to make observations on events. The *waki* conventionally belongs to one of three types—the official, the priest, or the more common social man (such as a soldier or a townsman). The traveling priest typically moves through the stage world as a student of life.[13]

The Noh drama *Rashomon* belongs to a unique category in which there is dramatic confrontation between *waki* and *shite*. The priest's motive as intermediary in the film *Rashomon* is to preserve his faith in human goodness. At one point, however, he reaches the same psychological position of refusal and denial that, for different reasons, the woodcutter assumes for the duration of other accounts. After the samurai-medium's version, the priest protests that he does not want to hear of any more horrible human deeds and he withdraws from the two men at the gate. Once the woodcutter has told his second version, the priest is drawn back into their dispute over the truth when he asserts his own *need* to have faith in humanity.

The commoner has dismantled the city gate further in scavenging wood for a small fire during the scenes of narration. With the conclusion of the woodcutter's second retelling, the commoner scatters the kindling into the rain. At this moment the cry of an infant is heard from a near distance and the scene of action at the gate begins. In events that follow, the commoner proves himself to be a thief and his accusations seem to confirm as well that the woodcutter committed a theft three days ago. The commoner is the first to search out the infant, with the purpose of taking its bedding and outer garment. (This theft of clothing from a defenseless victim is a story event transposed from the servant's attack on the old woman in "Rashomon.") In this action and in the cynical laughter with which he justifies it, the commoner resembles the bandit. Their motives center on the dictates of self-interest. For them there is no question of faith in humanity since obviously no individual is to be trusted.

Though the commoner has not irrefutably proven that a macabre theft of the dagger took place in the forest, the woodcutter's silence in the face of this accusation implicates him. The woodcutter's subsequent apology to the priest ("I'm the one who ought to be ashamed") seems like an admission, but the crime is not objectively verified. Even if true, as is likely, this theft does not reconcile the contradictory plots of the previous accounts. The woodcutter's capacity for goodness, on the other hand, is concretely demonstrated when he comes to the infant's defense. By the film's conclusion, his position has evolved from uninvolvement to commitment. As eyewitness to this charitable act, the priest is able to retain faith in humanity.

Closure to the scene of action at Rashomon is strongly encoded as a "message" movie ending. The rains have stopped, the dialogue and action affirm human trust, the infant stops

crying, priest and woodcutter bow respectfully to each other,
and the orchestral arrangement of a Japanese theme rises
steadily on the soundtrack. After the musical themes for the
film's opening credits, the only sound effects associated with
the gate setting have been environmental. But in the ending
naturalistic sound gives way to conventional movie music,
which reaches a crescendo when the woodcutter walks forward, out from the gate, cradling the infant protectively.

Many film critics express reservations about the film's closing action. That Kurosawa considered the concluding scene
unambiguously positive is suggested by his later design of a
prominent outer gate for the public medical clinic for *Red
Beard* to mark a path leading to hope. In interviews after that
film's release, the director spoke frankly of the heroism of his
doctor protagonist as a humanitarian dream and a social
wish fulfillment: "Red Beard is the prototype of a redeemer.
With all my heart I want this kind of man to stand as an example. Red Beard is an imaginary person, but in creating him
I represented the ideal of a being of good will."[14]

The most frequent objection to *Rashomon* is that the woodcutter's act of goodness comes as a hasty, sentimental, and
false gesture. The ending is discredited as inconsistent and
unpersuasive in the context of the craven egoism and moral
relativism shown in the course of the film. Presumably the
infant has remained hidden in a recess of the gate for the duration of the storytelling. With fortuitous timing, the infant
first cries at the point in the narrative where all hope for humanity seems lost. Reacting to such a last-minute plot artifice, the director Masahiro Shinoda has described *Rashomon* as a monument to Kurosawa's "simplistic humanism."[15]

The closing action brings an end to a paradoxical narrative
representative of fragmentation and multiplicity in human
experience, but by no means does it resolve or undo the powerful effects of that narrative. After the scene of narration becomes itself a scene of action in the film's final minutes, human truths of respect and compassion emerge. Within his
first account the woodcutter is often obstructed from view

by thick forest growth, and within the second he is completely absent, while at the conclusion to the gate scene he is in full, open view as he walks forward into the sunlight. The final event demonstrates a human capacity for goodness and offers an instance of it, but that instance does not negate the sense of human depravity that precedes it.

The woodcutter's charity comes as an unpredictable and chance act much as, presumably, his act of theft in the forest did. (The bandit had described his own actions as the consequence of a chance occurrence: a sudden breeze that parted the wife's veil and gave him a glimpse of her beauty.) To serve his own need, which may be described as one of simple humanism, the priest finds universal significance in one random act of kindness. By the film's conclusion, however, the audience is attuned to the narrative process by which a story element is transformed by plot into an argument that lays claim to truth.

The *Rashomon* gate scenes are the only ones to give film viewers their own objective perspective on events. Scenes in the prison courtyard, with the witnesses facing the camera squarely as they make statements to an unseen judicial authority, make film viewers conscious of their position as audience. In the setting of the gate as a scene of action, a new dynamic replaces the interactions of commoner as audience, priest as intermediary, and woodcutter as eyewitness or participant. Now film spectators are the sole audience and—without intermediaries—the commoner, priest, and woodcutter are participants. With the departure of the commoner, who has been uniformly cynical in his assessment of humankind, the audience is left to judge for itself the validity among contradictory story events, among five plots made of forest events and the one the priest now makes of events at the gate, and among the arguments posited through the varied combinations of story and plot. The truths of *Rashomon* will be no more and no less than what the individual film spectator makes of them.

The Wipe Cut

In 1950, as he was developing the script and the monumental gate set for *Rashomon*, Kurosawa contemplated the
loss to contemporary cinema of film traditions from the silent era:

> Since the advent of the talkies in the 1930s, I felt, we had
> misplaced and forgotten what was so wonderful about the
> old silent movies. I was aware of the aesthetic loss as a con-
> stant irritation. I sensed a need to go back to the origins
> of the motion picture to find this peculiar beauty again; I
> had to go back into the past. (*Autobiography*, 182)

In his work over the next several years Kurosawa was espe-
cially mindful of the spirit of pure visualization in the French
avant-garde cinema of the 1920s in the work of directors like
Alberto Cavalcanti, Germaine Dulac, Abel Gance, and Jean
Epstein, which he had seen over that decade upon his brother
Heigo's recommendations. Sergei Eisenstein's *Battleship Po-
temkin* and Vsevolod Pudovkin's *Mother* are two examples of
Soviet montage cinema he also remembered from that period.

The techniques of rapid montage prominent in the silent
films of Gance and Eisenstein are utilized freely in *Rashomon*. The woodcutter's walk through the forest recounted in
his first version of events is depicted by a sequence that is
three minutes fifty seconds in duration and contains twenty-
nine separate shots.[16] Though the average shot length in the
opening forest sequence, eight seconds, does not approach
the rapidity of montage in *Potemkin*, in which the average
shot length is close to two seconds for the entire film (inclusive of its intertitles), the *Rashomon* sequence employs unusual permutation and juxtaposition in its construction. Its
shot compositions vary from a long shot of an indistinct object lying among leaves, which lasts one second, to a twenty-
five second shot that opens with a woman's reed hat and veil
prominent in the foreground and the woodcutter standing in
the background, staring forward at the hat. This same shot

depicts the woodcutter's movement forward, to touch the veil in the foreground, and his movement away (captured by a pan of the camera) and deeper into the forest, until he is lost from view.

Another sequence shot in the opening forest setting consists of a choreographed travel and pan of the camera that in the span of fifteen seconds moves from a high angle perspective to a lateral perspective in following the woodcutter as he moves in and out of view through heavy foliage. The changing visibility of the woodcutter in such sequence shots is itself a kind of montage. In the construction of this forest segment there are extreme contrasts in shot scale as well, with distant long shots followed immediately by tight closeups.

In visual style, *Rashomon* also entails great variation in the logic of camera position and movement. In some shots the camera travels in reverse direction, without motivation by the dramatized screen geometry of a character's movement. Within the bandit's version, the wife's perspective suddenly emerges at the point where, by his account, the rape has become a consensual act. In his embrace, her head is bent back and her eyes remain open. Intercut with this action are shot compositions of sunlight piercing the forest canopy, as seen from her position below. The visual style employed for the forest scenes generally is one of such impressionism. For those scenes set in the prison courtyard and at the gate, it is one of realism, with the exception of the séance in which the medium summons the samurai's spirit.

Kurosawa's contemporary story films made in the 1940s experiment with the visual and dramatic possibilities of realism at the same time that the neorealist movement emerged in Italy with *Ossessione* (1942) and *La Terra Trema* (1948) directed by Luchino Visconti, *Rome, Open City* (1945) and *Paisan* (1946) by Roberto Rossellini, and *Shoeshine* (1946) and *Bicycle Thieves* (1948) by Vittorio DeSica. Italian neorealism constructs a powerful effect of reality through reportorial objectivity in camera and editing and through a dependence on actual locations and nonprofessional performers. As evidenced by the conclusion to *One Wonderful Sunday,* Kurosawa's experiments with the effect of reality are closer to the "poetic realism" to be found in the cinema of Jean Renoir during the 1930s, in films like *The Crime of Monsieur Lange* (1936), *La Bête Humaine* (1938), and *Rules of the Game* (1939).

Rashomon as well as *Ikiru* freely use the wipe cut, a visual device common in many traditions of silent film but generally suppressed within the classical sound cinema and its codes of realism. By means of this device one image is "wiped" off the movie screen by the movement of a new image onto the screen. The frame-line of this new image typically moves across the screen in a horizontal direction, but in the history of cinema there are several instances of wipes in a vertical direction. In *Rashomon* the wipe cut serves a number of visual and transitional functions. It is used in conjunction with traveling and pan shots as an optical means of accenting the momentum of screen action. In other instances the film's wipe cuts mark a shift in the contexts from which story events are related in the narrative's transitions to and from the prison courtyard setting. The wipe cut can also indicate a visual ellipsis that has eliminated connecting action within the same scene, as in the advancement from the conclusion of the woodcutter's testimony to the start of the priest's in the prison courtyard.

The significance of the wipe cut within Kurosawa's work is accounted for variously within film criticism. In distinguishing the components of film language, Christian Metz places the wipe cut within the code of *trucage,* which includes optical effects that constitute visual but not photographic material. That is, a *trucage* is not primarily photographic in itself but is rather a modification of the photographic. In Metz's estimation, a *trucage* signals the direct intervention by the filmmaker into a story, whereas a film's photographic material alone simply implies the filmmaker's point of view through the development of a story.

A *trucage* produces a manifest effect on the photographic

image simultaneously with the viewer's perception of that image. Metz gives as an example the kind of wipe cut Kurosawa uses in _Seven Samurai_, which involves and affects two sets of moving images, the images departing and the ones entering. Metz terms _trucage_ an "avowed machination," a rhetorical intervention which the viewer often subsumes into the unfolding story.[17] The apparent manipulation of the image is in these cases attended by the viewer's psychological denial of its artificiality. _Trucage_ is thus for Metz a double structure involving opposed qualities such as imaginary/real, distancing/identification, and recognition/denial. It is never totally one or the other quality from each pair of alternatives; it is rather an interfusion of the two. Without recourse to the term, Metz's account describes an optical intertextual figure.

Noel Burch assesses Kurosawa's employment of the wipe cut as a deliberate anachronism in view of the general evolution toward dissolves in film editing during the 1940s. According to Burch, by manifestly causing the frame-line to cross the spectator's field of vision, Kurosawa's wipe cuts expose elements that otherwise sustain the illusion of reality. Kurosawa thus acknowledges discontinuity and the screen's two-dimensionality as conditions of filmic representation, while conventional Western codes conceal these formal limitations. Burch's claims about the wipe cut in Kurosawa films accord with his book's more general argument about the unique reflexivity and intertextuality of Japanese cinema.[18] Burch argues that in regard to narrative structure, however, Kurosawa fully adheres to a Western linear development of visual information and to univocal resolution of dramatic conflict by constructing a one-dimensional realm of meaning.[19] Contrary to this last assertion, within Kurosawa's cinema there is often in fact resolution at the level of events while conflict at the level of meaning remains unresolved, as in the obvious cases of _Rashomon_, _Ikiru_, _The Idiot_, and _Red Beard_.

In the estimation of Gilles Deleuze, the wipe cut constitutes an imaginary Japanese character that serves as Kurosawa's cinematic signature. The imaginary character is composed of a thick vertical stroke that extends from top to bottom of the screen and is joined by thinner, variable horizontal strokes that move screen right to left and left to right, which are the photographic components of whatever images are involved in the wipe cut. This signature is a comprehensive movement-image that retraces both the film's segmentation and its wholeness. It is also a configuration that reiterates Kurosawa's thematic preoccupation with life at the high and low reaches of society and his camera's frequent exploration of scenic space in vertical and horizontal directions.[20] For all of Deleuze's ingenuity in fashioning this gestalt for Kurosawa, it remains an auteurist conjecture on the director's presence in the film work.

Donald Richie terms the wipe cut a "punctuation mark" in Kurosawa's cinema through which a "new image pushes off the old, as one lantern slide pushes off the other." Though Richie thinks the device signals a "definite meaning," he leaves that meaning largely to speculation: "Perhaps it is its finality that appeals, this single stroke canceling all that went before, questioning it, at the same time bringing in the new."[21] Richie believes Kurosawa's most frequent application of the wipe cut is to give an impression of the elapse of time, usually a short period of time. Its other uses include the abridgment of a related series of events into a few representative, essential actions and the designation of closure to the film drama's most important events. Richie's comparisons to the lantern slide and the punctuation mark indicate a conceptualization at the level of the still image and the sentence unit, while in fact Kurosawa's cinema manifestly employs the wipe cut as a mobile, narrative factor.

The wipe cut is present in Kurosawa's cinema from its inception. In his early script *Bravo, Tasuke Isshin!* (*Appare Isshin Tasuke*), later directed by Kiyoshi Saeki in 1945, a character is represented in a series of comic postures and humorous circumstances that are linked through a number of wipes

designated in the scenario itself. Another early script entitled
*Three Hundred Miles through Enemy Lines (Tekichu Odan
Sanbyaku Ri)*, later filmed in 1957 under the direction of Issei
Mori, conceives its storyline in a chase-action formula that
visually motivates use of the wipe cut.[22] In the first film under Kurosawa's direction, *Sanshiro Sugata*, its use is sparing
and unaffected. Rapid but unemphatic wipes, in both horizontal and vertical directions, either link actions within a scene
or relate successive events. In one innovative editing figure
that marks a change in scene, Kurosawa joins two shots that
contain swish pans, both in the same screen direction, that
simulate a wipe cut. In using the wipe cut along the horizontal axis Kurosawa does not privilege one direction over the
other, despite a Japanese directional bias of right-to-left found
in habits of reading print materials, of viewing traditional picture scrolls and other visual compositions, and of responding
to the scenic space in classical theater.[23]

With Kurosawa's reinvigorated interest in visual experimentation around 1950, the wipe cut is given greater importance and flexibility in his filmmaking. In segments of *Rashomon* and *Throne of Blood* it is used in conjunction with
traveling and pan shots as an optical means of rendering the
narrative sweep of events. Its uses in *Ikiru* are multiple in
meaning and tone, ranging from a comic figuration of bureaucratic futility to a figure for a newly gained, heroic momentum to life. In the films from this period to 1965 the wipe cut
functions often as an accented narrative connective to designate *ongoing* events.

In some cases, the wipe cut functions as a signifier of the
motility inherent in narrative form. In *Ikiru*, for example,
some wipe cuts signal the intertextual relation between story
elements and plot. In *The Hidden Fortress*, the opening sequence progresses through tracking and traveling shots as
two peasant soldiers wander down a road, bickering and in-
sulting each other along the way. Once the peasants split up
and go their separate ways, the film's first wipe cut is used to
follow the next adventure of one of them. The device inaugur-

ates the onset of events that rapidly lead to the reunion of the two peasants.

Editing technique in *The Lower Depths* is consciously restricted to the simple cut and the three fade-out to black/fade-in optical devices used to designate act divisions. But the director has ingeniously arranged physical properties and dramatic activity in order to slide new visual images in and out of view much as a wipe cut does. From behind a curtain drawn across his bunk the actor suddenly appears, as later he will withdraw from view behind it. The prostitute Osen will similarly emerge from her bedding and subsequently cover herself again. After the gambler falls down in a drunken stupor, he lies unnoticed on the floor until the landlord inadvertently kicks him and the gambler rises into view again. In the tenants' lodging as in the landlord's house, sliding doors and windows serve to interpose and to remove characters within both the visual field and the dramatic action. Kurosawa's use of architectural features for such purposes is evident as early as *Sanshiro Sugata*.

Ikiru

Kurosawa has made the general observation that "there is nothing more dangerous than a worthless bureaucrat who has fallen prey to the trends of the times" (*Autobiography*, 119). The breakup of large business trusts, or *zaibatsu*, and reform of the civil service bureaucracy were primary goals during the Allied occupation of Japan in the years 1945–52. By the late 1950s, however, the *zaibatsu* had regained significant financial control and exerted powerful influence on government, a situation Kurosawa dramatizes in *The Bad Sleep Well*. And despite its initial goals, the Allied occupation administration implemented reform of civilian government indirectly, through many of the same agencies in power during wartime. Consequently, a majority of the bureaucrats remained in place and those at the top were given responsibility for the restructuring that was originally intended to remove them from government.

The company vice president at Toho judged the last scenes in *Ikiru*, after the funeral and back in the government office, to be an unnecessary continuation in the criticism of bureaucracy, but Kurosawa refused to adhere to the studio's instructions to remove them. The director threatened that if those sequences were tampered with he would insist that all the office scenes be taken out. Two years earlier the president of Daiei studios had complained that *Rashomon* was incomprehensible, but he claimed credit for the film after its international success. These professional experiences confirmed Kurosawa's distrust of the power structure in contemporary Japan's bureaucracies. In a subsequent critique of power, Kurosawa intended that the original audience for *The Bad Sleep Well* would recognize that the corrupt company president receives instructions over the phone directly from Premier Nishi, who was in office at the time.

In *Ikiru*, the social ill that brings the housewives to the municipal Citizen's Section is an infested drainage area in their neighborhood. But at the municipal offices they are exposed to the far greater disease of a stagnant bureaucracy. The bureaucracy of Japan in the period of its reconstruction is shown to defeat the purpose of reform and to serve the purpose of self-promotion for a few higher officials. In its scenes concerning the office worker Toyo and Watanabe's son Mitsuo, *Ikiru* also finds that the younger generation's absorption in material life has made them indifferent to suffering and ungrateful for the sacrifices of their parents.

The X-ray image that opens *Ikiru* is accompanied by a narrator's explanation, in voice-over: "This is the stomach of the hero of our story. There is stomach cancer, . . . but the man himself doesn't know this yet."[24] From a clinical point of view, a tumor has been discovered inside this man. From ethical and philosophical points of view, there remains the unanswered question of what lies inside man. When the writer in the bar asks Watanabe if his stomach hurts, Watanabe replies that his pain is greater than that and he clutches at his chest. The gesture evokes an image of emotional and spiritual pain at the heart of humanity. In *Ikiru*, as in *Rashomon*, there is great frequency in the use of dramatic closeups. In both cases, two dimensions of meaning to the human face are made evident. One is the face as a social mask, the other is as a mirror to the individual's spirit. These two films treat the face in closeup as a social and psychological site. This usage contrasts with films where closeups appear infrequently, such as *Throne of Blood* and *The Lower Depths*, whose tone is by comparison distant and emotionally austere.

From an X-ray image that presents Watanabe as an apparition, the narrative is inaugurated with an account of his virtual nonexistence in his professional and social life. In the course of its duration, the narrative reiterates the statement that Watanabe has existed like a corpse or a mummy for over twenty-five years. Our understanding of Watanabe and his self-understanding advance by means of the existential paradox that this spiritless man will discover a meaning in life only on the brink of death. The paradox thus offers a promise and an argument that emerges from the narrative: even a nearly lifeless individual, such as this mummy within the bureaucracy, contains the potential for change and action as long as he is alive.

A modest thematic statement of this paradox is made through the Japanese love ballad popular among Watanabe's generation, "Life Is Short," a lyric commentary that evolves in meaning within the film. The refrain of this ballad states: "Life is so short / Fall in love . . . / Before you can no longer love." It is from the prospect of nonexistence that *Ikiru* draws existence into focus. Kurosawa explains the inception of this original film story as follows: "Sometimes I think of my death. I think of ceasing to be . . . and it is from these thoughts that *Ikiru* came."[25]

First seen in person, at his cramped desk at the municipal office, Watanabe appears mechanical and lifeless. There is a narrow, confined symmetry to his desk job, with its towering stacks of documents and forms prominent in both foreground and background. These tight compositions are restated in

shots of the small shrine at home that commemorates his
dead wife. They are reiterated in the opening scene at the funeral gathering, with the mourners lined to each side of the
altar, at the center of which is a black-bordered photograph of
Watanabe. Though central within the visual composition,
Watanabe and his experience are in these compositions marginal in dramatic and narrative importance. In the course of
the funeral sequence, however, where he is absent except for
his likeness on the memorial photograph, Watanabe is shown
to exert an unexpected margin of power within society. At
the end of life Watanabe comes into being. He belongs to the
type of "unformed characters" that deeply appeal to Kurosawa, who has stated: "no matter how old I get, I am still unformed myself; in any case, it is in watching someone unformed enter the path to perfection that my fascination
knows no bounds" (*Autobiography*, 129–30).

As an inquiry into character destiny, the narrative takes a
false start in the early scenes, as indicated by the narrator's
comment: "This is the main character of our story, but he's
not very interesting yet. He's just passing the time, wasting
it, rather. It would be difficult to say that he is really alive."
The narrator's commentary is dramatized at this point by a
joke the young office worker Toyo reads about a dutiful bureaucrat who is in fact entirely superfluous. The narrator continues, "This is pretty bad. He is like a corpse and actually he
has been dead for the past twenty-five years. Before that he
had some life in him. He even tried to work." The sequence
cuts to a desk drawer that contains a long-forgotten proposal
to increase office efficiency, which he now uses only as waste
paper to clean his fountain pen and ink stamp.

Opening explicitly as an inquiry into Watanabe's physical
condition and his state of being as a whole, the commentary
initiates a search for meaning through the instrument of narrative itself.[26] In his commentary the narrator goes on to observe about the purposelessness of Watanabe's working life:

His ambitions have been well smothered by City Hall. But, he's busy—oh, very busy. Still, he is doing little. He has to keep busy simply to stay where he is. Is this as it should be? [The sequence cuts to Watanabe swallowing tablets he has taken from a bottle.] But before he begins to think seriously, his stomach must get worse and more useless hours must accumulate.

Given the intertexts disclosed through *Something Like an Autobiography*, this narrator can be recognized as an adaptation of the benshi's functions. More intimately, the narrator of *Ikiru* (a word that translates "to live") can be recognized as Kurosawa's means of commemorating his brother Heigo, the negative image in counterpart to the positive image of continued life.

In addition to the investigation into Watanabe's life conducted by this unidentified, external narrator, the pursuit of meaning within the narrative takes many directions. These range from the comic insistence of Watanabe's brother Kiichi that he take a mistress, and Kiichi's final disappointment that apparently Watanabe had not after all done so, to the dawning conviction among fellow office workers that their chief realized he was mortally ill. To comprehend fully the varied results of such a search, the structural distinctions between story and plot within the narrative of *Ikiru* must be recognized. Clearly, the plot of *Ikiru* departs radically from the chronological order of its story components. And this plot restructuring constitutes an argument about the meaning of Watanabe's life story.

The film's structural variations between story and plot are indicated by the chart below. In *flashback* the forward flow of narrative time is broken to insert a scene from the past. Conventionally, a flashback entails some tangible editing cue, such as a dissolve, as a mark of alteration in the order of time. Rather than use stressed optical or editing devices, however, Kurosawa accents the emotional and visual stimuli that prompt Watanabe's memories. The memorial altar and photograph of his wife leads to recall of the funeral procession following her hearse. The baseball bat Watanabe uses to secure a sliding door is the link to a day on which he watched his son play in a baseball stadium.[27]

The narrative flow of events at the very outset is subtle in that the X-ray anticipates an event in the near future. The opening incidents in the office revert back in time to the routines before Watanabe visits the clinic for a diagnosis of his stomach pain. This reversion in time is conducted without the formal device of a flashback. In part, the initial office scene typifies the meaningless desk work that characterizes the existence of a bureaucrat throughout his career. The temporality of the scene in this regard is generic. Watanabe's official stamp has far more importance to his existence than anything he does until he finally takes action on behalf of the housewives.

The housewives who make an appeal at the Citizen's Section, where a prominent sign invites the public's inquiries, are given a quintessential bureaucratic runaround as they are sent off to be shuffled among fifteen different government agencies. A series of rapid wipe cuts, in both directions, shows them finally returned to the Citizen's Section without any progress having been made. The editing figure for this futile circularity is constructed of wipes in the following order: three wipe cuts that move from screen right to left, two from left to right, two from right to left, one from left to right, six from right to left, and a final wipe from right to left that brings the housewives back where they started.

Within the sequence of wipe cuts an appreciable period of time passes in the transition from a summer heat wave to conditions of heavy rain. On the narrative level of the housewives' efforts, the montage is a *synopsis* of their long, persistent, frustrating attempts to get government action. On the narrative level of Watanabe's physical and psychological condition, the montage of wipe cuts is an *ellipsis*, telescoping the time that passes before he begins to confront life.

Only after the angry outburst that ends their return visit

Ikiru: Story and Plot

Story Elements (events in the chronological order of their occurrence)

Watanabe's 30 Years as a Bureaucrat

"Plan for Efficiency"	The office "Mummy"				X-Ray	2 weeks' absence	Back at office	Park construction / Park in use	Office routine resumes
Wife's funeral	Conversation with brother about remarriage	Son's baseball game	Son's operation	Son's departure for war		Spree with writer / Pursuit of Toyo	Last 5 months	His death	Funeral

Watanabe's Personal Life

Narrative Plot (order in which events are presented)

[→ indicates narrative movement forward in time
← indicates narrative movement backward in time]

Voice-over narration	Dramatic action				(Voice-over narration)	Dramatic action	(Voice-over narration)	Dramatic action
X-Ray →	← Routines of office life, petition by housewives	→ Visit to clinic, Watanabe's conclusion that he has cancer	→ At home that night, Watanabe's memories, in flashback: Wife's funeral, Conversation with brother about remarriage, Son's baseball game, Son's operation, Son's departure for war		→2 weeks, away from office	→ First day back at office	Death, 5 months later	→ Funeral ← Memories, in flashback, of Watanabe's last 5 months	→Next week, office routine, the park in use

to the Citizen's Section is their human plight acknowledged. A clerk explains that the Section Chief is absent for the day and he suggests that they submit a written petition. The suggestion contains no promise of government action, of course, since the office is already full of pointless documents. The housewives' outburst and Watanabe's coincidental absence, however, mark a rupture to the routines of bureaucratized life for both these citizens and the office chief. The plot now begins to initiate change in the generic time of Watanabe's life story.

At the clinic, where a doctor examines the X-ray of Watanabe's stomach, the narrative reaches the starting point of the plot, the film's opening image. Watanabe is not informed directly by the doctor of the gravity of his condition. Rather, Watanabe infers the truth from the description of fatal symptoms made by another patient in the waiting room. The scene in the waiting room is a powerful instance of black comedy. The patient, who takes pleasure in considering the morbid condition of others at the clinic, presses Watanabe with graphic and horrifying details of the cancer's effects. As Watanabe changes his position on the sofa in growing discomfort, the patient leans further toward him. By the time Watanabe is called to the doctor's office he is in complete despair.

Watanabe will come to accept the truth of his sickness in spite of the doctor's lie that he suffers only from treatable stomach ulcers. Part of the process of gaining strength and self-knowledge is his own independent recognition of the degree of sickness within him. In private conversation after Watanabe leaves the clinic, the doctor, an intern, and a nurse speculate on what their own reactions to news of a mortal condition would be. They have silently conspired to withhold such news from Watanabe. In an offhand manner, the nurse indicates that she would commit suicide by taking strychnine. In the subsequent scene in the bar, Watanabe confesses that he has contemplated suicide through an overdose of the sleeping pills he gives to the writer. But he has decided against that alternative: "It's not that easy. I'd thought of end-

In *Ikiru*, Watanabe and a morbid fellow patient in the clinic waiting
room.

ing it all, but it's hard to die. And I can't die just yet. I don't
know what I've been living for all these years." In effect, Watanabe has initiated a quest to unravel a riddle that leads from
plot to life story.

An intimation of the proximity of death in everyday life is
made in three sequences that depict near-accidents in the
city streets. The first involves Watanabe when he walks heed-
lessly into heavy automobile traffic after leaving the clinic in
shock over the meaning of his condition. From the start of
this sequence the soundtrack remains completely silent in
order to suggest the paralysis that has stricken his consciousness, but the dissonance of city noise suddenly breaks through
when a truck narrowly misses Watanabe. The subsequent
two incidents are comic in tone. On a spree with the writer
through the city's pleasure quarter, Watanabe rushes into
nighttime traffic in his drunkenness and is miraculously un-
scathed. Toyo, in delight over her new silk stockings, rushes
from a store into the busy street and two city buses, passing

in opposite directions, just miss her. She reacts with laughter. After Watanabe has visited the clinic, he sits at home in complete darkness when Mitsuo and his wife enter. The young couple are involved in a discussion of how much money from his pension they can spend on the purchase of a modern house. After Mitsuo comments, "Even father wouldn't take his money to the grave," they discover Watanabe alone in the dark. The pathos of Watanabe's situation is a world apart from their material concerns and they will not come to know what he suffers. With the American popular tune "Too Young" heard from the couple's room upstairs, Watanabe opens the shrine to his wife in his room on the ground floor.

The photograph of his wife at the center of the altar is the psychological frame through which Watanabe begins to look into his past in narrative flashback.[28] The first perspective on the past is one from inside a car following the hearse with his wife's body. The sequence of shots identifies the point of view as that of Mitsuo as a child. Mitsuo is in turn regarded with concern by Watanabe, who is still a young man at the time. This identification of Watanabe's recollection with the perspective of his son as a child is an expression of the man's capacity for deep compassion. The boy worries that they will lose his mother if the limousine does not keep pace with the hearse. Metaphorically, the sequence places death as an immediate prospect within life and it suggests the narrative's own patterns of approach and withdrawal from its protagonist's death. Watanabe's compassion for Mitsuo is revealed further in the memory of his son's baseball game, which ends in a moment of defeat for the boy. The hospital flashback recalls a moment of the son's emotional need for his father. The last flashback in the series, set at a train station in wartime, focuses on the son's face and the anxiety evident there.

From these flashbacks, the narrative is advanced by several brief scenes in which Watanabe's absence from work is discussed by his family and by office clerks in the Citizen's Section. Watanabe physically reappears in the narrative at the small city bar where he meets the writer. This character becomes Watanabe's guide to the world of sensual indulgences, a self-declared tempter and Mephistopheles. While he proclaims a lust for life to be virtuous, the writer it turns out has nothing more in mind than dissipation and excess. In light of Watanabe's estrangement from his son and daughter-in-law, there is irony to the verse from an American popular tune rendered in English by two Japanese bargirls: "Come on'a my house." The night's adventures ultimately nauseate Watanabe, whose reaction signals the effects of both a sudden overindulgence in life's pleasures and an advancing stage of his cancer.

The transformation that Watanabe undergoes as a bureaucrat is first glimpsed in an incident involving a visit from Toyo when she presents her formal resignation from the municipal bureau. At home, where he has brought his government stamp, he starts to respond in an officious manner and he indicates that she has presented her petition on the wrong form. At the moment that he sees her look of disappointment, however, he overcomes his ingrained habits, disregards this irregularity, and approves the document. The exuberance of her gratitude startles Watanabe, who finds her vitality irresistibly attractive.

In escorting Toyo during the next several days, Watanabe is fascinated by her great hunger for life. This trait is literalized in the several scenes where, after finishing her own serving, she also eats the food that he has ordered for himself but cannot consume because of his stomach condition. Toyo is unresponsive, however, when faced with Watanabe's emotional starvation. At a sukiyaki restaurant, he starts to confess in a halting voice why he has existed as a mummy for nearly thirty years in the office. He did so for the sake of a son who now, Watanabe explains, is selfishly indifferent to his father. As the confession progresses, the camera gradually draws back, making Toyo more prominent in the foreground, diminishing Watanabe in the background. With her mouth full, she draws back from the table, further away from him, running her hands over her new stockings. She cuts short his confession with a reproach: "But you can't blame your son for that. . . . All parents are the same. . . . What's the matter with you. Why are you telling me your complaints about your son?" She abruptly closes this uncomfortable topic with the laughing accusation, "You love your son more than anyone else." A reaction shot shows Watanabe breaking into a smile of acknowledgment.

From the scene in the sukiyaki restaurant, the narrative shifts to a shot of Watanabe walking home alone that night, with a stricken look on his face. The juxtaposition of facial expressions suggests how fragile his emotional state is. When Watanabe later makes a surprise visit to Toyo at her new factory job, the qualities of joy and spontaneity have faded from her face. Her complaint at being taken away from the production line — "Every second wasted means less money" — reflects her annoyance over his continued attentions and hints that her youth is being expended for piece-work wages. Though at first she flatly refuses, Toyo relents and agrees to meet with Watanabe for one last evening.

Within many of its story events *Ikiru* employs visual figures of descent and ascent. In the clinic's examination room, for example, Watanabe's overcoat drops to the floor when the doctor explains his condition as only a case of stomach ulcers, the diagnosis that the other patient had warned will be given to disguise his terminal condition. When the doctor repeats this diagnosis in answer to a plea for the truth, Watanabe's head falls to a point nearly touching the desk in front of him. At home that night, Mitsuo and his wife find Watanabe sitting in the unlit room with his head still deeply bowed. In response to the son's call of "Father" from upstairs, Watanabe starts to climb the narrow staircase but he stops halfway up when the son calls down "Goodnight" and asks that the door and windows be locked. A camera point of view from upstairs shows Watanabe arrested in this position. The camera looks down on a bowed and stooped figure, the face not in view. In a subsequent family scene, after defeat in an effort to confide in his son, Watanabe leaves the upper floor in a daze and slowly climbs down the stairs to his own room.

Visual figures of descent, however, do not uniformly signify a broken spirit. Among his outings with Toyo is a visit to a skating rink where, in his inexperience, Watanabe falls to the ice and brings Toyo down with him, to their shared delight. In a flashback depicting an episode from his last months of life, Watanabe stumbles to the ground at the construction site where the park will be located. Unharmed, he is helped to his feet by one of the housewives. Water is brought to him from a neighborhood home and a look of wonder and pleasure comes over Watanabe's face. With the conclusion to this flashback, one of the mourners comments that his face held the expression of a man looking at his own grandchildren.

The scene of Watanabe and Toyo's last evening together, at a large, Western-style coffee shop, is a more complex figuration. During the scene the light recorded music heard (which includes "The March of the Wooden Soldiers") and the excitement of a children's birthday party in the background counterpoint the pathos of Watanabe's emotional dependence on Toyo. In a broken and confused voice he admits that he envies her high spirits. He confides further that when he realized he was dying he reexperienced the sensation of nearly drowning as a boy, an intertext Kurosawa has drawn from his own childhood. Watanabe's head is weighed down with despair by the thought that it is too late to accomplish anything in life. But his face abruptly lifts up and brightens with the thought that his last months can be useful. With a revived spirit, Watanabe descends the central stairway as the children's party guest of honor is greeted with a chorus in English of "Happy Birthday."

The next scene depicts Watanabe's return to the office, where he now functions with obvious purposefulness. To suggest that in the last months of life the man is reborn, the "Happy Birthday" melody is woven into the music track. At his desk, Watanabe's head nods up and down as he reads the written columns of a document. This gesture, which in the routines of office life had been a sign of ineffectual paper shuffling, is now preparatory to action. The document is identified as the housewives' petition, from which Watanabe tears a notation forwarding it to another municipal office. The noon lunch siren sounds as he heads out of the office to investigate the neighborhood's problem. At this point the narrator intervenes: "Five months later the hero of this story died."

The plot advances to Watanabe's funeral. With events over the last five months of his life narrated from this perspective, the film shifts to another context for investigation into his existence. One issue raised is that of the legacy Watanabe has left with his death, another is the narrative key that explains his transformation over the last months of life. The reporters and the mourners make diverse attempts to construct a convincing plot line from story events. Reporters stationed outside the funeral to interview the Deputy Mayor are developing the lead that Watanabe's death in the park was a suicide in symbolic protest over city hall's taking credit for the construction. The Deputy Mayor's revelation that the autopsy shows cause of death as cancer disqualifies that line of argument. This elected official is smugly confident that Watanabe had no knowledge of the disease. At the funeral gathering, all the section clerks nod their heads in obedient consent while the Deputy Mayor downplays Watanabe's role in creation of the park. The Deputy Mayor's plotting of events dispels any sense of riddle to the narrative and makes the meaning of Watanabe's changed behavior in the Citizen's Section irrelevant and immaterial.

With the arrival of the neighborhood housewives, the carefully managed formality of the funeral ceremony is disrupted, in much the same manner as these women had disrupted the routines of bureaucratic life. The first disruption they caused inaugurated the process of change in Watanabe's life story, this second one inaugurates a genuine search for the truth of his last five months of life. The narrative action of the funeral episode is in effect a search for the plot that contains the argument that answers the riddle of Watanabe's changed behavior.

The entry of the housewives brings to a standstill the officials' control over the occasion. The politicians are silenced as the women openly grieve and pay their sincere respects at the funeral altar. When the housewives leave, the sequence mounts three successive shots of the altar with Watanabe's photograph in the center. This photograph has been the transitional image marking the plot advancement from Watanabe's first day back in the office to his death five months later. Here, each successive shot enlarges the scale of the photograph until the last one fills the screen. This image is the positive counterpart to the X-ray negative that opens the narrative. The two photographic images are obvious intertexts. Made self-conscious by the outpouring of emotion, the Deputy Mayor and bureau chiefs awkwardly depart. With their departure, clerks from the Citizen's Section and those from other municipal bureaus draw closer together around the altar and interact with greater familiarity, especially as the drinking continues.

The previously linear and hierarchical symmetry of the funeral ceremony is broken down further as the mourners pursue an explanation for the cause underlying the change in Watanabe's life. Among the rationales they imagine are a love affair and the motive of self-advancement. The assistant Noguchi thinks that the park resulted from a set of political circumstances—such as upcoming city elections and the graft of local gangsters—that Watanabe could not have influenced at all. To the clerk Saito's speculation that his chief knew he had stomach cancer Mitsuo makes a categorical denial. The son expresses confidence that his father would have informed him in such a case, but the film audience has seen Watanabe fail in his attempts to overcome Mitsuo's indifference.

The mourners' persistence in seeking a clue to Watanabe's transformation results at this point in the scene's first flashback. Its focus is the Chief's new, light-colored hat, the source of several rumors about his behavior. Since the moment Watanabe acquired it on his nighttown odyssey with the writer, the hat has become a sign of his quest for a new approach to life. As a visual figure, the hat is an example of the rhetorical device *synecdoche*, through which a part of an object or a person is made to represent the whole. The closeup, a powerful and flexible element in film language, can readily create such figures. The Soviet director Eisenstein has explained this rhetorical property at length in his theoretical writings. His film *Battleship Potemkin* provides a famous example in the ship's doctor's pince-nez glasses, which dangle from an anchor line after the crew throws him overboard during a mutiny.

The order of the several flashbacks that follow in the plot is not necessarily equivalent to their chronological order in the story. What organizes them in the plot is a structure of *telling* details that gradually confirm the speculation that Watanabe acted like a man who knew he had only a few months left to live. Against the persistent skepticism of some office clerks, Kimura defends the heroism of Watanabe in overcoming bureaucratic obstacles and inertia to get the park built. As Watanabe's persistent efforts of the last months are recounted in flashback, the Chief's typically bowed posture changes in significance. Rather than humility and lifelessness, it is now a sign of respectful but resolute conviction. The camera depicts Watanabe in this posture now from a slightly lower angle that shows more of his face. As a consequence the film spectator can read from Watanabe's facial expression the realization that even a dying, unimportant man can exert influence if he is sufficiently determined. His liberation from the confined existence of the bureaucracy is indicated by the outdoor, open-air scenes prominent in the sequence of events resulting in construction of the park.

The flashbacks make apparent the existential paradoxes of Watanabe's life at its end. As his physical strength diminishes, his social effectiveness increases. The park to which he devotes his new-found energies becomes his tomb on the

**The policeman speaks at the funeral gathering for Watanabe in
Ikiru.**

snowy night when he dies. Seen in X-ray image as an apparition and a phantom in the beginning, Watanabe is revealed by the plot in the end as a pure and intense soul.

The policeman who returns Watanabe's new hat, now soiled and battered, reports that he had thought the old man was drunk on the night of his death in the park. With a sense of his own professional negligence, the policeman explains that he would have ordered Watanabe to leave the park but he finally did not want to disturb the old man as he contentedly sang "Life Is Short." The son clutches the hat as he leaves the ceremony, followed by his wife, to whom Mitsuo complains that he was wronged by his father in not being told about the cancer. Though his son cannot recognize the legacy embodied by the new hat, in the plot it has become a banner of the life Watanabe finally fulfilled.

In the last phase of the funeral wake, colleagues solemnly and drunkenly vow to uphold Watanabe's example as a civil servant. The concluding office scene, however, demonstrates that the bureaucratic status quo of ineffectiveness and futility remains unchanged. Watanabe's unprecedented activity and advocacy over the last months of life are a legacy lost on official society. In the concluding office scene Ono, the new Section Chief, instructs a clerk to send a citizen's complaint off on the first leg of a futile bureaucratic circuit. As he witnesses the incident, Kimura rises angrily from his desk, knocking over a chair in his haste. Kimura's reaction lasts only a few seconds; he leaves unvoiced any protest. In the face of Ono's blank stare, Kimura sits back down and resumes the busy work at his desk, obscured by a stack of documents in front of him. Kimura had been given the office nickname "Gelatin" by Toyo to indicate a personality that is fainthearted and always quivering. The brief rise and fall of his movement is the film's final iteration of the visual figure of ascent and descent; its meaning is already enfeebled. The argument maintained through the plot had been momentarily persuasive among the drunken, maudlin mourners but it proves powerless to change the norms of office life. The film's encompassing argument nonetheless sustains a potential and promise for human change.

Where the narrative to *Rashomon* leads to a charitable act taken in the face of humanity's corruption and deceptions, the narrative to *Ikiru* results in human inaction. But the finale to *Ikiru* is an image rather than a scene of events. In the closing sequence, Kimura visits the small city park Watanabe succeeded in having built. In the gathering darkness, just after the children are called home, the empty swings are still in movement. Their gentle, harmonic sway is a sign of the modest mark Watanabe has left on the world. This movement is a final iteration of the wipe cut figures, which have come to suggest the potential for change in the plot of a man's life. No monument marks this realized potential. Rather, Watanabe's legacy is contained in the humble, lyric beauty of the moving swings.

4

Tragedy without Heroes

In his *jidai-geki*, Kurosawa explores several distinctive types of heroism. In its representation of the warrior class, *Seven Samurai* depicts personalities that range from the dutiful apprentice Katsushiro and the consummate swordsman Kyuzo to the ingenious and spiritually wise leader Kambei (portrayed by Takashi Shimura). Numbered among the warriors is the renegade Kikuchiyo (played by Toshiro Mifune), who attempts to evade his fate as one born into the peasant class by posing as a samurai. Kikuchiyo's relationship to the genuine samurai is marginal until preparations for battle begin. By the time he has fallen in action, he dies a warrior hero.

The heroism of the male protagonists in *The Hidden Fortress* and *Red Beard* is relatively uncomplicated. The sixteenth-century general in the first and the nineteenth-century physician in the second, both portrayed by Toshiro Mifune, are epic types who soberly embody the highest moral qualities. In events that take place immediately prior to those onscreen in *The Hidden Fortress*, General Rokurota Makabe has sacrificed the life of his own sister to make possible the escape of Princess Yuki, whom he loyally protects.[1] But the disturbing implications of this act are raised only once and then are left unexamined. Comic inversions of the film's heroism are presented through the bickering companions Tahie and Matakishi, two peasants who are induced through greed to participate in the General's brave efforts to protect the Princess. This comic duo is the model for the robotic pair C3PO and R2D2 in George Lucas's *Star Wars* (1977), which draws additional story ideas from the Kurosawa epic. The doctor in *Red Beard* proves physically superior in a test of his fighting abilities when single-handedly he defeats armed attackers. This skill in battle serves his humanitarian ideals, for it enables him to rescue an abused adolescent girl.

The antiheroic elements associated with the Toshiro Mifune character in *Seven Samurai* are fully developed through his roles in the comic, action-adventure *jidai-geki Yojimbo* and *Sanjuro*.[2] As compared with the hero's idealized dignity, greatness, and power in the face of fate, the antihero often appears ignoble, small-minded, ineffectual, or passive. The Mifune character in each film is an antihero in appearance and in some of his behavior, but his character proves ultimately to have strength, integrity, and a personal code of justice. The antithetical construct of such heroism is dependent on intertextual dynamics of characterization that reverse codes of idealized heroic *appearance* but does not ultimately negate heroic ideals.

Yojimbo is set in 1860, at the end of the Edo era, to mark a point of exhaustion in the feudal system and in the traditional hierarchy that had placed the samurai completely above farmers, artisans, and merchants. Though some social forms in the film continue to refer to the feudal order, the infrastructure to its fictional town is clearly determined by modern commercial interests. The traditional elevation of the samurai class has been reduced to a point where unemployed samurai have become thugs hired to protect the merchant class. Lawlessness and disloyalty are the rule in this new age. Farmers have become powerless victims.

In an intended parallel to the collusion between business and *yakuza* in postwar Japan, the town's merchants in the mid-nineteenth-century setting of *Yojimbo* are dependent upon criminals to protect their business interests. In the midst of their fierce competition, however, the only tradesman to prosper is the coffin-maker. The masterless samurai Sanjuro, using the name he has fabricated on the spot, appears to offer his services to the highest bidder among the battling parties. Sanjuro's clever tactics lead the competitors onto a path of mutual destruction until he is obliged to take a more direct role. Once forced into action, his sword is the swift instrument of his superiority. Sanjuro restores peace to the town and a possibility for order, then he saunters away. In the sequel *Sanjuro*, the character continues his antic, antiheroic ways and in the end is compelled to discourage the worshipful loyalty of nine young samurai. *Sanjuro* consistently parodies the clichéd idealizations of *bushido* common to Japanese period films.

Kurosawa's solitary, anonymous human agent of justice is the basis for Sergio Leone's Westerns featuring Clint Eastwood as the hero with no name later in the 1960s. The Japanese director recognized from the first the correlations of his two films with the Western genre: "Good Westerns are liked by everyone. Since humans are weak they want to see good people and great heroes. Westerns have been done over and over again and in the process a kind of grammar has evolved."[3] In visual language, *Yojimbo* and *Sanjuro* fully employ the film grammar developed by John Ford, Howard Hawks, and other Hollywood directors, but in storyline, characterization, and tone they treat the hero with comic, reductive familiarity.

Beyond the expediency of money, Sanjuro embarks on a campaign against corruption and injustice as an indulgence to his own whims. In these respects, the character is a direct parody of the selfless, pure motives of an ideal hero. But the characterization of Sanjuro still conveys an unlikely heroism. It is an example of the "hybrid construction" Bakhtin identifies in his analysis of the novel. In explanation of this textual property, Bakhtin offers as a primary example parody, which "actually contains mixed within it two utterances, two speech manners, two styles, two 'languages,' two semantic and axiological belief systems."[4] In such a doubled structure there is no internal formal boundary that separates the languages and belief systems. Rather, the text is a field of interaction among them.

In the contemporary stories *The Bad Sleep Well* and *High and Low*, heroic action for the protagonists, again portrayed by Toshiro Mifune, is complex and contradictory as the result of textual factors other than parody. In the first film, motives of revenge have led Koichi Nishi to assume a false identity, serve dutifully for five years as secretary to the business executive who has destroyed his father, and to marry that executive's daughter. As a consequence of his methods, Nishi nearly commits the same crimes that he attempts to redress. Nishi recognizes that obsessive vengeance has made him as merciless as the company bosses, and he relents. At the point where he is ready to abandon his scheme and to accept his wife with love, the momentum of events sweeps forward and Nishi is compelled to kidnap a business administrator in an attempt to make the company's crimes public. In the end, however, he falls victim to company intrigue and to his own duplicity. Nishi is killed near his hideout in an automobile accident staged by the executive's agents.

The protagonist Kingo Gondo of *High and Low* is coerced into a heroic sacrifice when a kidnapper who intended to ransom his son takes the son of Gondo's chauffeur by mistake. A successful production manager who is about to gain control of his company, Gondo is convinced by police to raise the ransom sum. This action leads to the return of the kidnap victim, but it ruins Gondo's business fortunes. In the aftermath, Gondo leaves the hilltop where his mansion stands and wanders through the same city streets frequented by the kidnapper, who is being trailed by police. The kidnapper, a poor medical student, subsequently murders an innocent drug addict by intentionally administering an overdose.

After the kidnapper has been sentenced to execution, Gondo visits the condemned man in prison. The kidnapper confesses to a profound hatred for Gondo's conspicuous wealth and to great satisfaction over its loss. The reflection of each man's face is cast in the plate glass partition that separates them. Gondo is unnerved by the encounter. As the sequence dramatizes their conversation, the reflected image of one man overlaps and matches the face of the other, and the pattern is reversed in the alternations among shot-reaction shot. The pattern conveys a profound psychological intimacy and doubleness.

Kurosawa has found a rich source for his explorations of heroism in Shakespeare's tragedies, particularly *Hamlet* (to which *The Bad Sleep Well* bears strong parallels), *Macbeth*, and *King Lear*. It is most accurate to describe *Macbeth* as the primary intertext for *Throne of Blood* rather than as the basis for a Shakespeare adaptation by Kurosawa. In similar fashion, *King Lear* can be considered one of two principal intertexts for *Ran*. In taking material from the Renaissance tragic repertory, however, Kurosawa disrupts and contests conventions of the genre. The individual, tragic worldview in the Shakespeare plays is reconceived in the Kurosawa films and becomes a tragic world without heroism. The condition of tragedy without heroism is inevitable from a modern, absurdist perspective on human experience.

Throne of Blood

Macbeth, like Richard III, is one of Shakespeare's most problematic tragic heroes. Masculine heroism conventionally offers an elevated if not idealized set of values in the hero's personality and social role. In the context of tragedy, the masculine hero by convention possesses uncommon greatness even while he is flawed or vulnerable in some profound way. Macbeth's heroic stature is established initially in an account by a wounded captain who has just returned from the battlefront. Faced in succession by rebel forces and Norway's invading army, Macbeth "carved out his passage" with a sword and "doubly redoubled strokes upon the foe" to "bathe in reeking wounds" the king's enemies (1.2.19, 38–39).[5] Upon hearing this report of slaughter, King Duncan praises Macbeth as a "valiant [and] Worthy gentleman" (1.2.24). Yet when Macbeth hesitates to commit similar acts to acquire the throne of Scotland, Lady Macbeth ridicules his lack of courage and resolve. In attacking his manliness and the strength of his love, Lady Macbeth shames her husband into resolving to fulfill his ambition through treachery.

Macbeth is confronted with a world of profound equivocation in which values and conditions that are normally op-

posed are now in a state of conjunction and interpenetration. The paradoxical context for the play's tragic events is announced at the opening in the witches' exchange, "the battle's
lost and won. . . . Fair is foul, and foul is fair" (1.1.4, 10). Such
equivocal conditions rapidly overtake both the social and natural orders. The political title given by Duncan to Macbeth
in reward for his battlefield success, thane of Cawdor, is a position just vacated with the king's execution of a traitor. The
title confirms Macbeth's legitimate rise in political fortunes
and it provokes his treasonous ambitions for the throne.

One Duncan is assassinated, an eclipse brings night to
the daylight hours and the king's horses turn into predators.
The fulfillment of Macbeth's ambition, once he occupies the
throne, destroys entirely his capacity to enjoy that fulfillment. His brief exercise of royal power only serves to destroy
his kingdom. In a final paradoxical situation, Macbeth's defeat comes when he is faced with an opponent "not born of
woman" (5.7.3). The degree of the play's negations is conveyed
in Macbeth's early observation that "nothing is / But what is
not" (1.3.141–42) and in his ultimate conclusion that life "is a
tale / Told by an idiot, full of sound and fury / Signifying nothing" (5.5.26–28). Such nihilism has gained new significance
in contemporary thought through the imaginative works and
philosophical inquiries of existentialists and absurdists.[6]

One difficulty in identifying Macbeth's situation and actions as tragically heroic lies in the character's conscious choice
of evil means in the pursuit of power. In a modern account of
Shakespearean tragedy that has long stood as a standard assessment, A. C. Bradley credits Macbeth as a man of honor,
conscience, and humanity at his core.[7] Tragedy ensues from
his sacrifice of this innate goodness for ambition and from the
catastrophic emotional and mental effects that follow. His
victimization is initiated through the influence of Lady Macbeth's ruthless will and pitiless scheming. Bradley finds in
Macbeth's last speeches both recognition and remorse in the
face of his short-lived annihilation of human values.

In another account of Shakespearean tragedy, Cleanth

Brooks identifies the heroic qualities that redeem Macbeth as a soldier's courage, great imagination, and his quest to master the future.[8] The audience's tragic identification with the hero comes in its recognition of an inevitable human struggle with fate. In this view, Macbeth's innate sense of pity and terror in the face of his own inhumanity is to be found in the vestiges of loyalty and compassion that remain in him as he faces defeat.

Within the play's framework of profound equivocations, however, Macbeth's redemptive human potential is recognized to be inseparable from his inhuman deeds. From a perspective of the play's nihilism and absurdism, its paradoxes are irresolvably cruel, for in several respects Macbeth fulfills his humanity through murder. Even with Duncan lawfully in power at the outset, human affairs are defined by their violence. As the play progresses, tragic paradox is revealed through the commission of inhuman acts in pursuit of human aims. In bloody times, murder empowers man. Conscience, which in better times might govern humanity, now threatens to incapacitate man.

Conventional accounts of Macbeth's tragic heroism consider his individual exercise of conscience weaker than the appeals to ambition provoked by the witches and Lady Macbeth. Yet, Macbeth's first extended self-examination (1.7) is based on calculated self-interest and pragmatic fear rather than a sense of conscience, honor, or compassion. Macbeth withdraws from the alternative of assassination after deliberating its negative consequences, which he envisions in terms of inevitable retribution against himself and of the pity Duncan's death will provoke among his subjects. Once Macbeth is in power, humane values such as justice and loyalty can no longer even be defined. The nobleman Ross, himself suspected of treachery by some interpreters of the play, states this condition of moral and political uncertainty: "cruel are the times, when we are traitors / And do not know ourselves" (4.2.18–19).

The characters and plot in *Macbeth*, Shakespeare's most condensed and abbreviated tragedy, are distilled for *Throne of Blood* into an even more concentrated and intense drama. The script has pared down action and speech to focus events exclusively on the Macbeth couple, Washizu and Lady Asaji. The Film Characters section at the back of this book provides the cast of characters in *Throne of Blood* and the corresponding Shakespeare roles, though in many significant respects the correspondence is limited. The film eliminates scenes devoted to the lords and leaders allied in the liberation of Scotland from Macbeth's tyranny. The most important of these in Shakespeare (4.3) is a demonstration of the integrity and patriotism of Malcolm, legitimate heir to the throne. It also contains, in references to the English king Edward the Confessor, a portrait of benevolent rule under a monarch who nurtures and heals the body politic of society.

Discussion by other nobles and by the doctor of the murderous events under Macbeth's reign (such as in 3.6 and 5.1) is removed. The script replaces such scenes with brief dialogues among samurai and soldiers about the course of their fortunes in service to Washizu. Their rise is measured by an advancement from outpost fort to North Castle and ultimately to Forest Castle. With the anarchy of Washizu's reign, his men observe that the castle foundations are rotting and that even the rats seek refuge elsewhere. Washizu's downfall will come at the hands of such men. Thus, the film's dramatic commentary on the course of destiny is made by a collective, anonymous voice rather than by heroic nobles. The script also removes the porter scene (2.3), which serves Shakespeare as a comic grotesque restatement of the play's imagery of infernal conditions and chaotic equivocation.

Most consequentially, the film has greatly reduced the role of Noriyasu, the counterpart to Macduff. With the slaughter of his innocent wife and young children under Macbeth's orders, a scene that has no equivalent in the film, Macduff is given the most immediate and sympathetic motives for ending tyranny. Macduff alone fulfills the prophecy about a man "not born of woman." With Macduff's ultimate revenge for these outrages in single combat with Macbeth, the audience is provided a sense of poetic justice. In the play's resolution, Macduff and Malcolm perform as the agents of a fate that restores order to the throne and thus to society.

The film dialogue makes no attempt to transpose Shakespeare's poetry into Japanese. Instead, the visuals create the film's metaphoric imagery. The film characters speak only from the necessity of a present situation. They are not developed through the reflective thought Shakespeare provides in asides and monologues. As a next step in his consolidation of power in the play, for example, Macbeth deliberates the assassination of Banquo in a soliloquy (3.1) that discloses his conscious effort to master destiny. In deleting such material, the film removes essential elements of heroic self-awareness and psychological conflict. Macbeth's climactic recognition, which includes his admission that "all our yesterdays have lighted fools / The way to dusty death" (5.5.22–23), is reduced to Washizu's frenzied exclamation "Fool!" The deletions also greatly change the dynamics of the conspiratorial partnership between husband and wife.

Throne of Blood condenses the dramatic settings to events into three locales: Forest Castle and the surrounding terrain, the dense and confusing Cobweb Forest that stands before the castle, and North Castle. Kurosawa and his script collaborators recognized that Forres, the location of Duncan's palace, is a place-name that designates a forest. Thus, in transposing the Birnam wood prophecy, they have brought the instrument of fate into closer proximity to the principal seat of power. In their respective rises to power, Washizu and Miki (Banquo) will each in turn occupy North Castle—Washizu first through his promotion by Lord Tsuzuki (King Duncan), and Miki through Washizu's assassination of Tsuzuki. North Castle had been commanded by Fujimaki, who had been urged to rebel by Inui, the ruler of an adjoining province. After this initial rebellion is defeated, Fujimaki commits *hara-kiri* in North Castle before Tsuzuki's orders for his execution can be carried out.

In its representation of the Forest Castle setting, the film's compositions are designed to foreshorten and compress vis-

ual perspective. Extensive use of the telephoto lens was favored by Kurosawa to achieve an effect that "effaces distance,
cancels all perspective and gives to the image a weight, a presence almost hallucinatory, making the rhythms of movement emerge."[9] In collaboration with scenic designer Yoshiro Muraki, the director decided that for Forest Castle

> the location should be high on Mount Fuji, because of the
> fog and the black volcanic soil. But . . . we created something
> which never came from any single historical period. To em-
> phasize the psychology of the hero, driven by compulsion,
> we made the interiors wide with low ceilings and squat pil-
> lars to create the effect of oppression.[10]

In its modulations of compositional scale, the film depicts
events as progressively larger than the individual's power to
control them.

The photographic texture of the image is often reduced to
strong contrasts between black and white. In interior scenes
this effect is gained primarily through set design and key
lighting; in exterior scenes it results from deep shadows,
blank mists, and nighttime settings. For such visualization
of the drama, the film draws from traditions of *suiboku-ga*
(ink-painting), in which empty expanses of white separate intense black brushstrokes. In terms of both composition and
drama, there is often onscreen an expanse of blankness, silence, and inaction that stands as a space for spectators' absorption and contemplation, for them to watch "with a detached gaze."

The passage of time, which is extraordinarily accelerated
in the Shakespeare play, is hastened further in *Throne of
Blood*. As messengers report to Tsuzuki and his war council
at the outset, the wipe cut is utilized as a visual figure for pre-
cipitous change in the course of events. In another example
of compression in time, Washizu's assassination plot against
Miki and his son Yoshiteru is presented without the play's
scenes of Macbeth's interview with the murderers or of their
attack on Banquo and Fleance. Instead, at the moment Wa-

shizu is persuaded to order the assassination, there is an abrupt and disorienting cut to the close view of a white horse in a panicked gallop within a castle courtyard. After a series of such shots, the viewer gathers that the horse resists being saddled for Miki and that the location is North Castle. The latter information derives from visual cues to an earlier scene at North Castle, when Washizu occupied it, and from a *deduction* in narrative logic, since Miki's promotion to the castle has not been depicted or reported. Through a powerful narrative ellipsis, the ambush is implied by the return of Miki's horse, now riderless, that same night to North Castle.

Political intrigues that undermine legitimate authority persist through the entire dramatic action in *Throne of Blood*, in contrast to their ultimate resolution in Shakespeare's tragedy. With victory over the rebels, Tsuzuki orders Noriyasu to monitor the activities of Inui in the border regions, but the sweep of events prevents action against this danger from being carried out. Lord Tsuzuki makes an unannounced visit to North Castle once it is under Washizu's command. When a lookout reports the approach of the Lord's armed retinue, Washizu suspects a trap and reacts initially to the report as an indication of an imminent threat against himself. Washizu is reassured in council when the Lord explains that he has resorted to the pretense of a hunting excursion to disguise his intentions of a surprise attack against Inui. Ironically, the presumed haven of North Castle becomes the scene of Tsuzuki's assassination. The assassination leaves the issue of the border threat from Inui unresolved.

After the murder of Tsuzuki, Noriyasu comes to the defense of the Lord's son, Kunimaru, and they take flight. Subsequently, Miki warns Washizu of a continued external threat posed by Inui. A rumor circulates among Forest Castle guards that Noriyasu and Kunimaru are joined by Yoshiteru and that they are all given sanctuary by Inui. The rumor is not confirmed by subsequent events, however, and Inui presumably remains a menace stationed on the border. The film drama concludes at the death of Washizu, but without any ceremony that confers power to one of the liberators such as Kunimaru and without the reassurances of order conveyed by Malcolm's regal promise, "this, and what needful else / That calls upon us, by the grace of Grace / We will perform in measure, time, and place" (5.8.71–73). In fact, a legitimate line of succession was never established by Tsuzuki, who had himself usurped power by murdering his lord.

Kurosawa has stated that his intentions for *Seven Samurai* and for this film were to present *jidai-geki* that are historically informed at the same time that they are visualized in a completely modern and dynamic manner. His concern for history, however, is not limited to matters of authenticity in sets and costumes. In all his *jidai-geki* Kurosawa demonstrates a preference for eras of disruption in samurai culture, of massive social upheaval, or of civil war. For *Throne of Blood* he had in mind the Sengoku period of civil wars (1467–1568) when there were frequent incidents of *gekokujo*, the overthrow of a superior by his own retainers.

In the prologue to *Throne of Blood* the camera surveys a vacant expanse of terrain as a male chorus chants:

Behold, within this place
Now desolate stood
Once a mighty fortress.
Lived a proud warrior
Murdered by ambition,
His spirit walking still.
Vain pride then as now will
Lead ambition to the kill.[11]

The arrangement and verse style in this chant are modeled on the traditions of Noh songs. Through a shroud of mist and fog, barren embankments and empty foundations of earth are visible in the landscape. The camera surveys the empty scene and comes to rest finally on a small group of low, undistinguished mounds and a solitary wooden marker that bears the place-name *Kumonosu-ju* ("Castle of the Spider's Web"). This desolate site is all that remains of human ambition.

The chant reiterates a Buddhist teaching on *mujokan,* the impermanence and brevity of worldly aims. Its restatement in the spinner-prophet's incantation, in the singer's performances during the banquet scene, and in the final chorus conveys the dominant truth of this teaching. Not even the ruins of a society are detectable in the opening shots. In the moments after the chant, the mists and fog dissipate to reveal a substance to human actions and a history that are absent from the greater order of time. With this sense of inevitability, the empty, eternal stage is filled for a period by human events and in the end returns to emptiness. Kurosawa develops this quality of *mu* (nothingness) through an adaptation from traditional Japanese dramatic and pictorial arts of the properties of *ku,* or empty space. *Ku* is to be found in such varied art forms as Noh, haiku, the garden, and the tea ceremony.

Another indication of Kurosawa's reorientation of tragic meaning in the film is its elimination of nearly all the scenes of *pathos* and acknowledged guilt in *Macbeth.* In the context of a conclusive pattern of defeated ambition and vain effort, of absolute futility, heroic fate is impossible. Tragedy in this film is mankind's general heritage rather than an individual destiny. From the distant, almost geologic, perspective in time that the prologue and epilogue establish, dramatic action becomes less experiential and more elemental, more emblematic.

In the film's first dramatic scene, two messengers deliver completely contradictory reports of Washizu's military fortunes whereas the Captain in Shakespeare's play brings a reassuring report of Macbeth's complete success in his defense of Duncan's kingdom. This difference is an early indication of how differently *plotted* events are in the two works. Once the assassination of Tsuzuki is committed, shouts of "Murder!" by Asaji and Washizu in the stillness of an inner courtyard to North Castle, and Washizu's curse, "Traitor," as he slays an innocent guard, lead immediately to a massive scene of troops and samurai in chaotic movement. At the end of the film drama the cycle of treachery remains unstopped. In a major revision of the source, Washizu is assassinated by his own soldiers, in a collective act of betrayal.

Washizu is forewarned about the futility of ambition. The initial movement of Washizu and Miki in their ride through Cobweb Forest is swift and determined, as accented through camera tracks and pans in a consistent direction from screen left to right. In a subsequent shot, however, they enter from screen right. Realizing that after two hours in the forest their ride has taken them full circle, Washizu and Miki fear they are held captive by a spirit. In trying to break the spell, Washizu rides on with bow drawn, an action suggestive of a Buddhist ceremony in which priest-archers shoot arrows to ward off evil spirits. The two samurai are led to a ghostly hut containing a mysterious old woman at a spinning wheel.

As the spinner works at her device, an image that suggests the thread of fate and a tragic wheel of fortune, her soft chant warns

> Nothing in this world will save
> Or measure up man's actions here
> Nor in the next, for there is none.
> This life must end in fear.

In her prediction of the rise in his political fortunes, the spinner dismisses Washizu's show of loyalty to Tsuzuki as a self-deception. The spinner scolds Washizu for denying his deeper ambitions for power. (In the subsequent reunion with her husband, Asaji expresses the same criticism of him.) When she gives voice to his inner desires, the spinner accelerates her movements and speech. Several visual analogies between this spirit and Asaji are developed, but one fundamental distinction between them is the spinner's cautions on the vanity of ambition. In leaving the forest, Washizu and Miki pass mounds of unburied human skeletons still dressed in battle gear. On his second visit to the forest spirits, Washizu will vow to leave a mountain of slain enemies, yet the only death that follows is his own.

Cobweb Forest is a paradoxical environment that contains utter contrasts in physical conditions. In the midst of sunlight there is a rainstorm, and though it is daytime there is immense darkness. The ride of Washizu and Miki is rapid and unimpeded, but in the foreground of each successive shot appears a tangle of tree trunks, branches, and undergrowth. They drive their horses furiously through a tempest but they find absolute calm around the mysterious hut. The forest offers the greatest strategic defense for Tsuzuki's forces, yet his two leading commanders become lost in it. Even when they have left the forest, Washizu and Miki remain lost. Though in completely open terrain, a dense fog protracts the labyrinthian confusion of their ride towards Forest Castle. Sparse, repetitive chords of music measure the futility of their ride in the fog. Once visibility is restored, they find themselves in front of the castle at a distance of only several hundred yards.

From that vantage point, Washizu and Miki dismount to rest their horses and to consider the encounter in the forest. Tsuzuki's Forest Castle fills the background that lies between them as they sit facing each other. Once Washizu restates the prediction of his rise to Lord and Miki weighs the promised reign for his son, they share a hearty laugh. There is a distinct "stage" quality, however, to their laughter. In this situation it serves them as a display of unbelief and disinterest in such great political fortunes. Washizu's laughter over the prophecy persists in later scenes as he attempts to guard against provocations to his ambition. He will laugh initially as well at Asaji's suspicions of Tsuzuki and Miki and, in the end, at the likelihood of the Forest approaching the castle.

In receiving new titles from Tsuzuki for their victory in battle, Washizu and Miki are shown in closeups that register mutual reactions of uncertainty and fear with this first fulfillment of the prophecies. Asaji, in contrast, greets her husband's rise in power with iron determination and ruthlessness, advising him that "In this world you must strike first if you do not want to be killed" and provoking him, "Without

Washizu and Miki are confused by the paradoxical environment of Cobweb Forest in *Throne of Blood*.

ambition man is not a man." In a visual moment that su-
premely conveys Lady Macbeth's invocation "Come, thick
night, / And pall thee in the dunnest smoke" (1.5.51–52), Asaji
disappears into total darkness in leaving to bring drugged
wine for the Lord's bodyguards. Washizu never makes the
same open, conscious commitment to the assassination that
Macbeth makes by the conclusion of Act 1. Asaji manipu-
lates her husband much further in treachery than Lady Macbeth does.

   With Lord Tsuzuki's unannounced stay at North Castle,
Washizu and Asaji will occupy another private chamber, the
"forbidden" one where the former castle commander, the
traitor Fujimaki, committed *hara-kiri*. The chamber remains deeply stained with his blood, even after Washizu's
men have washed it vigorously. From this chamber the murder of Tsuzuki is staged. Once Washizu is prepared to act,
neither of them speak. But Washizu is passive until Asaji
places a weapon in his grasp. In his brief absence, Asaji moves

about the room in a fretful dance as she regards its blood-stained surfaces, with the drums and flute of Noh played on the soundtrack. In the chaos that immediately follows the murder, Asaji engineers the political maneuver that enables her husband to occupy Forest Castle. She arranges to send the Lord's coffin ahead to Forest Castle, thus forcing Miki to open its gates to the procession Washizu leads.

Asaji instigates the murder plan against Miki and his son. Her initiative marks a major departure from the Shakespeare tragedy, where Macbeth alone plots their murder and proudly intends to keep Lady Macbeth "innocent of the knowledge" until its success (3.2.45). At the point where Washizu has refused to listen further to Asaji's incitements against Miki, she announces suddenly, "I am with child." With Washizu's shocked exclamation, the scene ends abruptly and the elliptical representation of Miki's murder follows. Her announcement is a shock as well to the viewer, who may be understandably suspicious of its truth. Nowhere in the film is there visual evidence of Asaji's pregnancy. It receives no further dramatic attention until her attendant reports that the child is stillborn. In Asaji's madness, there is no specific indication of grief over this loss.

Asaji is present when the outcome of the ambush on Miki and Yoshiteru is reported and she prompts the disclosure of the son's escape. That news provokes Washizu into executing the murderer on the spot. While Asaji is almost always impassive in expression, still in posture, and gradual in her movements, she is the principal moving force behind Washizu's agitated, unsure, and reckless actions. There is no caution in her prompting of his ambitions. To goad him into action, she forewarns him that "Arrows will seek your life not only from the front but from the rear" at the orders of Tsuzuki and Miki. She insists that Washizu murder first, before any plot against him can be initiated. At the end of the film narrative, her specific forewarning is seen to possess an ironically predictive accuracy.

Lady Macbeth's presumed self-slaughter is received in the

Asaji and Washizu in the "forbidden," blood-stained chamber of North Castle, in *Throne of Blood*.

Shakespeare tragedy as a sign of violent retribution for her "fiendlike" influence and actions (5.8.69). Her damnation is redoubled and moral balance is regained in this commission of the cardinal sin suicide. In contrast, Asaji is not reported dead at the conclusion. Within the samurai context, suicide is an honorable ritual that makes possible individual moral resolution after profound defeat, shame, or loss. It is a recourse taken by Lord Tsuzuki's wife after his assassination, but it is not one the plot allows for Asaji.

The film brilliantly reconceives the play's elaborate bird imagery, which is inaugurated by Lady Macbeth's murderous allusion, "The raven himself is hoarse / That croaks the fatal entrance of Duncan / Under my battlements" (1.4.40–42). Dialogue references, sound effects, and filmic images are combined to form similar metaphors that encompass the film drama. When Washizu's men prepare the forbidden chamber for their master and lady, a passing crow's cry is heard over visuals dominated by the room's walls, discolored by blood. The crow is a symbol of death within traditional Japanese culture, and Washizu's men react to the cry as an omen of evil.

In urging her husband toward the first murder, Asaji hears a similar cry and assures her husband that the crow has signaled, "The throne is yours." Just before Washizu goes to commit the assassination, the visuals cut away to a night sky. Prominent in the sky is a crescent moon, which is the symbol of Tsuzuki's reign. Across this night sky a crow flies and sharply caws.

Against all logic, Washizu insists at his last war council that the sudden, unexplained flight of forest birds into the castle's chambers is a good omen. After making this assertion he sits down in a show of defiance, but a bird then calmly perches on his shoulder. The frightened screams of women draw Washizu from the council chamber. In the corridor he encounters attendants in terrified flight from Lady Asaji.

When the forest finally approaches the castle, Washizu's soldiers turn against their master. With a sustained barrage of arrows, they entrap him within Forest Castle. The protracted death scene is an ironic manifestation of Washizu's tenacity and firm will to power, attained, finally, at the point of his own destruction. The baroque prolongation and overstatement of this event is a culmination of the visual figures for forces—the spinner-prophet's exposure of his inner ambitions, Asaji's manipulations, a heritage of political intrigue—that ultimately ensnare him.

Without the play's poetic characterization, Washizu is more reactive than reflective. He does not engage in the intellectual mediation between desire and action that occurs, in intense but brief speeches, in the play. Nor, after power has begun to unravel, does he contemplate the destructive logic of his acts. In resisting his wife's first provocations, Washizu protests that samurai honor prohibits such actions, but she easily persuades him that their world does not in fact adhere to *bushido*. With the report that Asaji's pregnancy has ended in stillbirth, Washizu returns to the castle's throne room and shouts in disbelief "Fool!" while regarding his helmet and sword. After that point, with the exception of a pleading repetition of his wife's name in trying to retrieve her from madness, Washizu's words are devoted solely toward proving his invincibility.

As Washizu's prolonged death agony occurs, low fogs begin to spread and obscure the human scene. Upon his death and from a perspective just outside the forest, the castle is finally obliterated from view by mists. This "dissolve" in the film's scenic and temporal contexts is handled as an environmental effect, while it functions also as an optical and formal device of narrative transition. The subsequent era to which place and time are advanced is devoid of any remnant of the reigns of Tsuzuki and Washizu except for the small memorial site. The expression of this geologic, inhuman passage of time in *Throne of Blood* renders the play's sense of humankind's meaningless progress as recognized by Macbeth at the end: "Tomorrow, and tomorrow, and tomorrow / Creeps in this petty pace from day to day, / To the last syllable of recorded time; / And all our yesterdays have lighted fools / The way to dusty death" (5.5.19–23).

The empty expanses in *Throne of Blood* are not a space vacant of meaning. Their nothingness—as in both Japanese pictorial conventions and European absurdist theater—has substance and significance. The film's extraordinary uses of silence and blankness (in both dark tones and light ones) have much in common with Japanese aesthetic conventions of *ma* and Buddhist concepts of *mu*. According to its contexts, *ma* can be translated as space, interval, gap, blank, time, pause, rest, or opening. Often its spatial and temporal meanings are combined, especially in relation to Noh theater. In Noh, *ma* can indicate the conditions of emptiness and stillness just before or after an event is performed on stage. By compositional design in the arts more generally, *ma* is negative space and negative time that have their own dimensions and functions. *Mu*, in Buddhism, is a state of nothingness that possesses its own order of meaning. It is a paradoxical state wherein absence is a quality of presence.

Speaking about form in the screenplay generally, Kurosawa has suggested as a model "the Noh play with its three-

Defeated by his own soldiers, Washizu is reduced to nothing by encroaching fogs in *Throne of Blood*.

part structure: *jo* (introduction), *ha* (destruction) and *kyu* (haste)" (*Autobiography*, 193). This sequential, rhythmic principle also underpins *renga*, or linked poetry, and other kinds of Japanese literature.[12] *Jo* can be further defined as preparation or beginning, and it often has the property of an elevated and refined style. *Ha* has the additional meaning of break or disorder, and it has properties of agitation and multiplicity. *Kyu* indicates a sudden finale to resolve the dramatic action, although it normally concludes in a condition of poise or rest. These three elements are a paradigm in Noh with respect to dramatic construction in each play and in the cycle of plays in a program, in the components of the performance space, in the pace of performance, and in the phrasing of both chants and musical instrumentation.

In relation to the full dramatic action of *Throne of Blood*, the introductory chant constitutes its *jo*, dramatic events from Tsuzuki's opening war council to the report of Cobweb

Forest's movement constitute its *ha*, and the betrayal of Washizu by his men and the closing chant, its *kyu*. Understood from this perspective, the film plot is profoundly ironic since Washizu's military successes and political rise are from the outset merely phases of destruction (*ha*). The paradigm also applies to construction among the film's scenes. The ride by Washizu and Miki through Cobweb Forest, for example, is preparatory (*jo*) to their fateful encounter with the spinner-prophet. Her prophecies are a disordering element (*ha*) and reach their first culmination in the brief, intense scene of the ceremony in which Tsuzuki honors Washizu and Miki (*kyu*).

The first shots of the scene that follows this ceremony depict life in North Castle as peaceful and orderly for Washizu's men. The scene is the introductory *jo* to another cycle of destruction and hasty resolution. Within the Shakespeare material itself there are many such drastic shifts in the pace and tenor of events, creating a pattern of alternation between ceremonial formality and murderous terror. One example in *Macbeth* is the juxtaposition between the state occasion at Forres, where Duncan confers honors on Macbeth and Banquo (1.4), and the reunion of Macbeth and Lady Macbeth, when she vows Duncan will not leave their castle alive (1.5). Another example is the transition from the meeting in England between Malcolm and Macduff, who forge an alliance against Macbeth (4.3), and the scene at Dunsinane where Lady Macbeth, in her madness, exhibits her blood guilt (5.1).

Filmic construction within a sequence can also reflect the properties *jo-ha-kyu*, as in the case of the ghostly spinner. Her soft chant restates the film story's *jo*. Tranquility is ruptured, however, when she speaks on the future of Washizu and Miki. Her movements are accelerated (in part through fast motion processing of the footage), a demonic expression emerges on her face, and her voice changes to unearthly tones. The sudden disappearance of both the spinner and her hut brings *kyu*, which is completed by the ride of Washizu and Miki through blinding fogs and their pause before returning to Forest Castle.

The five categories of Noh plays are traditionally designated by the identity of the main character: god, warrior, woman, lunatic, or demon. A full program of Noh includes a play in each category. In its dramatic scope *Throne of Blood* encompasses events that fall within each of these categories, with the divine expressed through the chant that frames the film drama. In creating a time perspective more expansive than recorded history itself, the film adapts from Noh the unique structure *mugen* (phantasm, dream, vision), which provides the theater great flexibility in time and space. Representation through the technique of *mugen* entails a reversal of the flow in time, from future to past.

For the encounter in Cobweb Forest with a ghostly prophet, Kurosawa had specifically in mind *Kurozuka*, which is presented in the *mugen* mode.[13] In the play's first part, a group of traveling monks encounter an old woman at her spinning wheel. In speaking to them, she curses her fate as a mortal. After the monks stay in the shelter of her thatch hut for the night, the old woman is revealed to be a demon. She is defeated after a struggle with the monks, an outcome Kurosawa significantly deletes. In other *mugen*, a common occurrence at the thatch hut setting is for both the hut and its inhabitant to vanish, thus confirming its ghostly identity.

Kurosawa values Noh for its symbolic range, dramatic compression, manner of understatement, and its fusion of form and substance. Noh has taught the film director much about the dramatic impact of economy in acting, set design, and sound accompaniment:

> In Noh there is a certain hieratic property: one moves as little as possible. Also, the smallest gesture, the smallest displacement produces an effect truly intense and violent.
> Now, Noh actors are all veritable acrobats. . . . But in general the actors conserve their energy, they avoid all unnecessary actions. There, to my mind, lies one of the secrets of Noh.[14]

Through its ceremonial, elemental, and contrastive method of presentation, Noh makes the properties of stillness and vehemence coexist on the stage. *Throne of Blood* achieves similar visual and dramatic rhythms that measure blank expanses against character movement, stillness against recklessness, passivity against vitality, and sparse sound signals or silence against shouts and sounds of battle.

Kurosawa's uses of Noh forms and sources remain modern and deliberately intertextual in his film. An entirely different sensibility toward Noh is exhibited by a contemporary to Kurosawa, the famous Japanese writer Jun'ichiro Tanizaki. Reflecting in 1933 on his love for Noh, Tanizaki observed:

> I find the thought fascinating: to imagine how very handsome, by comparison with us today, the Japanese of the past must have been in their resplendent dress—particularly the warriors of the fifteenth and sixteenth centuries. The Noh sets before us the beauty of Japanese manhood at its finest. What grand figures those warriors who traversed the battlefields of old must have cut in their full regalia emblazoned with family crests, the somber ground and gleaming embroidery setting off strong-boned faces burnished a deep bronze by wind and rain. Every devotee of the Noh finds a certain portion of his pleasure in speculations of this sort, for the thought that the highly colored world on the stage once existed just as we see it imparts to the Noh a historical fascination quite apart from the drama.[15]

On the powerful evidence of the uses of Noh conventions and *jidai-geki* subject matter in *Throne of Blood* and *Ran*, it is clear that Kurosawa opposes any such antiquarian idealization that posits a golden age of heroism and beauty in feudal Japan.

Noh stylization in the presentation of Asaji is quite evident in her masklike facial expression, her frozen postures, and her constricted, unnatural movement. Donald Richie has argued that her personality is contrasted with her husband's through its unique Noh references.[16] But Washizu is conceived as well through extensive Noh stylization. Kurosawa prepared each principal actor by assigning a Noh mask for the basis of characterization. For Toshiro Mifune's performance as Washizu the model was the *Heida* mask, by tradition the face of a warrior in his prime. In the context of *Throne of Blood*, there is an ironic discrepancy in this image, since the *Heida* mask indicates a man of greatness who conquers evil spirits. The mask named *Mika-zuki* (crescent moon) is the face of a wrathful warrior and it may have inspired Kurosawa's choice of the symbolic crescent moon to mark Washizu's reign.

The expressions on Washizu's face are extremely changeable but remain frozen at the points of greatest dramatic tension, as in the early scene when he listens intently to the spinner-prophet's warnings and predictions. The gaping laughter on his face in the scene just prior to his return to Forest Castle is replaced by dumbfounded wonder in receiving his promotion from Tsuzuki. In the end the deathblow delivered to Washizu, by a final arrow that pierces his neck, paralyzes his face in an agonized grimace. His expression of horrified defeat suggests the *Yase-ototo*, the Noh mask of man on the verge of death.

The use of facial closeups in *Throne of Blood* is noticeably sparing, particularly in comparison to psychological interpretations of Shakespeare such as Roman Polanski's *Macbeth* (1971). Polanski relies on the closeup to visualize a play of emotion and consciousness on the faces of Macbeth and Lady Macbeth, often while their most revealing thoughts are delivered through voice-over. In his own cinema of the early 1950s — particularly in *The Idiot* and *Ikiru* — there is great dependence on the closeup and the reaction shot in dialogue scenes for the disclosure of character psychology. The human face in *Throne of Blood*, most often seen at a distance that objectifies its appearance, is a social mask. The character motives behind such a mask are to control the social meaning of one's presence and to control the interpersonal situation.

Kurosawa recognized that in *Throne of Blood* he violated the norms of intimate drama:

I tried to show everything using the full-shot. Japanese almost never make films in this way and I remember I confused my staff thoroughly with my instructions. They were
so used to moving up for moments of emotion, and I told
them to move farther back. In this way I suppose you would
call the film experimental.[17]

Such experimentation with the camera's remoteness from
the dramatic center of action had been by that time conducted rigorously in the cinema of Kenji Mizoguchi. When a
sequence in *Throne of Blood* does cut to closeup, the face is
fixed in expression in the character's reaction to events for
the duration of the shot.

Kurosawa has described characterization on the basis of
the mask as "the opposite of acting."[18] In Western theatrical
traditions that follow the methods of Constantin Stanislavsky, the actor develops and impersonates the unique individuality of the character through analysis of the psychology of
that particular personality. The Noh actor, through study of
the *omote* ("outside") or dramatic mask, expresses an exterior image of the spirit or essence of character. The mask represents a transformation of character into symbol. In assum-
ing the mask, the Noh actor places a symbolic image on the
surface of character. As a consequence, the presentation of a
Noh character's experience is based upon ideas rather than
personality and upon an image of emotion rather than raw
emotion itself. Masked drama produces a "distancing effect"
between character and audience, and this quality has figured
prominently in modern Western cultural innovation by writers as dissimilar as Ezra Pound and Bertolt Brecht.[19]

Kurosawa's adoption of Noh methods for *Throne of Blood*
facilitates the creation of an unheroic film tragedy. Its protagonist is not depicted as the sole or even primary agent of dramatic events. Audience understanding of his character is developed through objective, external means rather than through
emotional identification. Washizu is not possessed of any
greatness, either inward or outward, that would enable him

to withstand and govern the forces that propel him. Not once does he voice his inner drives. The spinner-prophet and Lady Asaji dictate to him the urgings of ambition that *they* attribute to his own desires. The stature of Washizu's feelings, thoughts, and actions is further diminished by the film's impersonal scale of events and the unworldly scope of time.

Ran

In 1980 Kurosawa remarked that his current projects — *Dersu Uzala, Kagemusha,* and *Ran* — in each case present the death of the protagonist as a reflection of his own historical pessimism. The settings of these films in eras of profound social change afforded the director dramatic situations that reveal the individual amidst his failed ambitions, ambitions that do not yield tragic greatness. In the director's reinvention of the *jidai-geki* genre, the canonized legends and heroes of Japan's past — such as the Loyal Forty-seven Ronin or the great warrior Motonari Mori — are passed over in favor of material developed from anecdotes or incidents secondary to legend and history. Kurosawa's period films offer variations on legend and footnotes to history that contradict orthodox, institutionalized culture.

With both period and contemporary stories, Kurosawa often creates "shadow heroes" by having the plot begin after the protagonist's death (as in *Throne of Blood*) or in anticipation of his death *(Ikiru)*. Subsequent to a foreglimpse of the narrative outcome in these two films, the plot returns to earlier story events to develop the causes of this final effect, in ways similar to the modern experiments in narrative by William Faulkner. *Dersu Uzala* opens in 1910 on the site of a new Siberian settlement. Only three years have passed since the Russian explorer and surveyor Vladimir Arseniev buried an old friend there, the native Goldi hunter Dersu. The forest trees that marked the grave site have been cleared away. From a position of Dersu's total absence, the plot turns back to 1902 and the first meeting between Arseniev and Dersu, in a virgin forest. By the film's conclusion, the narrative has advanced to

1907, when Arseniev returns to Siberia to arrange a burial after Dersu has been murdered for his valuable rifle, a gift from the Russian. The plot thus encloses the life of Dersu within story elements that convey his extinction as a result of modernization and the advance of society into nature.

Kurosawa's interest in the material that evolved into the *Kagemusha* screenplay came through his awareness that in the late sixteenth century there was a battle in which an entire army with all its *taisho* (generals) was massacred. In 1575 the Battle of Nagashino brought total collapse upon the Takeda clan, whose war motto had been adopted from the classical Chinese military strategist Sun Tsu: "Swift as the wind, silent as the forest, ravaging as fire, immovable as the mountain." The Takeda army had remained undefeated until the engagement with rival war clans at Nagashino. Kurosawa was also intrigued by historical indications that the clan leader Shingen Takeda, who died in 1573, had used a number of *kagemusha* ("shadow warriors," or doubles) to impersonate himself in order to deceive enemies and spies.

Kagemusha is set precisely in the years 1573–75, a period between the conclusion in 1568 to the *sengoku-jidai* ("era of the provinces at war") and the inauguration in 1603 of the Tokugawa reign, which brought two and a half centuries of national unity and stability to Japan. The nature of samurai warfare changed profoundly in this interim. In the 1570s, musket corps were regularly placed on the battlelines along with conventional footsoldiers, pikemen, and archers. At Nagashino the army led by Nobunaga Oda included 3,000 experienced musket soldiers who laid down a barrage of fire from their concealed positions as the Takeda force attacked in successive waves. The entire Takeda army, estimated at 16,000 men, was destroyed. Through such disastrous events the new technology of mechanized warfare began to displace the heroic ideals of a samurai warrior's skills. Battles over the consolidation of power in Japan continued until a decisive victory in 1600 by Ieyasu Tokugawa, who assumed the title of Shogun three years later.

Both Oda and Tokugawa are represented in *Kagemusha*, but its protagonist is a common criminal who impersonates Shingen Takeda. Through the screenplay's invention, this unnamed criminal continues successfully in the role for over two years after the actual clan leader is dead. While historical accounts of the circumstances underlying Shingen's death vary, the film depicts it as the result of a sniper's precise marksmanship. The dramatic emphasis in events surrounding Shingen's death is not on the moment of his mortal wounding but rather on a demonstration some time later of the methods a Tokugawa soldier employed to aim his musket in the darkness of night at the victim. Kurosawa's period films make such fictive interventions into the documented record to dramatize the nature of historical transformation within Japanese political power and warfare. His *jidai-geki* function as interpretative hypotheses about the course of history.

Kurosawa's tragicomic intentions with the material are clear from the fact that he conceived the dual role of Shingen and the shadow warrior with the actor Shintaro Katsu in mind. Katsu was immensely popular in Japan for his film performances as the blind swordsman Zatoichi. In that role, Katsu's screen personality is farcical, spontaneous, eccentric, and free-spirited. This actor left the production as filming began, however, when differences with Kurosawa over acting the part arose. With Tatsuya Nakadai newly cast in the role, the character's comic independence gives way to growing devotion to Shingen. In the process, the film nonetheless fosters emotional distance from the pathos of his situation by narrative and visual disruptions of any intimate representation of his experience. It persistently emphasizes the criminal's insignificance as a person in his own right.

In structuring the representation of an epic period of Japanese history around the political strategy of a double, the film paradoxically centers events on a nonentity. By definition a shadowy presence within society, the criminal is reputed to have committed many unsolved crimes, including murder. The criminal's life has been spared from capital pun-

ishment in the form of crucifixion. The man who spares him
is Shingen's brother Nobukado, who has himself impersonated the Takeda leader on the battlefield. Shingen is bemused
by the irony that a condemned criminal should bear such a
complete resemblance to himself.

During their first meeting, the prisoner interrupts his lord
with accusations that the noble is a far worse criminal than
himself. With candor that wins the criminal's respect, Shingen replies, "I am as wicked as you believe. I am a scoundrel.
I banished my father and killed my own son. I will do anything to rule over this land. War is everywhere and unless
someone unifies the nation and reigns over it we will see
more rivers of blood and more mountains of the dead."[20]
Since the land is not unified within Shingen's rule, this last
remark will be seen to be brutally predictive. It is also an
ironic corrective to the seemingly valiant battle plan "immovable as the mountain." Some critics have seen the criminal's
deepening identification with Shingen as proof of the common man's great heroism, but such an interpretation ignores
the lord's frank admission of ruthlessness.

Dedication by the common criminal to the noble role
comes after he fails in an attempt at thievery from the Takeda clan. He breaks into a huge ceramic jar in the belief that
it contains a precious treasure but discovers instead the body
of the dead Lord Shingen, dressed in full armor and preserved
in lacquer. After this incident, the clan warlords grant the
thief his freedom. In witnessing their profound grief over the
lord's loss, the criminal insists on carrying through the impersonation. After close instruction and surveillance, the
double can occupy the seat of power as convincingly as Lord
Shingen. Ultimately the disguise fails when he falls from the
lord's favorite horse. Once his false identity is revealed and he
is banished, the double—who is never identified by a given
name or family surname—returns to being a mere shadow,
without social substance.

He secretly follows the Takeda army, only to witness in horror its utter defeat at Nagashino. The final battle is depicted

through imagery of the army's obedient march into destruction and of the shadow warrior's reactions to the slaughter. The enemy troops who cause the debacle are merely glimpsed. In the aftermath, the shadow warrior enters the battlefield to pick up a lance and charge the enemy. Like all the others, he is felled by a distant musket shot. The criminal has been spared execution under Takeda authority only to die senselessly in defense of the lost Takeda cause. He falls dying into a river. In grasping for the Takeda battle standard as both float down river, the double is spread into a posture that suggests the body of a man crucified.

Kagemusha is Kurosawa's third work to be filmed in color. In the 1960s the director had remained opposed to the color process. His reasons for dissatisfaction with color extended from technical limitations such as the difficulty of maintaining a sharp depth of field with long camera lenses, which he regularly uses, to an aesthetic judgment that the color range traditional in Japanese culture had yet to be reproduced in motion picture photography. His own aspirations to convey such colors underlie much of the design and cinematography in *Kagemusha* and *Ran*. In the dream of the shadow warrior, however, the compositions turn to the nightmare extremes of expressionist painters like Oskar Kokoschka, Chaim Soutine, and Emile Nolde.

Knowing that Kurosawa had no confidence in color technique or in its dramatic suitability, Henri Langlois, head of the Cinémathèque Française, screened the extraordinary banquet scene from Sergei Eisenstein's *Ivan the Terrible* (Part Two, 1946) for the Japanese director during a visit to Paris. One lesson to be learned from the Eisenstein example is that color can function in film as a distinctive element of meaning and not simply as the medium for a seemingly transparent reproduction of appearances. Kurosawa indicates that his interest was stimulated by Langlois's encouragement and the demonstration in *Ivan the Terrible* of artistic possibilities for color film.

Kurosawa had contemplated using a color segment within

Sanjuro in conjunction with the plot device of sending a signal with red camellias, but except for the touch of showing pink smoke in one sequence of *High and Low* he worked exclusively within black and white cinematography until the production of *Dodeskaden*. He conceived of the slum setting for *Dodeskaden* in terms diametrically opposed to naturalism. In creating a large wasteground for the principal exterior location, Kurosawa cleared off all vegetation. The setting was then painted in a distinctly inorganic color scheme. For scenes that reflect the retarded boy Rokuchan's perceptions, a childlike, intense, and simplified coloration is evident. In *Dersu Uzala*, on the other hand, the color design is primarily naturalistic and it entails the many effects of weather and the seasons appropriate to the story.

Kurosawa began writing the script for *Ran* in 1976 and completed a first version around 1978. With the collaboration of Hideo Oguni and Masato Ide, the script continued to evolve over the next seven years.[21] *Ran*, which has been translated as "chaos," conveys additional connotations of revolt, upheaval, discord, turmoil, and anarchy. Inspiration for the story came first through Kurosawa's notion to invert the legend of Motonari Mori (1497–1571), whose three sons are admired in Japan as the ideal of family loyalty. In a fabled incident attributed to him, Mori gives each son a single arrow to break in order to show the fragile condition that would result from any personal ambitions or political rivalry among them. The father then hands each one a bundle of three arrows to demonstrate that in combination power cannot be broken by an individual son. Motonari Mori is also remembered, however, for the political maxim that a leader should not trust anyone, particularly not family members.

Ran is a *sengoku-jidai* like *Seven Samurai* and *Throne of Blood* and, like these films, it represents ironically the historical conditions of samurai power. The irony in *Seven Samurai* is primarily one of obsolescence. The warriors train peasants to defend their village against bandits and together the two classes restore peace and security. Through this success, however, the samurai make themselves unnecessary in the end. Once Kurosawa had begun scripting *Ran*'s story of a feared yet aging ruler deposed by disloyal sons, similarities to *King Lear* became apparent to him. In Shakespeare's tragedy, Goneril, Regan, and Edmund rebel against the dominion held by patriarchs. Regan's motives are barely concealed in a show of concern toward her father: "O, sir, you are old, / Nature in you stands on the very verge / Of his confine. You should be ruled" (2.4.145–47).[22]

In considering *King Lear*, Kurosawa was puzzled that Shakespeare had given his characters no past:

> We are plunged directly into the agonies of their present dilemmas without knowing how they came to this point. How did Lear acquire the power that, as an old man, he abuses with such disastrous effects? Without knowing his past, I have never really understood the ferocity of his daughters' response to Lear's feeble attempts to shed his royal power.[23]

In the script to *Ran*, the answer to such questions is to create a past political career for the ruler and to set events in a specific era. Since the story is set in medieval Japan, the fictional Great Lord Hidetora Ichimonji's line of descent had to be male. To divide a realm among daughters would have contradicted history completely. Though plot elements, important incidents, and central metaphors are drawn from Shakespeare's tragedy, the textual treatment of adapted material is governed by Kurosawa's original conception of an inversion to Japanese ideals of family and political loyalty.

In his film adaptation of *King Lear* released in 1970, Peter Brook responds to the absence of history and a personal past in the play with an anthropological approach. Reasoning that Shakespeare derives the play from legend rather than history, Brook bases his interpretation on imagery of the elemental human needs of shelter, clothing, food, and warmth. His visual and dramatic design was achieved through a process of elimination in language, action, and setting to focus primarily on the inner, essential experience of characters. The film's senses of time and place are defined by an emptiness and blankness derived from absurdist theater. The Shakespeare play for Brook is less about the fate of royal power than about the vulnerable existence of an individual, irrespective of social position, in danger of becoming and meaning nothing. In its figurations of nothingness the Brook film has affinities with the conventions of *ma* and concepts of *mu* in *Throne of Blood*.

The Soviet film director Grigori Kozintsev, in a 1971 adaptation of *King Lear*, treats the play as a social tragedy and a visual epic. In an extensive discussion of the play and his film treatment, Kozintsev offers this interpretation:

> *Lear* is not only the drama of a particular group of people
> who are linked by the plot, but also a stream of history.
> Whole structures of life [and] social situations are carried
> along and tumbled together. Not only single voices are heard
> in the din of tragedy (lifelike in the fullest sense of the word)
> but combined and mighty ensembles, whole choruses.[24]

From Kozintsev's perspective on Russian and Soviet history, absolute dictatorship is both a cultural legacy (the tsars) and a living historical memory (Stalin). His film represents the life of a willful ruler through its reflection in the lives of his subjects. The tragic destiny of Lear expresses at the same time the destiny of a people.

In Kurosawa's perspective on the era of Japanese history in which he sets the events of *Ran*, absolute power is based on a legacy of ruthlessness. After a lifetime of brutality, Hidetora unwisely plans for peace through a scheme of shared power with the eldest son Taro established in First Castle, the next son Jiro in Second Castle, and the youngest son Saburo in Third Castle. The Japanese meaning of these given names —"first son" (Taro), "second son" (Jiro), and "third son" (Saburo) — reiterates this hierarchical arrangement. Amidst the suffering and chaos that results from his ill-conceived plan, Hidetora encounters the surviving victims of his own savage conquest of the realm many years earlier. This dramatic movement through the ruins left by past ambition and war is quite different in structure from the immediacy of the tragedy that follows from King Lear's demand for professions of love and from his rash temper, both of which a theater audience directly witnesses.

Since much criticism has insisted on treating *Ran* as a Shakespeare adaptation, it is necessary to clarify the film's relationship to *King Lear*. The play is a rich intertextual source for the film but it is not the basis for a film interpretation of Shakespeare. The differences of *Ran* from a Shakespeare film adaptation are evident in the scene of the royal hunt. In *King Lear*, the hunt is the first activity the King engages in after stepping down from the throne. It is reported (1.3) before his re-entrance at the palace of Goneril and the Duke of Albany (1.4). The Brook and Kozintsev adaptations develop connecting action between early scenes on the basis of this information in order to convey the size and vigor of Lear's retinue of one hundred knights.

The play's reported action of the hunt has extensive metaphoric implications, for it intimates the predation and animal terror that rapidly overtake human events. Within the family as well as within the state, individuals lay snares and traps and give chase to others, irrespective of their personal and social bonds. The violent means that have given humanity mastery over nature are in the tragedy used to master other humans. *Ran* incorporates this profound poetic conceit and gives it great dramatic presence. As in the case of *Throne of Blood*, this film has a stronger intertextual relation to Shakespeare in terms of the play's figurative language rather than in terms of incident, characterization, or description.

In *Ran* a ceremonial hunt *precedes* the council in which Hidetora retires from power. With a knowing laugh, the Lord compares himself to an old male boar, the prey he has just felled. He questions whether the two invited, rival lords Fujimaki and Ayabe would consume an old warlord like himself. Hidetora cautions them that he is tough and indigestible. The hunting weapon, the arrow, will figure in the justifica-

tion for his planned relinquishment of power and responsibility. It is also one weapon with which the armies of Taro and
Jiro will hunt down Hidetora. The council ends in disarray
with Saburo's protest that, as a result of Hidetora's own savagery, humanity lives in a world without conscience or justice.
Hidetora has made the capacity for violence and the exercise
of superior strength society's governing principle.

In Shakespeare's tragedy, once Lear releases his tight grip
on the reins of power he loses the substance of his royal person. To the King's protestation, "Who is it that can tell me
who I am?" the Fool retorts, "Lear's shadow" (1.4.236–37). In
Ran, through both visual and narrative means, Hidetora is
quickly revealed to be a shadow warrior. His social substance
as Lord and family patriarch dissipates.

In addition to such broad analogies in the main plot, *Ran*
contains important particulars adapted from the play. These
include the crown of weeds and flowers fashioned for the
ruined King by his Fool (4.4) and the King's lamentation upon
being drawn back from madness to conscious life, "You do
me wrong to take me out o' th' grave" (4.7.45). The dramatic
action is narrowed, however, to exclude the Gloucester subplot and its tragic parallels. Some elements are transposed
from the subplot, such as Edgar's act of kindness in shading
his father Gloucester under a tree (5.2), an action Saburo
takes toward Hidetora in the film's opening scene.

After division of the realm, the first open disrespect shown
toward Lear comes from the steward Oswald who, in doing
so, follows Goneril's instructions. Subsequently, Regan and
her husband Cornwall travel at night to the Duke of Gloucester so as to be absent from their own castle when the king
and his entourage arrive. These specific intrigues and ploys
are not retained in the film plot. In *Ran* the first insults to
Hidetora's dignity come at First Castle directly from Lady
Kaede, his daughter-in-law through her marriage to Taro. His
son Jiro is present at Second Castle and there denies Hidetora proper respect and hospitality. Another transposition
involves the Duke of Albany's denunciation of his wife Gon-

Hidetora on the ceremonial hunt prior to his abdication of sovereignty in *Ran*.

eril as a fiend (4.2), a charge made in the film by Kurogane, a warlord under Jiro, against Lady Kaede, who is Taro's widow and Jiro's mistress at that point in the film plot.

In its intertextual treatment of material found in the Shakespeare play, the film typically condenses, abbreviates, or intensifies events and character traits. Lady Kaede possesses the same savage ambition as Edmund, but she has a motive of revenge that he does not. She was born and raised at First Castle, when her father ruled from there. Kaede left to marry Taro, an alliance that led her family to trust Hidetora, who soon overtook First Castle and murdered the men of her family. Other elements from the play are completely reimagined, such as the absurd pantomime of Gloucester's fall from a cliff at Dover, which becomes an actual fall that Hidetora takes in the ruins of a castle he had destroyed.

Still loyal to Lear, the banished Earl of Kent adopts a disguise and rejoins the king's retinue in an effort to protect his master from ruin. His counterpart in *Ran* is the faithful re-

tainer Tango, who begins the journey to exile with Saburo
but returns to defend Hidetora upon the urging of the banished son. Tango adopts a disguise in order to pass undetected
by the forces of Taro and Jiro, but his identity is quickly made
known to Hidetora once Tango rejoins the Great Lord's small
retinue. Ikoma, the other most trusted retainer, has remained
with Hidetora's retinue but he does so as a spy, for Ikoma is
in league with Jiro against the Lord.

In *King Lear*, the Duke of Albany is inclined toward compassion for Lear, but in the face of Goneril's mistrust and manipulations he has no will to act from compassion until Act
4. At the play's close Albany oversees the restoration of political order. The only rough equivalent to Albany in terms of
both family relationship and personality is Lady Sué, but the
great differences in characterization indicate the film's degree of independence from the play. On the strength of Buddhist devotion, Lady Sué is selfless and pure in her acceptance of suffering. Her forgiving soul compounds Hidetora's
sense of guilt for the siege he led against her family's castle
and the murder of all but two family members. After this victory Sué was bound in marriage to Jiro. Lord Hidetora confesses that her hatred would make him feel easier. In the end,
when Lady Sué is assassinated at the orders of Kaede, she
falls as another victim of the chaos Hidetora had initiated decades earlier.

Ran reverses the logic that underpins the tragic course of
events in *King Lear*. In Hidetora's past quest for power he
blinded Tsurumaru, Lady Sué's brother, in exchange for sparing the boy's life. In the play, the blinding of Gloucester, committed by Cornwall with the incitement of Regan, is an act of
pure evil against an innocent man. In the film, the blinding
of an innocent is reported as an atrocity committed by the
Lord himself earlier in his rise to power. Rather than the
tragedy's expression of a greatness of spirit in Gloucester and
Lear born of their suffering, the film presents the political
greatness Hidetora has achieved as the consequence of the
horrible suffering he has brought upon others. By no means

can Hidetora make the same claim to pathos heard from Lear as he wails in contention with the storm, "I am a man / More sinned against than sinning" (3.2.59–60).

One draft of the *Ran* script includes a nightmare vision wherein Hidetora is haunted by all those he has killed. Indications are that the vision was to be subjective and stylized in treatment, in a manner similar to the dream sequences in *Drunken Angel, Kagemusha,* and sections of *Dreams.* A notation in the published *Ran* script states that the idea for the sequence is drawn from the famous Noh play *Funa Benkei,* in which a samurai traveling by ship sees in the waves the ghosts of his victims.

Social chaos persistently threatens in *King Lear,* as rumors of possible civil war between the dukes of Albany and Cornwall are repeated (2.1 and 3.1), but the treacherous alliance of Goneril and Regan against Lear forestalls it. The sisters' conspiracies against one another for the favors of Edmund bring their own destruction before society is brought to ruin. Within *Ran,* however, social and political order quickly unravels. Total war against Hidetora is waged soon after his rejection by Taro and Jiro. Such chaos is an inevitable legacy of his patriarchy, as Saburo warns during the family council in the first scene:

> What kind of world do we live in? One barren of loyalty and feeling. . . . You spilled an ocean of blood. You showed no mercy, no pity. We too are children of this age, weaned on strife and chaos. We are your sons, yet you count on our fidelity. In my eyes, that makes you a fool. A senile old fool!

Indeed, Hidetora had waged war for over fifty years, since age seventeen, to expand the realm now protected by three main castles. In seeking refuge in Third Castle now, however, the Lord is besieged by the armies of Taro and Jiro, mobilized from Castles One and Two.

The logic of events in *Ran* approaches the rationale for brutality and treachery asserted by Edmund: "men / Are as the time is: to be tender-minded / Does not become a sword"

(5.3.31–33). On the first occasion that he is alone onstage, Edmund proclaims opposition to any belief that would exonerate the individual. Edmund holds humanity responsible for evil in the world and he rejects the rationale that misfortune is providential:

> This is the excellent foppery of the world, that when we are sick in fortune, often the surfeits of our own behavior, we make guilty of our disasters the sun, the moon, and stars; as if we were villains on necessity; fools by heavenly compulsion; knaves, thieves, and treachers by spherical predominance; drunkards, liars, and adulterers by an enforced obedience of planetary influence; and all that we are evil in, by a divine thrusting on. (1.2.128–36)

Ran concludes, however, without the ceremonial act of justice fulfilled when Edgar advances a challenge to battle against Edmund. In defeat, Edmund acknowledges his evil again and finally acts in compassion in warning of the secret execution order against Lear and Cordelia (5.3).

The royal property used in *Ran* to announce the Lord's voluntary renunciation of power is not a map but arrows, the weapon with which Hidetora has just slain a boar on the hunt. The policy the Great Lord demonstrates is designed to bind the realm under the leadership of Taro. As an implement of the hunt and war, the arrow contradicts the symbolism Hidetora intends. In breaking the bundled arrows over his knee, Saburo seems to be the first member to violate the family bond. In banishment, the loyal Saburo will be allied through marriage to Lord Fujimaki. (Through an ironic coincidence, this ally bears the same family name as the traitor in *Throne of Blood* whose blood indelibly stains the walls of the chamber Washizu and Asaji occupy.) Later, with Fujimaki's troops amassed just across the border, Saburo objects that this support—though well-intended—will provoke a battle with his brother Jiro that he wishes to avoid. When the troops of Saburo and Jiro do engage in war, the other neighboring warlord Ayabe initiates an attack on First Castle.

In the film's opening scene, Saburo's kindness toward Hidetora is overcome by uncertainty when his father awakens from a nightmare of being stranded in the wilderness. Taro and Jiro come to their father's side to give him physical support and reassurance, but Saburo recoils from his outstretched hand. Saburo becomes disoriented, unreasonable, and unkind in reaction to the unfamiliar weakness and terror he has just witnessed in his father. Nor is he accustomed to any dependency by Hidetora upon his sons. Hidetora, unlike Lear, first displays a *need* rather than a demand for filial love. There is in Saburo's behavior at this point a suggestion of the disturbingly perverse element to Edgar's actions toward his father Gloucester late in *King Lear* (4.1, 4.6). In guiding and protecting the blinded Gloucester, even to the extent of preventing him from a suicide attempted in despair, Edgar maintains a disguised identity.

Hidetora's royal emblem is a radiant sun against a black background. This image is reiterated in the meeting on the ramparts of Second Castle between Hidetora and Sué as the sun sets. It is suggested as well in the scroll containing an icon of the Buddha Amida that Sué leaves as security with Tsurumaru just before she is assassinated. The Buddha Amida, or Amitabha, is the Buddha of Boundless Light whose great powers will bring believers rebirth in paradise. (The sect has had broad mass appeal in Japan.) The royal emblem is also suggested, however, in the infernal scene of attack on Third Castle during which the forces of Taro and Jiro besiege Hidetora. The slaughter advances to the main keep, where Hidetora has sought refuge. Flaming arrows and the flashes from musket fire create a hellish radiance. His retinue, concubines, and guards are all destroyed. The fool Kyoami and the loyal retainer Tango escape slaughter only because they have not joined in seeking refuge in Third Castle.

In the last minutes of the attack, several men and women in the Lord's retinue commit suicide, but Hidetora cannot find a serviceable sword with which to bring an honorable death through hara-kiri. With flames advancing through the castle keep, his awareness and determination are overcome with shock and Hidetora walks out from the holocaust in a trance. As Hidetora descends mechanically and vacantly down an exterior flight of steps, enemy troops are awestruck. Hundreds of men mobilized by Taro and Jiro to destroy Hidetora bring their weapons to rest. With a frozen, crazed expression on his face, Hidetora continues on a straight path between the parting army ranks, and the Lord gains safe passage out from Third Castle. In the chaos of the siege, Kurogane has assassinated Taro, thus giving Jiro absolute authority. But Jiro is immobilized and powerless at the sight of his father. Madness preserves Hidetora at this moment.

In appearance, Hidetora has become less a man than the mask of a man. Following Kurosawa's instructions, the makeup on Tatsuya Nakadai has passed through three phases, with each phase based on specific images in the repertory of Noh masks. In the first, the makeup is lightest and most naturalistic in suggesting the face of a vigorous but aged leader. With banishment, anxiety and exhaustion deeply mark Hidetora. For the final stage of terror and madness, the makeup becomes an impasto that sculpts a rigid image on the face. The Lord's facial coloration has turned emphatically unnatural.

Madness ultimately brings insight for Hidetora. In horror, Hidetora recoils from an inner image prompted by the sight of tall grasses swirled into waves by a harsh wind and the Lord moans, "Forgive me." Kyoami recognizes the reaction as one of guilt over past atrocities, and the Fool recites a grotesque variation on lines from the Noh play *Funa Benkei*:

The wonder of it!
I see on this withered plain
All those I destroyed.
A phantom army,
One by one they come floating,
Rising before me.

There are many visual intertexts to the sequence's imagery within Kurosawa's cinema, dating back to his first film *San-*

shiro Sugata and the climactic fight scene that takes place on grassy slopes amidst a gale.

While researching Japanese culture of the historical period in which *Ran* is set, Kurosawa made discoveries that shaped his conception of the social ambiguities in the fool Kyoami's role:

> Warlords of the period had people in their entourage of very low birth. Depending on their particular skills, they would dance, tell jokes, entertain. But their main function was to be a conversationalist. Through them, the warlord would learn about what the people he governed were really thinking. And since they were not of samurai class—you will notice that Kyoami doesn't wear a sword—they were exempted from the majority of the rules of etiquette. So Kyoami can say anything he wants.[25]

The social psychology of this characterization largely accords with the freedom of the "all-licensed Fool" in *Lear* (1.4.206). Kyoami's dialogue is written in the script to suggest the farcical language of the *kyogen* pieces in Noh. Kurosawa was also mindful of the *vox populi* expressed through the carnival and the fool in feudal societies and its inversions of normative social rules and official truths.

With Kyoami and Tsurumaru, the film develops two characters who manifest great ambiguity in gender. Such ambiguity may have been suggested in part by correlations in *King Lear* between the Fool, whose costume features a coxcomb as a symbol of masculinity, and Cordelia who, in death, is called by Lear "my poor fool" (5.3.307). Issues of sexuality are essential in Kurosawa's characterization of the Fool:

> In the time of the samurai, when the warriors were away at battle most of the time and the women were hiding out in the castle, the "fool" was something like a page who waited on them and with whom they had sexual relations. They were treated with great affection. My feeling about the relationship between Hidetora and Kyoami was that they prob-

ably had that relationship in the past when Hidetora was a younger man out on the battlefield a lot of the time.[26]

Peter, the actor who plays Kyoami, was an icon in Japanese popular culture at the time of his casting in *Ran*. A singer, dancer, and television entertainer, Peter's public personality was celebrated for its childlike temperament, outrageous behavior, and its transvestism.

Within the domain of the patriarch Hidetora, Kyoami has an indeterminate social and sexual identity. Kyoami is placed within the noble hierarchy but he is without a place in the rigid feudal system of class. Though Kyoami is an intimate within the most powerful inner circle of warriors, he is unarmed and defenseless. By samurai standards of masculinity, Kyoami is effeminate. By comparison to the first impressions of Hidetora as venerable and restrained, the Fool is ageless and extravagant. The ambiguities within Kyoami's personality are indicative of the more general truth that there are no intrinsic or fixed traits that define gender. The same conclusion must be reached in consideration of a female character like Lady Kaede. The only quality she has in common with Lady Sué, another survivor of Hidetora's reign of terror, is that of gender, which is thus disqualified as a determinant of personality. Lady Kaede's will to rule is far greater than that of Lord Jiro, whom she easily overpowers, seduces, and commands. Kurosawa, like Shakespeare, accepts the possibility that ruthless intentions can be harbored by men and women equally.

Aspects of Gloucester and Edgar are to be found in the film's characterization of Tsurumaru as a blinded victim living like a hermit in exile. More pronounced in *Ran*'s characterization, however, are certain androgynous traits. When Hidetora is taken from the storm by Kyoami and Tango to the shelter of a rural thatch hut, they encounter a delicate-voiced stranger inside. The stranger has physical attributes that resemble the ghost figures traditional to Noh theater. Tango first addresses the stranger as a woman, on the basis of the long hair and style of kimono, though these features are only half visible in the darkness. Within minutes, Hidetora regains his senses and reflects upon the betrayal and slaughter that has surrounded him. After Hidetora's admission that his own survival is unjust, the stranger is revealed to be Tsurumaru, grown to manhood since his blinding by the Lord.

Though Tsurumaru's identity is clarified, his feminine appearance is not altered or lessened for the remainder of the film story. Like Gloucester, he is a sufferer who now sees feelingly. The film adds with this character, as a surviving victim, a paradoxical witness to Hidetora's wretchedness. The expression of Tsurumaru's pathos at this moment is through the *nohkan*, or Noh flute. It is the only wind instrument used in Noh theater's musical accompaniment and it conventionally expresses the main character's state of mind. The *nohkan* is capable of reaching an intensely shrill and eerie pitch. Tsurumaru offers to play the instrument as a gesture of his "hospitality of the heart." His deeply ironic comment that the music "is the only pleasure left to me" is followed by flute notes that rise to a pitch of hysteria. Hidetora reacts with horror and he tumbles through the hut's wall out into a furious storm. Kurosawa's conception of this dramatic moment can be understood as a brilliant restructuring of Lear's instruction to the blind Gloucester: "A man may see how the world goes with no eyes. Look with thine ears" (4.6.152–53).

In such moments, Hidetora faces the human cost of his political career. The destruction of the Great Lord's family and his own ultimate destruction repeat the pattern of destruction that brought him to power in the first place. This course of events satisfies Lady Kaede's lust for vengeance, which is fully revealed at the film's close, but it cannot be calculated as the result of her will alone. Her vengeance, like Sué's piety, is the product of Hidetora's merciless ambitions. His past reign has left a legacy of cruel inevitability.

In his alliance with Taro against their father, Jiro kills many in his brother's troops and in his own ranks and has Taro assassinated at the same time. Lady Sué escapes an assassination ordered by Lady Kaede once, when Kurogane refuses to follow

instructions and instead warns Lord Jiro against his fiend-
ish mistress. Sué is slaughtered nevertheless in a second attempt. With the discovery of this ultimate treachery, Kurogane butchers Lady Kaede. His act of vengeance is by no
means a purifying act of justice, since Kurogane is the assassin of Taro.

Ran is structured extensively through a visual iconography
of humanity's descent into chaos. After the transfer of power,
Hidetora's perspective is first represented from his position in
a tower within the outworks to First Castle. The Lord looks
down upon his own concubines and household servants as
they relocate to an outer building. Their departure from the
donjon interferes with Lady Kaede's retinue and the new Lady
of the castle is indignant. Hidetora angrily watches as his entourage kneels in deference to Lady Kaede. Kaede is much like
Lady Asaji in her physical bearing. Both women give the appearance of immobility and passivity while violent intentions surge within them. Lady Kaede is seen early in the film
with her head bowed and her regard deflected in accord with
Japanese customs of the respect to be shown by a wife to her
husband and in-laws. But these customs also serve her as strat-
agems in her manipulation through indirection.

The next elevated perspective is from Taro's position at the
top of First Castle's donjon. He has an unobstructed pano-
rama of the realm. With great satisfaction over his rise in the
world, he commends the view to Kaede. Her attention, however, is focused on the ceremonial platform within the council chamber, which is now empty of the Lord's armor, helmet, and family standard. They have been transported to
the Lord's chambers in the outworks. Lady Kaede warns her
husband that without possession of the family banner—the
foremost regalia of clan rule—Taro will remain a "shadow." A
struggle between factions of castle guards over this banner
ends when an arrow kills one of Jiro's men. Hidetora has shot
the arrow from his position above. This proves to be the Lord's
last act of violence. The rapid descent from power begins
when Hidetora is coerced into signing a pledge of absolute

obedience to Taro. Though he seals the written pledge with blood, the Great Lord renounces his first son and departs First Castle in a fury.

After Jiro's refusal to accept the Lord's full retinue at Second Castle, Hidetora is betrayed into seeking haven in Third Castle. During the siege that ensues, the noise of battle is entirely mute under the film's music track. In regard to the sequence's audiovisual montage, Kurosawa has explained: "In eliminating the sounds from the scene of battle I wanted to indicate that the perspective was that of the heavens: the heavens watch such unthinkable and bloody battles and become literally mute."[27] In the arrangement of instrumental music for scenes of battle, Kurosawa instructed his music director Toru Takemitsu to develop counterpoint through the symphonic orchestration of traditional Japanese themes. The director had attempted to add a female chorus to the soundtrack music for this sequence, but in his experiments with the montage he could not find a vocal sound that reached a pitch high enough to convey the intended impression of heavenly despair.

The visual and symphonic résumé of battle at Third Castle is broken by the sound of a single gunshot as the assassination of Taro succeeds amidst the brothers' armed attack against their father. The chaos of battle is devoid of a heroic center. Hidetora's last attempt at violence is his failed intention to commit hara-kiri. Strife ends when the Great Lord emerges, in a trance of shock and madness, from his refuge in the main tower. Hidetora's descent from the tower is a deranged and perverse ceremony that takes place before an assembly of enemy troops who formerly held allegiance to him.

At the extreme of his suffering, Hidetora regards the world from a mental inferno. The terrain across which he wanders in exile features a volcanic wasteland and the burned ruins of Azusa Castle, which once belonged to Sué's family. On a rampart within the castle ruins, Hidetora remarks weakly, "I'm lost." The fool Kyoami replies: "Such is the human condition. . . . Men always travel the same road. If you're tired of it, jump!" Carrying through this ultimatum, Hidetora jumps from the outer wall. From a height that could have brought death, he falls unharmed into a sand pit.

From this position he looks up to see Sué, then Tsurumaru, and he comes back to complete consciousness with the recognition of where he is and of the ruin he brought to the family and Azusa Castle. Upon making this realization he exclaims, "Is this a dream? No, this is hell! The lowest level of hell!" From his original perspective down upon the world, Hidetora has fallen to a depth from which he fully perceives the consequences of the chaos he has brought upon his victims.

Hidetora is lost in an ashen, volcanic landscape before he is discovered by Saburo. At this lower depth of despair, Hidetora hopes he is dead and in the otherworld already. The paradox of such hope in the midst of despair is registered in *King Lear* by Edgar's thought, spoken alone on the heath: "To be worst, / The lowest and most dejected thing of fortune, / Stands still in esperance, lives not in fear" (4.1.2–4). Kurosawa considers his film more hopeful than Shakespeare's tragedy:

> I believe my film to be less pessimistic than *King Lear*; in any case, it is with this sense that I made the film. In contrast to King Lear, who has no regrets, who does not contemplate his past, who needlessly falls in this terrifying drama, Hidetora reflects on his past and regrets it. In this sense, I think my work is less tragic.[28]

Ran lacks the archetypal pattern of Western tragedy's sacrifice of the hero and promise of redemption for the society that survives him. A principal consequence of the film's creation of a detailed past of misdeeds by the character is to make Hidetora not only less tragic but also less heroic than Lear.

As the forces of Jiro and Saburo poise for battle, the regiments of Ayabe and Fujimaki are mobilized into positions along the ridges just outside the boundaries to the Ichimonji realm. In deciding to violate his peace pact with Saburo and to engage in total war with the two rival lords, Jiro acts upon the same urges of treachery, opportunism, and fatalism that drove his father's political and military career. In the climactic military events, Saburo is not present on the battlefield to lead his troops in victory over Jiro. At the time when victory comes, Saburo is killed by an assassin's bullet.

Through its remarkable costumes, sets, location scenes, and cinematography, *Ran* treats color not as a transparent or naturalistic element but as a denatured, motivated set of signs imposed by humanity on reality. The most obvious example of color as a cultural sign is in the military gear of warring armies. The color used in the soldiers' pennants and helmets is an index to their political identity: the troops of Taro are in yellow, those of Jiro in red, Saburo in blue, Fujimaki in white, Ayabe in black. After its introduction in early scenes, Hidetora's royal emblem does not remain conspicuous. In this sense, Hidetora becomes a lord without political identity once he concedes power over an army and retains only his immediate retinue.

In many instances a specific color does not prove to have a fixed, one-dimensional meaning. As befits his title, Hidetora is attired in early scenes with luxuriant robes that contain much gold woven into their patterns. The Lord's chamber in First Castle is adorned with gold panels. This golden chamber is the scene of Hidetora's official suppression by Taro and Lady Kaede. Later it is the scene of Lady Kaede's mastery over Jiro. Gold also adorns, however, the scroll bearing the radiant image of Buddha Amida. Here its brilliance and allure is a symbol of spiritual enlightenment and heavenly promise. The radiance of the setting sun contains a paradoxical brilliance in its associations with Sué. It positions her on a brink of the same darkness Hidetora forced Tsurumaru into by blinding him.

The film's most ironic uses of color are in the case of green, which dominates many scenes set in nature. In its natural settings, however, *Ran* often dissociates green from the mythic conventions of spring and summer as restorative or redemptive of humanity's spirit. A plain lush with tall grasses and wildflowers is the landscape of Hidetora's derangement. During the storm, he fears that winds have turned this plain into a violent sea that will submerge him. The corpses of Lady Sué and her attendant lie on grasses and wildflowers crushed by their weight. Opposing armies amass on a field and surrounding hills lush with summer grasses. The field becomes a battleground and the scene of slaughter.

In *King Lear,* the human understanding born of suffering is conveyed by the tragic hero Lear to Gloucester, his counterpart in pain and banishment:

> I know thee well enough; thy name is Gloucester:
> Thou must be patient; we came crying hither:
> . . . .
> When we are born, we cry that we are come
> To this great stage of fools.
>
> (4.6.179–85)

In *Ran* the expression of a similar understanding is left to the fool Kyoami: "Man is born crying. When he has cried enough he dies." With the murder of Saburo by an assassin's bullet, Hidetora falls lifelessly beside his son. The scene is without the lament or protestations Lear makes over the slain Cordelia.

Though Saburo's troops have won one campaign, victory will not end chaos in the realm since an assault against First Castle has already been undertaken by Ayabe's army. In the last scene at First Castle, its donjon is in flames and Kurogane instructs Jiro to prepare to commit suicide now that Ayabe's soldiers have penetrated the fortifications. War ultimately brings new social order in the heroic tragic worlds of *Macbeth* and *King Lear,* but it does not do so in the world of *Ran.* Peace and new order is formalized in *Macbeth* through the ceremonial inauguration of a successor and in *King Lear* through funeral rites that honor the legacy of the king's suffering and through a rational division of power between Edgar and Kent. At the conclusion of *Ran,* war has only further intensified the disorder within family and society.

At the depth of his despair, Gloucester muses: "As flies to wanton boys, are we to th' gods, / They kill us for their sport"

Tsurumaru blindly approaches a precipice, in an image of the human condition from *Ran*.

(4.1.36–37). A similar reflection is made by Kyoami in the face of the deaths of Saburo and Hidetora. Tango contradicts this belief in a statement that has no direct counterpart in *King Lear:* "Do not blaspheme! It is the gods who weep. They see us killing each other over and over since time began. They can't save us from ourselves." The sun has begun to set over Azusa Field with the murder of Saburo and the death of Hidetora. Within this place, the film's remaining images are silhouettes cast by the gathering darkness.

Tsurumaru is left unattended at the ruins of his family home, Azusa Castle. Sué has returned to the primitive hut to see what happened to her attendant, who had gone back to retrieve the flute. After imagery of the cumulative slaughter that takes these two lives along with those of Saburo, of Jiro's soldiers, and of Lady Kaede, darkness gathers around Tsurumaru as he stands on a high outer rampart. Through the continued ambiguity of appearances in regard to this character's gender, the impression made is that this sightless figure is not a man or a woman but humanity. And in the end humanity is seen as unprotected and blind while standing near the edge of a precipice.

With a reed cane as guide, Tsurumaru tentatively moves forward. When the cane tip leaves the stone rampart and reaches into thin air, Tsurumaru is so startled that he drops the scroll of Buddha Amida, which was intended to secure him from harm. The only comforts left to these two victims of Hidetora's past brutality—Tsurumaru's flute and Sué's scroll—are lost. The world that the survivor Tsurumaru blindly faces is not graced by Buddha's enlightenment or a promise of deliverance to paradise. The situation is a final indication that human suffering has entirely human origins. There is no otherworldly cause, answer, or meaning to suffering. The tragedy is historical, existential, and unheroic.

The final images in *Ran* are edited in a progression closer toward Tsurumaru until the moment when he nearly plummets into the abyss, when the order of the images is reversed and the perspective increases in distance from him. This progression and recession in the scale of the human figure at the center of a darkening world is accompanied by the *nohkan*'s anguished notes. The sequence is a summation of Kurosawa's vision of what humanity is, in having brought itself to the brink of extinction. The prospect of nonexistence, which shapes meaning in each of the major films studied here, can appall or inspire. Humanity gauged by the measure of history, as in the case of *Throne of Blood* and *Ran*, is a source of pessimism. By the measure of individual existence, as in *The Idiot*, *Ikiru*, and the ending to *Rashomon*, humanity can be the source of hope.

Conclusion

Repeated patterns of themes and of visual style in Kurosawa's cinema have been widely analyzed by film critics. Donald Richie documents a thematic preoccupation with conflicts between illusion and reality in the individual's experience of the world. Richie has also charted an underlying "sonata form" in the narrative structure to many films.[1] Stephen Prince valuably traces the director's continued engagement with issues of group norms, social duties, and individual responsibilities. In the matter of stylistics, he notes a characteristic acknowledgment of artifice within Kurosawa's film language. For Noel Burch, one thematic constant is the trait of "masochistic perseverance in the fulfillment of complex social obligations" by the director's protagonists. The formal constants in imagery and dramaturgy Burch identifies are "disjunctiveness, pathos and excess."[2]

Within Kurosawa's cinema, as the present study has found, there is also a deep structure of inquiry and internal dialogue that motivates the narrative and the visual text. In several cases, a later Kurosawa film returns to the problematics in theme and style of an earlier one in order to explore an alternative contextualization and visual approach. David Desser has accounted for this process in the case of *Ikiru* and its relationship to *Drunken Angel* and *Rashomon*.[3] *Ikiru* returns to the question of heroism within the ordinary, fallible man, an issue prominent in the two earlier films. In structure, *Ikiru* adapts *Rashomon*'s reflexive properties and narrative relativism for purposes appropriate to the modern story's contexts.

Dodeskaden presents another case of intertextual response within Kurosawa's cinema. This film returns to an environment and to social issues related to those in *The Lower Depths*. The contemporary film story was adapted in collaboration with Hideo Oguni and Shinobu Hashimoto from a collection of stories by Shugoro Yamamoto. Its setting is a wasteground shantytown outside Tokyo. The setting is established, however, as a fictional space rather than as an urban reality documented by the camera. While *The Lower Depths* presents its substratum of society as confined from the surrounding, mainstream reality, *Dodeskaden* does not. The shantytown opens onto the broader social world and it is linked directly to modern, urban Japan. The most obvious link is the trolley line. A commuter train that passes near the slum is heard but remains unseen. The imaginary trolley that the adolescent Rokuchan conducts is heard in the complete details of its operation. As a result of Rokuchan's consuming illusions, this vehicle is present in a sense for the film viewer even though it remains invisible.

Another prominent link to a broader social reality is the automobile. In the slum, the hollow shell of a European compact car provides shelter for the dreamer and his small son. Later, the boy is dwarfed by the city's automobiles when he travels the streets to beg food from restaurant kitchens. In a departure from *The Lower Depths*, fantasy or kindness makes possible transcendence for a few inhabitants of the shantytown in *Dodeskaden*. Despite the taunts of passing schoolboys and his mother's distress, the retarded Rokuchan can exist blissfully in his imaginary world of trolley cars. Through a pure paternal heart, the brushmaker Ryo loves the five children in his home even though he can recognize in their faces the evidence of his wife's betrayals. Though his wife is illtempered and rude, Mr. Shima is able to remain content with life through a trust in her fundamental loyalty.

For one old man, exhausted by the sorrow and emptiness of his life since the loss of his sons, his livelihood, and finally his wife, suicide seems to be the only promise left. Mr. Tanba, a generous and wise craftsman, offers a strong poison in answer to the man's despair. Mr. Tanba has in fact provided only a harmless stomach remedy. In the course of their conversation as the man awaits death, Mr. Tanba enables him to recognize the continued value of life. Frantic, the old man now demands an antidote, and Mr. Tanba reveals the truth of the situation. The fake poison has cured the desperate man of his preoccupation with suicide. The scene possesses a quality suggestive of the absurdism in Samuel Beckett's drama in its contradictory introduction and negation of the idea of suicide as a resolution to the suffering and contradictions of life.

Fantasy or kindness are meaningless, however, in the lives of other inhabitants. Through neglect the homeless father, who obsessively designs a dream house in his mind, loses his son. His fixation makes him incapable of perceiving the obvious severity of his son's illness, caused in the first place by the father's distracted state of mind. The ragpicker Hei is consumed by contempt for his wife. Her love and regret cannot overcome his condemnation of her for a sexual indiscretion she committed in the past. She patiently attempts to resume domestic life with him, but his terrifying silence and disregard drive her away. The futility and hopelessness contained in these storylines alternate with the compassion and resilience shown in other characters. As a result, the shantytown world of *Dodeskaden* does not sustain the profound absurdity or the atmosphere of existential dread created in Kurosawa's *The Lower Depths*.

The slum in *Dodeskaden* is a denatured world. Though *Dodeskaden* is Kurosawa's first color film, in designing it he selected predominantly inorganic materials. For the exterior locations all trees, shrubbery, and ground cover were removed and a color scheme was artificially applied. Even shadows were painted in, using darker hues. Kurosawa approached the film as a "color experiment": "I tried all kinds of things — even painting the ground, not to mention the sets. To deal with these characters in their very restricted setting, I had to use color as much as possible to bring out this setting."[4] The setting often functions in relation to characters as a mind screen. Emotionally blinded and deadened, Hei occupies a colorless world. Inside his shanty, the faint light reduces all appearances to a flat, dun monochrome. Even the space out-doors around his shelter appears dispirited. The one distinguishing feature is a thin, barren, and forked tree that stands nearby. Upon her departure, having forsaken all effort at reconciliation, his wife comments that this shape cannot even be called a tree since it has no life.

As the dreamer looks on helplessly, his son's life ebbs. Both their faces have turned to ghastly hues of green and gray. They are illuminated, however, by colors from a brightly painted sunset on the horizon. This noticeably artificial image of a natural phenomenon suggests the remoteness of a man-made world from the order of nature. A painter enters briefly into the narrative to *Dodeskaden*. He has set up his easel in the middle of the slum wasteland, which he studies carefully. But his position stands in the path of Rokuchan's imaginary trolley line and the boy's determined approach quickly forces the painter to flee. The film viewer never sees his artistic impression of the setting. The only paintings that enter the dramatic context are the childlike, brilliantly colored images of trolleys that decorate the walls and sliding panels of the shack Rokuchan occupies with his mother.

Figuratively, and ironically, the painter in *Dodeskaden* is seen as standing in the way of pure imagination. Painting is surprisingly not a prominent intertext in *Scandal*, the one Kurosawa film story with a painter as its protagonist (in a role performed by Toshiro Mifune). Though *Scandal's* painter is shown at work at a few points in the narrative, the creative process and the artist's composition have no dramatic import. In fact, they are only briefly glimpsed in the film. From what can be seen of the work in his studio, he is a Western-style artist of no particular originality. Perhaps Kurosawa added this visual hint about the painter in *Scandal* as a wry commentary on his own derivative imitations of Western masters as an art student.

In the museum episode of *Dreams*, the vivid power of Van Gogh's art transports the young Japanese man into the era when it was created. Transposition from a painted canvas to a duplicate film scene marks the entry into that era. The brief meeting with Van Gogh ends when the painter explains, "The sun . . . it compels me to paint." The young man wanders in search of the artist through a full-scale world of his drawings and paintings. He is compelled onward by the sheer force of line and color in the Van Gogh compositions. Here, Kurosawa pursues to the furthest extent the earlier screen experiments with painterly images made in *Drunken Angel, Dodeskaden,* and *Kagemusha.*

Kurosawa has explained that when he began a career in film he "intended to forget painting once and for all." In pursuit of this end, he destroyed all the pictures he had painted to that time. With film directing, however, Kurosawa recognized the effectiveness of his sketches in communicating ideas to his production team. In preparation for *Kagemusha* and *Ran,* Kurosawa freely developed his ideas for the films through numerous, elaborate color images he drew and painted. Some of these images were subsequently exhibited and published. They are by no means merely storyboard illustrations. As in the case of Eisenstein's graphic art, the Kurosawa drawings and paintings are full visualizations of the imaginary world in each film. Kurosawa assesses the pictures, which are truly beautiful and powerful in their own right, with characteristic humility and irony:

> Are they worthy of being called art? My purpose was not to paint well. I made free use of various materials that happened to be at hand. At best, they are remnants left from making the films. . . .
> I cannot help but be fascinated by the fact that when I tried to paint well, I could only produce mediocre pictures. But when I concentrated on delineating the ideas for my films, I unconsciously produced works that people find interesting.[5]

Music has also functioned in Kurosawa's cinema as a strong intertext, beyond the purposes of accompaniment and audio-

visual montage. The director has stipulated a fundamental relationship between the two art forms: "A good structure for a
screenplay is that of the symphony, with its three or four
movements and differing tempos" (*Autobiography*, 193). Franz
Schubert's *Unfinished Symphony* in several respects provided
the story structure to *One Wonderful Sunday*. Though in poverty and suffering intense pain at the time he composed the
symphony, Schubert created an inspired and, in its second
movement, serene work of art. Such contradictions between
a person's material and physical conditions and his emotional
and imaginative potential is a basis for the film's characterization of the young lovers. In addition to its use on the soundtrack
as coloration to scenes, the *Unfinished Symphony* serves an
explicit narrative function at the story's conclusion, in the
young man's efforts to conduct an imaginary orchestra in a performance of the musical score.

Music in Kurosawa's cinema has thus fulfilled a concep-
tual role in the creation of narrative and visuals. Toru Takemitsu, the composer on *Ran*, describes a process of intertextuality in the collaboration with the director on film music:

> The difficulty with Kurosawa is that he already has in mind
> a very strong acoustic image for each scene; unfortunately,
> the musical reference does not necessarily correspond with
> his other decisions. It is from this discrepancy that our dis-
> cussions begin.
>
> Moreover, each film director possesses a musical memory
> that is uniquely his own. Fellini and Visconti work in musi-
> cal registers that do not resemble each other and that give
> their films a very personal quality. In the case of *Ran*, Kuro-
> sawa thought specifically of musical passages from Mahler
> and Grieg. Often I had to rewrite the score to certain se-
> quences until they corresponded.[6]

As the result of their collaboration on *Ran*, the music is ap-
propriately epic and tragic. In the case of *Dodeskaden*, for
which Takemitsu also composed the soundtrack, the film's
theme music is distractingly frothy and commercial. During

the production of *Kagemusha*, the creative argumentation involved in collaboration with Kurosawa led finally to the departure of Masaru Sato, the music composer for all the films in the decade 1955–65. The extraordinary visuals of *Kagemusha* are ultimately disserved by the clichés of its heroic movie music, composed by Sato's replacement, Shinichiro Ikebe.

Kurosawa offered an explanation of the nature of the collaboration with Hideo Oguni in the script and production of a film: "Sometimes I pay too much attention to the images, to aesthetic effects, and I forget my subject matter. Oguni, who is a genuine scenarist, redirects me; it is the pilot fish that points out the right way."[7] This statement is relevant to the dialogic writing process at work in the four decades 1946–85, and that has fundamentally shaped the intertextual structure within Kurosawa's cinema. The absence of that process in the production of *Dreams* and *Rhapsody in August* has left the two films largely without forceful characters or story situations despite the eloquence of many stunning visuals in them. These two films are solitary explorations into the processes of imagination and memory and are shaped as monologues.

Actors' performances provide unique intertexts to Kurosawa's cinema. Codes of characterization and screen behavior are brought into the film through the director's rigorous preparation, rehearsal, and supervision of the actor. The codes for screen performances in *Rashomon*, for example, are distinct and contrastive. Its styles of acting vary among the animalistic eccentricity of the bandit, the refinement and restraint of the samurai couple seen traveling on the road, the theatrically stylized torment of the spirit-medium, and the quiet interior drama of the priest. The performance codes vary further within a single actor's characterization as the narrative discloses conflicts and shifts in perspective. One comic variation comes when the unruly bandit imagines himself riding skillfully, like a movie hero, against a vast, open horizon.

Kazuo Miyagawa, the cinematographer on *Rashomon* as well as on *Yojimbo* and *Kagemusha*, has compared Kurosawa's

directing method with actors to that of Mizoguchi, another
master with whom Miyagawa worked:

> Mizoguchi was strict; he was obsessed. Everyone would try
> to follow along, without any kind of explanation. Kurosawa
> was also like that in some ways—seizing the initiative. . . .
>   I would hear Mizoguchi say over and over: "You're the ac-
> tor, right? I'm in charge of the production. You can add your
> own interpretation." Kurosawa was different. He created
> with a certain actor or actress in mind, and he would often
> demonstrate what he wanted from them. Mizoguchi *never*
> did that—he'd just say "Once again," and then remain silent.
> No one knew what aspect of the performance was good or
> bad—he'd never say "Stop! Right there—that's wrong!" With-
> out giving any explanation, he'd sit glaring at the actors,
> with his arms crossed and his face growing red. Kurosawa
> would stop them sharply in the middle of their performance
> and say: "There!"[8]

Mizoguchi adopted a relatively passive role in the direction of
actors in sending them only reactive signals in response to
their performances. His working method required of the actor
perceptiveness in grasping the director's aesthetic, reflection
on the script material, and discipline in preparing the role.
     At the time *Ran* was released, Kurosawa explained his rela-
tionship on the set with actors as follows:

> I push. Some directors seem to "pull" performances out of
> actors, but I'm always pushing them, nudging them to try
> new or different things. We rehearse a scene or bit of action
> over and over again, and with each rehearsal something new
> jumps forward and they get better and better. Rehearsing is
> like making a sculpture of papier-mâché; each repetition lays
> on a new sheet of paper, so that in the end the performance
> has a shape completely different from when we started. I
> make actors rehearse in full costume and makeup whenever
> possible, and we rehearse on the set. . . . In costume, the
> work has an onstage tension that vanishes whenever we try
> rehearsing out of costume.[9]

While Kurosawa requires some qualities in the performance ultimately similar to those required by Mizoguchi, Kurosawa's method is always directive, aggressive, and interactive. He makes the actor in a sense the respondent in a dialogic process of characterization. In the filming and in the editing phases, Kurosawa further shapes the role as material in the film text.

Many of the same properties of intertextuality analyzed in previous chapters in terms of a few films are to be found with frequency in Kurosawa's cinema. Paradoxical heroism, for example, also characterizes the protagonist of *The Quiet Duel*, the doctor Kyoji Fujisaki. Infected by syphilis from a patient, Kyoji refrains from physical intimacy. Yet he derides his own professional and ethical behavior: "My abstinence is comical and sentimental." Kyoji's confession of anguish to the nurse Rui is captured in one continuous shot, which orchestrates the press of emotions upon him. This sequence shot, the longest in duration of all the film's shots, ends abruptly when the doctor assumes his customary stoic attitude.

Though called a saint by colleagues in medicine, the doctor is a hero with a sense of the ridiculousness, if not the absurdity, of his own purity. The paradoxical structure of value and meaning in the film is given visual form through a use of wipe cuts. By chance Kyoji encounters his wartime syphilitic patient, Tatsuo Nakata, at the police station, where the doctor has treated a patrolman injured by the veteran. A wipe cut transposes the action to a bar, where the doctor and the veteran are engaged in conversation. It is clear from his manner that the veteran has become a success as a criminal in the postwar economy. A wipe cut in the opposite direction transposes the scene to the clinic, where the doctor is alone and deep in thought.

In a subsequent meeting with Nakata, the doctor is impassive about the consequences to him of the infection, but he urgently seeks to persuade the veteran to undertake full treatment for a cure. Nakata becomes enraged when the doctor discloses that he became infected with syphilis in operating on him during the war. The doctor's disclosure is not made in an accusatory manner. The unrepentant syphilitic nonetheless refuses to acknowledge his own responsibility in endangering others—including his wife and unborn child as well as the doctor—and he attributes the doctor's infection to immorality.

Such perversion in logic and ethics is one additional indication of humanity's paradoxical nature. The opening scenes of *The Quiet Duel* are set in wartime at a battlefield hospital in the tropics. It is in this context that the infection is passed from soldier to doctor. In the initial shots, a torrential rain pours down, much as in the gate scenes of *Rashomon*. In subsequent daylight and nighttime scenes in this tropical setting, visibility is mottled and broken, as in the forest scenes of *Rashomon*. In daytime, the effect is produced by camouflage netting and reed roofing. At night, it is caused by deep shadows that overtake the limited light sources. The implication of these visuals is that the war is a time of fragmentation, obscurity, and relativism.

Intertextual structures between story and plot, and between narrative and argument, are also widely present in Kurosawa's cinema. In *Red Beard*, the outpatient waiting room and the wards of the hospital are settings of narration, where the meaning of patients' suffering is conveyed. Their suffering contains a redemptive power for the living. The patients heal the arrogance and prejudices of the well-educated but inexperienced intern Yasumoto. The first lesson in humanity for the reluctant Yasumoto is a bedside vigil over a speechless terminal patient. After the patient dies, Red Beard instructs Yasumoto that the man's silence concealed great misfortune.

Yasumoto's full instruction in the pain and loneliness many people endure comes with a vigil by Sahachi, who has returned to his home village to die. With Yasumoto in attendance and the villagers gathered around, Sahachi narrates the events that explain the identity of a skeleton recently uncovered in a landslide nearby. The body was that of Onaka, to whom Sahachi was once married. Their blissful marriage did not protect them from the disasters of an earthquake, separation, and her remarriage. Their reunion, years later, drove Onaka into despair and suicide.

The narrative context of Sahachi's account is thus a form of *memento mori*. Sahachi's deathbed is the setting in which story events from his life are reconstructed and in which they enter the film plot. The narrative technique is similar to that in *Ikiru*, but the narrative material reaches beyond the principal protagonists (Red Beard and Yasumoto). Like *Ikiru, Red Beard* employs synopsis and ellipsis to telescope events in the film plot. The account of Yasumoto's treatment of Otoyo, the compulsive young girl rescued from a brothel, is given in diary form. Otoyo's cure is achieved when she, in her turn, ministers to Yasumoto through his serious illness. These narrative interventions and variations within the film serve the functions of its humanist arguments about poverty, suffering, humility, and compassion.

In *Dodeskaden* there is an interpolation that serves similar purposes. In an otherwise linear narrative, one brief subplot is told from two temporal perspectives. It begins as a new scene, in the dramatic present, within the succession of vignettes of shantytown life. In the open space outside his shack, the drunken Kichi is terrorizing family and neighbors with a drawn sword. Mr. Tanba walks calmly toward him and says something to Kichi that quickly subdues him. The camera's distance from the two men and a heavy rain during the scene prevent the neighbors or the film viewer from overhearing Mr. Tanba's words. A subsequent shot in this subplot advances the perspective to a moment in time that the viewer can judge to be at least a day later. In this time frame Kichi is asked by the grocer So what Mr. Tanba had said that day. The subplot returns to the original scene, with the camera now close in, and we see and hear Mr. Tanba offer Kichi to relieve him, to take on his threatening tirade for a while. The subplot then returns to the later conversation with the grocer, and Kichi explains that the offer so surprised and embarrassed him that it defused his anger. The narrative in this minor subplot to *Dodeskaden* thus defers the substance of the encounter between Kichi and Tanba to a subsequent time period in order to suggest how experience can function to instruct humanity.

Often, within the main narrative to a Kurosawa film significant experience is glimpsed or a minor character's life story is summarized. The main narrative then moves on with its principal concerns and it pays no further direct attention to the interpolated material. While it serves no subsequent narrative purpose, this incidental material continues to function as part of the film's argument. *Dersu Uzala* contains one such instance when Dersu and the Russians encounter in the remote forests a Chinese hermit named Li Tsung-ping. The hermit speaks only once, in a brief exchange of formal greetings with Arseniev. Dersu explains that this quiet man has lived alone for forty years, having retreated from society when his wife became involved with his brother. In this manner, the main narrative retains the trace of an untold epic of personal experience.

Many biographemes that Kurosawa designates in *Something Like an Autobiography*, beyond those I have analyzed in Chapter 1, are manifest in his film texts as well. The autobiography understands Heigo's guidance through the ruins of Tokyo after the 1923 earthquake as a lesson intended to overcome ignorance and anxiety about human suffering. Kurosawa recounts the excursion through this hell on earth with gratitude toward his brother: "It had been an expedition to conquer fear" (*Autobiography*, 54). The thematic of human inquiry in the face of destruction, corruption, and death is reinscribed in films like *The Quiet Duel, Stray Dog, Rashomon, Ikiru,* and *Red Beard.*

In the constant and varied reading he did as a youth, Kurosawa remained captivated by a descriptive passage from Ivan Turgenev's "The Rendezvous," a story in the Russian writer's collection, *Sketches from a Hunter's Album* (1852): "The seasons could be determined from nothing more than the sound

of the leaves on the trees in the forest" (*Autobiography*, 46).
In citing the passage from memory, Kurosawa remarks that
in those years he understood more about nature than about
people. The conception acquired through this reading experience developed into a visual paradigm for the representation
of nature. In many passages within Kurosawa's cinema, nature is endowed with a dramatic impact as great as that made
by the film's principal characters.

The torrent of rain at Rasho gate and the wind and shadows of the forest, for example, are determinants in the viewer's responses to character conflict and narrative logic in
Rashomon. The obliterating fog and labyrinthian Cobweb
Forest in *Throne of Blood* are figurations of a worldview on
human ambitions and the will to power. In its expanse of virgin woods and vast, frozen marshes, *Dersu Uzala* visualizes
an existential stage on which an exploration into the nature
of humanity is dramatized.

Another biographeme concerning natural forces took form
when Kurosawa worked as assistant director to Eisuke Takizawa on *Saga of the Vagabonds* (*Sengoku Guntoden*, 1937).
On location for the film, he developed a deep affinity for the
Hakone region of mountains and lakes and for the barren
plains at the base of Mount Fuji. The 1937 film's heroic action scenes in such settings left a definitive impression: "My
experience of the spirited charge of horses in *Saga* so im-
pressed me that I revived it in *Seven Samurai*, *Throne of
Blood*, and most recently in *Kagemusha*" (*Autobiography*,
115). With *Ran*, the film that followed *Kagemusha*, Kurosawa stages the most elaborate and epic horse charges and battles in his cinema.

Horse, Kurosawa's last film as assistant director, should
also be added to the list given in *Something Like an Autobiography*. Its scenes of horses in movement become a visual
elegy onscreen. In editing these scenes in 1941, he sought
guidance from the director Kajiro Yamamoto, who stated simply: "Kurosawa, this sequence isn't drama. It's *mono no
aware*" (*Autobiography*, 105). *Aware*, which in its origins de-

noted an exclamation of intense feeling, is a term dating back to the Heian period. The phrase *mono no aware* came to express "sadness at the fleeting nature of things." The sensation is, in a sense, an intertext of affects that binds nostalgia, sorrow, beauty, and pleasure. Kurosawa reports that Yamamoto's guidance was incisive: "When I heard this ancient poetic term, I was suddenly struck by enlightenment as if waking from a dream" (*Autobiography*, 106).

At the start of Japan's war period (1937–45), Kurosawa recognized the superficiality of his cultural knowledge and he turned to the study of traditional Japanese dramatic and plastic arts. His dedicated study of these arts was prompted by the pure beauty Kurosawa found in haiku. Up to this time he had not seen a Noh performance. The mature study of traditional culture instilled an attitude of artistic humility: "I recognized my lack of education and talent; and I felt deeply ashamed. There must be many such things I thought I understood and yet really knew nothing about" (*Autobiography*, 147). In reflections on cinema published in 1975, Kurosawa emphasizes the beauty and power of "kiln changes" in the creation of a film (*Autobiography*, 193). Through this analogy to the unique glazes on traditional ceramic art, the director refers to elements of improvisation, aleatory effects, and fortuitous discovery involved in the filmmaking process.

Within the "defeated Japan" context of the contemporary story films Kurosawa made in the period 1947–55, the specific issue of the American use of atomic bombs is raised in *Record of a Living Being*. The unprecedented destructiveness of these weapons is reflected in two *jidai-geki* of the 1950s as well. The historical period of *Rashomon* is depicted as an era of devastation to Japan's cities and of threatened social chaos. The narrative context to *Throne of Blood* is set in a time after the obliteration of a center of Japanese life and political power. The vacant plains and blinding fogs of the film's prologue and epilogue suggest some historical ground zero in Japan's feudal past.

Controversy over the means by which Japan was defeated

in World War II intensified in the postwar period with the testing of atomic weapons by Western powers in the northern Pacific region. Over the years 1946–58 the United States conducted atmospheric tests of these bombs at the Eniwetok and Bikini atolls in the Marshall Islands. The Korean war (1950–53) raised the possibility of American deployment of atomic weapons again in Asia. In 1954 over twenty men on the Japanese fishing vessel *Fukuryu Maru* ("Lucky Dragon") were severely contaminated by radioactive fallout from the Pacific tests. One fisherman died by the end of the year. A series of Japanese monster movies that are worst-case scenarios about the effects of atomic testing in the Pacific was inaugurated with *Godzilla* (*Gojira*, 1954), directed by Ishiro Honda (who later assisted Kurosawa on *Ran* and *Rhapsody in August*).

Record of a Living Being is a family, psychological drama centered on a man's rising anxiety about nuclear destruction. The high-pitched, nervous noise on the soundtrack for the film's opening credits is an effect drawn deliberately from the science fiction screen genre of the 1950s. The protagonist is a successful businessman and manufacturer, with a large family and two mistresses to support. His fears about the dangers of nuclear weapons have a rational basis, given cold war politics and atmospheric testing in the Pacific. Common environmental factors—such as lightning strikes and thunderclaps—seem menacing in the context of his fears. The refusal of most people in Japanese society to take atomic danger seriously leads ultimately to his confinement in a mental asylum. In 1990 Kurosawa returned to the issue with the two episodes in *Dreams* that imagine an apocalypse caused by an accident at a nuclear power station. *Rhapsody in August* contemplates the contemporary legacy that remains from the 1945 atomic bombs dropped on Japan.

The dynamics of intertextuality are apparent in many periods of film history and in many national cinemas. In *Narrated Films: Storytelling Situations in Cinema History*, Avrom Fleishman has examined a specific dynamic, the incorporation of acts of storytelling into film narrative. His book offers a broad taxonomy of storytelling situations in the fiction film. Its taxonomy indicates the diverse applications and cultural contexts of such situations, in examples that range from *The Cabinet of Dr. Caligari* and Jean Cocteau's *Orpheus* to *Rashomon* and Woody Allen's *Zelig*. In Fleishman's account, cinema is a narrative form receptive to many properties from modernist movements in the arts, such as the mixed temporalities and atonal experiments in symphonic music, the new discontinuity and subjectivity in drama, and the multiple perspectives of cubist painting.

Fleishman joins the critics Claude-Edmonde Magny, Alan Spiegel, and Keith Cohen in locating cinema's most potent narrative resource within the modern novel.[10] Under its example, cinema has experimented with various discursive modes in an effort to communicate the kinds of narrative perspectives possible in literature. Modern fiction has motivated filmmakers to pursue the narrative project in various directions, one of which Fleishman delineates as a move "from nonfocalized to internal presentation, conveying limited or subjective views of events within a more encompassing, quasi-authorial perspective."[11] Further possibilities for fragmented, unreliable, or provisional perspectives come with this increased subjectivity in the film narrative.

With the study *Ecraniques: Le film du texte,* Marie-Claire Ropars-Wuilleumier proposes a process of intertextual interpretation that gives "filmic" readings of modernist literary texts. As one example, "the references, the citations, interferences, short-circuits or false echoes" Godard renders in his cinema are a filmic foundation for reading "other forms that exist only in the condition of traces, altered and alternating."[12] In cinematic, literary, and theatrical forms equally, *écriture* can place in doubt the referentiality of a sign and it can set in motion an extravagant play of meaning. The specificity of cinema as a medium derives, paradoxically, from the heterogeneity of the materials it incorporates. Its heterogeneity can reopen the literary text, which has an appearance of homogeneity as the result of its derivation from purely linguistic material. For the literary interpreter, Ropars-Wuilleumier advocates an application of the principle of filmic montage in the deconstruction of the text. The dynamic forms of construction in cinema are an effective reminder to readers of the literary text's semiotic activity and multiplicity. Intertextual cinema initiates new interpretation of other forms of culture. In its uses of classic works of literature, theater, music, and painting from both Western culture and Japanese traditions, Akira Kurosawa's cinema fully engages in such cultural rereading. The existentialism and absurdism Kurosawa derives in his interpretations of Dostoevsky and Gorky he applies in Japanese contexts in the adoption of material from Shakespeare's drama and in formulating a response to the Western conventions of a tragic world view. His cinema has the power to restructure our perceptions of Western and Japanese cultures and to make us recognize a new domain of intercultural meanings.

Notes

Introduction: Film Text, the Intercultural Film Text, and an Intertextual Cinema

1. Umberto Eco, *A Theory of Semiotics* (Bloomington: Indiana University Press, 1976), 274. A full consideration of the aesthetic text and semiotic invention is contained on pp. 261–76.

2. Christian Metz, *Language and Cinema*, trans. Donna Jean Umiker-Sebeok (The Hague: Mouton, 1974), 92–93. The discussion of film textuality appears on pp. 91–160.

3. David Desser, *The Samurai Films of Akira Kurosawa* (Ann Arbor: UMI Research Press, 1983), 5. Desser has turned attention to Kurosawa within a perspective of traditional Japanese narrative in "Narrating the Human Condition: *High and Low* and the Dilemma of Personal Responsibility," in Kevin K. W. Chang, ed., *Kurosawa: Perceptions on Life, An Anthology of Essays* (Honolulu: Honolulu Academy of Arts, 1991), 6–15.

4. Lev Kuleshov, *Kuleshov on Film*, ed. and trans. Ronald Levaco (Berkeley: University of California Press, 1974), 127–30, 144–45.

5. Jean-Luc Godard, *Godard on Godard*, ed. Jean Narboni and Tom Milne, trans. Tom Milne (New York: Viking, 1972), 172–77.

6. Metz, *Language and Cinema*, 124.

7. See Alain Silver, *The Samurai Film* (New York: Barnes, 1977), 13–42, and Desser, *Samurai Films of Kurosawa*, 20–22, 31–55.

8. The property of mutability within genre and among genres is explored in Jacques Derrida, "The Law of Genre," trans. Avital Ronell, *Glyph*, no. 7 (1980): 202–29.

9. See the discussion of *Yojimbo* in Desser, *Samurai Films of Kurosawa*, 97–105, 133–37. Desser explores the uses of the Western genre in another Kurosawa film in his essay "Kurosawa's Eastern 'Western': *Sanjuro* and the Influence of *Shane*," *Film Criticism* 8, no. 1 (Fall 1983): 54–65.

10. Noel Burch, *To the Distant Observer: Form and Meaning in the Japanese Cinema*, rev. and ed. Annette Michelson (Berkeley: University of California Press, 1979), 26. A restatement of this position is made in Noel Burch, "Approaching Japanese Film," in *Cinema and Language*, ed. Stephen Heath and Patricia Mellencamp (Frederick, Md.: University Publications of America, 1983): 79–96. For further discussion of the cultural uniqueness of Japanese cinema, see Donald Richie, "Viewing Japanese

Film: Some Considerations," *East-West Film Journal* 1, no. 1 (December 1986): 23–35.

11. In a critique of the Burch thesis, David Bordwell outlines many of the intercultural conditions of Japanese film production from the 1920s onward in his essay "Our Dream Cinema: Western Historiography and the Japanese Film," *Film Reader*, no. 4 (1979): 45–62. Other critiques of the Burch thesis are to be found in Robert Cohen, "Towards a Theory of Japanese Narrative," *Quarterly Review of Film Studies* 6, no. 2 (Spring 1981): 181–200; David Desser, *Eros plus Massacre* (Bloomington: Indiana University Press, 1988), 13–15; and Scott L. Malcomson, "The Pure Land Beyond the Seas: Barthes, Burch and the Uses of Japan," *Screen* 26, no. 3–4 (May–August 1985): 23–33. An illuminating discussion of intercultural interpretation in film studies is available in Scott Nygren, "Doubleness and Idiosyncrasy in Cross-Cultural Analysis," *Quarterly Review of Film and Video* 13, no. 1–3 (1991): 173–87.

12. David Bordwell, *Ozu and the Poetics of Cinema* (Princeton: Princeton University Press, 1988), 8–9.

13. This biographical information is drawn from Dudley Andrew and Paul Andrew, *Kenji Mizoguchi: A Guide to References and Resources* (Boston: G. K. Hall, 1981).

14. Emmanuel Decaux and Bruno Villien, "Entretien avec Akira Kurosawa," *Cinématographe*, no. 88 (1983): 62.

15. The quotation is contained in Donald Richie, "A Personal Record," *Film Quarterly* 14, no. 1 (Fall 1960): 22.

16. Two helpful surveys of the critical thought on intertextuality are Jonathan Culler, *The Pursuit of Signs: Semiotics, Literature, Deconstruction* (Ithaca: Cornell University Press, 1981), 100–118; and Thaïs E. Morgan, "Is There an Intertext in this Text?: Literary and Interdisciplinary Approaches to Intertextuality," *American Journal of Semiotics* 3, no. 4 (1985): 1–40.

17. Eco, *Semiotics*, 133–35, 149.

18. Julia Kristeva, *Desire in Language*, trans. Thomas Gora, Alice Jardine, and Leon S. Roudiez (New York: Columbia University Press, 1980), 64–91.

19. Roland Barthes, "Theory of the Text," trans. Ian McLeod, in Robert Young, ed., *Untying the Text: A Post-Structuralist Reader* (Boston: Routledge & Kegan Paul, 1981), 39; another exposition of these ideas is presented in "From Work to Text" in Roland Barthes, *Image-Music-Text*, trans. Stephen Heath (New York: Hill & Wang, 1977), 155–64.

20. Akira Kurosawa, *Something Like an Autobiography*, trans. Audie E. Bock (New York: Vintage, 1983), 191. Subsequent references to this book will be made in the text using the short title *Autobiography*.

21. Metz, *Language and Cinema*, 151.

22. Ibid., 182.

23. Stephen Heath, *Questions of Cinema* (Bloomington: Indiana University Press, 1981), 132.

24. Bruce Morrissette, *Novel and Film: Essays in Two Genres* (Chicago: University of Chicago Press, 1985), 1–10, 141–56. These issues are also examined in Morrissette, *Intertextual Assemblage in Robbe-Grillet from Topology to the Golden Triangle* (Fredericton, New Brunswick: York Press, 1979).

25. André Bazin, *What Is Cinema?*, vol. 1, ed. and trans. Hugh Gray (Berkeley: University of California Press, 1967), 128.

26. Nick Browne, "Film Form/Voice-Over: Bresson's *The Diary of a Country Priest,*" *Yale French Studies*, no. 60 (1980): 233.

27. See "Private Scribblings: The Crux in the Margins around *Diary of a Country Priest*" in Dudley Andrew, *Film in the Aura of Art* (Princeton: Princeton University Press, 1984), 112–30.

28. Marie-Claire Ropars-Wuilleumier, *De la littérature au cinéma: genèse d'une écriture* (Paris: Armand Colin, 1970), 145. For further analysis of these directors, see her study *L'écran de la mémoire: essais de lecture cinématographique* (Paris: Seuil, 1970).

29. T. Jefferson Kline, *Screening the Text: Intertextuality in New Wave French Cinema* (Baltimore: Johns Hopkins University Press, 1992), 225.

30. Seymour Chatman, *Coming to Terms: The Rhetoric of Narrative in Fiction and Film* (Ithaca: Cornell University Press, 1990), 6–21.

31. Metz, *Language and Cinema*, 285–86.

32. Burch, *To the Distant Observer*, 47, 49.

33. Roland Barthes, *Empire of Signs*, trans. Richard Howard (New York: Hill & Wang, 1982).

34. Frank Lloyd Wright, *The Japanese Print: An Interpretation* (New York: Horizon Press, 1967), 32.

35. Burch, *To the Distant Observer*, 298; the complete discussion of Kurosawa appears on pp. 291–323. Burch restates this thesis in his article "Akira Kurosawa" in Richard Roud, ed., *Cinema: A Critical Dictionary* (New York: Viking Press, 1980), 571–82.

36. J. L. Anderson and Loren Hoekzen, "The Spaces Between: American Criticism of Japanese Film," *Wide Angle* 1, no. 4 (1977): 4.

37. For the principal examples of auteur criticism, two useful anthologies are John Caughie, ed., *Theories of Authorship* (Boston: Routledge & Kegan Paul, 1981), and Bill Nichols, ed., *Movies and Methods*, vol. 1 (Berkeley: University of California Press, 1976).

38. Donald Richie, *The Films of Akira Kurosawa*, rev. ed. (Berkeley: University of California Press, 1984), 228–29.

39. Stephen Prince, *The Warrior's Camera: The Cinema of Akira Kurosawa* (Princeton: Princeton University Press, 1991), xxi.

40. Audie Bock, *Japanese Film Directors* (San Francisco: Kodansha

International, 1985), 138, 140; her discussion of Kurosawa and a filmography appear on pp. 161–88.

41. Audie Bock, "The Moralistic Cinema of Kurosawa," in Chang, *Kurosawa*, 16–23.

42. Tadao Sato, *Currents in Japanese Cinema*, trans. Gregory Barrett (Tokyo: Kodansha International, 1982), 28–30, 116–31.

43. Keiko I. McDonald, *Cinema East: A Critical Study of Major Japanese Films* (Rutherford, N.J.: Fairleigh Dickinson University Press, 1983), 155; her discussion of *Rashomon* appears on pp. 23–35, of *Red Beard* on pp. 71–87, and of *Throne of Blood* on pp. 154–67.

44. Joan Mellen, *The Waves at Genji's Door: Japan through Its Cinema* (New York: Pantheon, 1976), 229–35, and "The Epic Cinema of Kurosawa," *Take One* 3, no. 4 (March–April 1971): 16–19.

45. Mellen, *Waves at Genji's Door*, 41–56.

46. Richie, *Films of Kurosawa*, 214.

47. Michel Foucault, "What Is an Author?" in *Language, Counter-Memory, Practice*, ed. Donald F. Bouchard, trans. Donald F. Bouchard and Sherry Simon (Ithaca: Cornell University Press, 1977), 113–38; Roland Barthes, "The Death of the Author" in *Image-Music-Text*, 142–48; Jacques Derrida, "Signature Event Context," trans. Samuel Weber and Jeffrey Mehlman, in *Margins of Philosophy* (Chicago: University of Chicago Press, 1982), 307–30.

48. Peter Brunette and David Wills, *Screen/Play: Derrida and Film Theory* (Princeton: Princeton University Press, 1989), 64.

49. Richie, "Personal Record," 21.

I. A Life and Its Intertexts

1. Jacques Derrida, *The Ear of the Other: Otobiography, Transference, Translation*, trans. Peggy Kamuf (New York: Schocken, 1985), 5–14.

2. Roland Barthes, *Sade, Fourier, Loyola*, trans. Richard Miller (New York: Hill & Wang, 1976), 8–9.

3. In a comprehensive discussion of the subject, J. L. Anderson identifies *katsuben* as the more accurate historical term: "Spoken Silents in the Japanese Cinema; or, Talking to Pictures: Essaying the *Katsuben*, Contexturalizing the Texts," in *Reframing Japanese Cinema: Authorship, Genre, History*, ed. Arthur Nolletti and David Desser (Bloomington: Indiana University Press, 1992), 259–311. My additional sources for information on the benshi are: Peter B. High, "The Dawn of Cinema in Japan," *Journal of Contemporary History* 19, no. 1 (January 1984): 23–57; Donald Kirihara, "A Reconsideration of the Institution of the Benshi," *Film Reader*, no. 6 (1985): 41–53; Hiroshi Komatsu and Charles Musser, "Benshi Search," *Wide Angle* 9, no. 2 (1987): 72–90.

4. This description of Bunraku is based on the discussion in Barthes, *Empire of Signs*, 48–62.

5. Burch, *To the Distant Observer*, 72, 75–81.

6. From a 1972 interview published in Joan Mellen, *Voices from the Japanese Cinema* (New York: Liveright, 1975), 45.

7. This account of the early scripts is based on information in Tadao Sato, "The World of Akira Kurosawa," trans. Goro Iiri, in *The Study of the History of Cinema* (Tokyo), no. 1 (1973): 79–96.

8. Georges Sadoul, "Entretien avec Akira Kurosawa," *Cinéma*, no. 92 (janvier 1965): 83.

9. Mark Roskill, ed., *The Letters of Vincent Van Gogh* (New York: Atheneum, 1963), 296.

2. Russian Intertexts

1. Mikhail Bakhtin, *The Dialogic Imagination*, ed. and trans. Michael Holquist and Caryl Emerson (Austin: University of Texas Press, 1981), and *Problems of Dostoevsky's Poetics*, ed. and trans. Caryl Emerson (Minneapolis: University of Minnesota Press, 1984). There is discussion of the relevance of Bakhtin to film studies, but not to Kurosawa specifically, in Robert Stam, *Subversive Pleasures: Bakhtin, Cultural Criticism, and Film* (Baltimore: Johns Hopkins University Press, 1989).

2. Richie, *Films of Kurosawa*, 81.

3. See Donald Richie, "Dostoevsky with a Japanese Camera," in Lewis Jacobs, ed., *The Emergence of Film Art* (New York: Hopkinson & Blake, 1969), 328–35; Richie, *Films of Kurosawa*, 68–69, 95, 177, 197; and Burch, *To the Distant Observer*, 294–301.

4. Prince, *Warrior's Camera* (94–95, 135–41), extends the analogies between Dostoevsky and Kurosawa in a few of the same directions pursued here.

5. Georges Simenon, *Maigret's Memoirs* (1951), trans. Jean Stewart (New York: Avon, 1963), 100.

6. Yoshio Shirai, Hayao Shibata, and Koichi Yamada, "'L'Empereur': Entretien avec Kurosawa Akira," *Cahiers du Cinéma*, no. 182 (septembre 1966): 37.

7. Feodor Dostoevsky, *The Idiot*, trans. Constance Garnett (New York: Modern Library, 1935), 545. Subsequent references to the novel will be indicated in the text.

8. Richie, *Films of Kurosawa*, 85.

9. From an interview with Donald Richie, "Kurosawa on Kurosawa," reprinted in Andrew Sarris, ed., *Interviews with Film Directors* (New York: Avon, 1967), 298.

10. My principal sources for the discussion of Japanese drama that follows are these: Paul Arnold, *Le Théâtre japonais: Nô, Kabuki, Shimpa, Shingeki* (Paris: L'Arche, 1957); Earle Ernst, *The Kabuki Theatre* (1956; reprint, Honolulu: University Press of Hawaii, 1974); Donald Keene, *Dawn to the West: Japanese Literature of the Modern Era*, vol. 2, *Poetry, Drama, Criticism* (New York: Holt, Rinehart & Winston, 1984); Earl Miner, Hiroko Odagiri, and Robert E. Morrell, *The Princeton Compan-*

ion to Classical Japanese Literature (Princeton: Princeton University Press, 1985); and J. Thomas Rimer, *Toward a Modern Japanese Theatre: Kishida Kunio* (Princeton: Princeton University Press, 1974).

11. One production still of *The Lower Depths* is published in Arnold, *Le Théâtre japonais*, 273.

12. Sarris, *Interviews*, 303–4.

13. Maxim Gorky, *The Lower Depths*, trans. Alexander Bakshy (New Haven: Yale University Press, 1945), 16. Subsequent references to the play will be made in the text.

14. Mellen, *Voices from the Japanese Cinema*, 43.

15. Sato, *Currents in Japanese Cinema*, 222.

16. Donald Richie, *Japanese Cinema: Film Style and National Character* (Garden City, N.Y.: Doubleday, 1971), 43.

3. Modernist Narrative and Intertextuality

1. Shirai, Shibata, and Yamata, "'L'Empereur,'" 76.

2. Roy Armes, *The Ambiguous Image: Narrative Style in Modern European Cinema* (Bloomington: Indiana University Press, 1976), 237. Stephen Prince reasons that *Rashomon* is not modernist, since it limits fragmentation and relativity to the content of narrative and does not extend these properties to its structure (*Warrior's Camera*, 135), a conclusion my analysis does not share.

3. David Bordwell, *Narration in the Fiction Film* (Madison: University of Wisconsin Press, 1985), 207–8.

4. Yuri Tynyanov, "Plot and Story-line in the Cinema," trans. Ann Shukman, *Russian Poetics in Translation*, no. 5 (1978): 20. In film studies, Formalist models have been elaborated in Seymour Chatman, *Story and Discourse: Narrative Structure in Fiction and Film* (Ithaca: Cornell University Press, 1978), and Kristin Thompson, *Breaking the Glass Armor: Neoformalist Film Analysis* (Princeton: Princeton University Press, 1988).

5. Chatman, *Coming to Terms*, 6–10.

6. Desser, *Eros Plus Massacre*, 15–25.

7. The three *Konjaku* tales that are sources for Akutagawa's two stories are translated in Marian Ury, trans., *Tales of Times Now Past* (Berkeley: University of California Press, 1979), 183–86, 197–98.

8. This quote from a tribute by Akutagawa to *Konjaku* is taken from Hiroko Kobayashi, *The Human Comedy of Heian Japan* (Tokyo: Centre for East Asian Cultural Studies, 1979), 262.

9. The Akutagawa stories are available in translation in Donald Richie, ed., *Rashomon* (New Brunswick: Rutgers University Press, 1987), 95–109, which is the source for the quotations here.

10. Shirai, Shibata, and Yamata, "'L'Empereur,'" 37.

11. For the convenience of readers, my quotation of dialogue conforms to the *Rashomon* filmscript edited by Donald Richie, which varies

slightly in places from the subtitle translations on the print of the film currently available on video.

12. Another approach to analysis of the narrative structure in *Rashomon* is taken in Richie, *Kurosawa,* 70–76. In his book *Narrated Films: Storytelling Situations in Cinema History* (Baltimore: Johns Hopkins University Press, 1992), 128–41, Avrom Fleishman refines the narrative system Richie charts, and he reaches the conclusion that "it is thus not only multiple versions of the story that *Rashomon* presents, but also multiple ideologies of storytelling itself" (136).

13. A thorough account of Noh traditions is available in Kunio Komparu, *The Noh Theater: Principles and Perspectives,* trans. Jane Corddry (New York: Weatherhill/Tankosha, 1983), from which the information here is drawn.

14. Shirai, Shibata, and Yamata, "'L'Empereur,'" 78.

15. Mellen, *Voices from the Japanese Cinema,* 252.

16. These figures are based on the shot-by-shot description in Donald Richie, ed. and trans., *Rashomon* (New York: Grove, 1969).

17. Christian Metz, "*Trucage* and the Film," trans. Françoise Meltzer, *Critical Inquiry* 3, no. 4 (Summer 1977): 664.

18. Burch, *To the Distant Observer,* 120, 298–99; Burch, "Kurosawa," 576.

19. Burch, *To the Distant Observer,* 299.

20. Gilles Deleuze, *Cinema 1: The Movement Image,* trans. Hugh Tomlinson and Barbara Habberjam (Minneapolis: University of Minnesota Press, 1986), 21, 188–93.

21. Richie, *Kurosawa,* 15, 78.

22. This information is taken from Sato, "World of Kurosawa," 89–92.

23. For discussion of the matter of directional bias, see Richie, "Viewing Japanese Film."

24. Quotations from the film dialogue are based on Akira Kurosawa, *Ikiru,* trans. Donald Richie (New York: Simon & Schuster, 1969), and on the print now in general circulation in videocassette, with the translation also by Donald Richie.

25. Richie, *Kurosawa,* 86.

26. This property is also analyzed in David Desser, "*Ikiru:* Narration as a Moral Act," in Nolletti and Desser, *Reframing Japanese Cinema,* 56–68.

27. This narrative linkage was first observed by Burch, *To the Distant Observer,* 302–3.

28. Burch is the first to identify the "visual rhymes" among flashbacks in this sequence in *To the Distant Observer,* 301–3, and "Kurosawa," 580–81.

4. Tragedy without Heroes

1. The qualities of super heroism in *The Hidden Fortress* are fully explored in Desser, *Samurai Films of Kurosawa*, 92–97.

2. My discussion of these two films is indebted to the analysis of story formula, heroism, and black comedy in Desser, *Samurai Films of Kurosawa*, 97–116.

3. Richie, *Kurosawa*, 147.

4. Bakhtin, *Dialogic Imagination*, 304. *Quarterly Review of Film and Video* 12, no. 1–2 (1990), a special issue on parody edited by Ronald Gottesman, contains several informative essays on this topic.

5. All quotations and line citations are based on William Shakespeare, *Macbeth*, ed. Sylvan Barnet (New York: Signet, 1987).

6. My understanding of *Macbeth* in these modern contexts is indebted to the discussion in Jan Kott, *Shakespeare Our Contemporary*, trans. Boleslaw Taborski (New York: Doubleday, 1964), 75–86.

7. A. C. Bradley, *Shakespearean Tragedy* (1902; rpt. New York: World, 1961), 17–33, 51–54, 264–317.

8. Cleanth Brooks, *The Well-Wrought Urn* (New York: Harcourt, 1947), 21–46.

9. Shirai, Shibata, and Yamata, "'L'Empereur,'" 76.

10. Richie, *Kurosawa*, 122–23.

11. All quotations of dialogue are based on the translation into English by Donald Richie on the videocassette release of *Throne of Blood* (copyright 1961 by Brandon Films) currently in distribution.

12. My account of specific properties in Noh is based on information in Komparu, *The Noh Theater*; Zeami, *On the Art of the No Drama*, trans. J. Thomas Rimer and Yamazaki Masakazu (Princeton: Princeton University Press, 1984); and Miner, Odagiri, and Morrell, *Princeton Companion to Classical Japanese Literature*. Other analyses of Noh properties in *Throne of Blood* are to be found in Richie, *Kurosawa*, 115–25; McDonald, *Cinema East*, 154–67; and Prince, *Warrior's Camera*, 144–49.

13. Keiko McDonald fully discusses the analogues between this play and the film in her essay, "The Noh Conventions in *The Throne of Blood* and *Ran*," in Chang, *Kurosawa*, 24–32.

14. Shirai, Shibata, and Yamata, "'L'Empereur,'" 75.

15. Jun'ichiro Tanizaki, *In Praise of Shadows*, trans. Thomas J. Harper and Edward G. Seidensticker (New Haven, Conn.: Leete's Island Books, 1977), 26–27.

16. Richie, *Kurosawa*, 117–20.

17. Sarris, *Interviews*, 303.

18. Shirai, Shibata, and Yamata, "'L'Empereur,'" 75.

19. See the discussion in Ezra Pound and Ernest Fenollosa, *The Classic Noh Theatre of Japan* (1917; rpt. New York: New Directions, 1959), 26–36; and the ideas on "Alienation-effect" and masked theater in Bertolt

Brecht, *Brecht on Theatre,* ed. and trans. John Willett (New York: Hill & Wang, 1964), 91–99, 179–205.

20. Quotations from *Kagemusha* are based on subtitles to the release print currently available on videotape, released through 20th Century–Fox.

21. The published script *Ran,* trans. Tadashi Shishido (Boston: Shambhala, 1986), differs from the released film in many significant respects. Quotations of film dialogue from *Ran* are based on the videocassette in general release (CBS/Fox, 1986), whose subtitle translations were prepared by Anne Brau. Another valuable resource is Bertrand Raison and Serge Toubiana, eds., *Le Livre de Ran* (Paris: Cahiers du Cinéma/Seuil, 1985).

22. All quotations and line citations are based on William Shakespeare, *King Lear,* ed. Russell Fraser (New York: Signet, 1963).

23. Peter Grilli, "Kurosawa Directs a Cinematic *Lear,*" *New York Times,* 15 December 1985, sec. 2, 17.

24. Grigori Kozintsev, *King Lear: The Space of Tragedy,* trans. Mary Mackintosh (Berkeley: University of California Press, 1977), 117.

25. John Powers, "Kurosawa: An Audience with the Emperor," trans. Audie Bock, *L.A. Weekly,* 4 April 1986, 45.

26. Ibid.

27. Max Tessier, "Propos d'Akira Kurosawa," *Revue du Cinéma,* no. 408 (septembre 1985): 69.

28. Ibid.

Conclusion

1. Richie, *Kurosawa,* 215–18.

2. Burch, *To the Distant Observer,* 296.

3. Desser, *"Ikiru:* Narration as a Moral Act."

4. Dan Yakir, "The Warrior Returns," *Film Comment* 16, no. 6 (November–December 1980): 57.

5. All quotations in this paragraph are taken from Akira Kurosawa, "Drawing and Directing: Some Thoughts Commemorating the Publication of This Collection," trans. Margaret Benton, in Kurosawa, *Ran,* 6.

6. Raison and Toubiana, eds., *Le Livre de Ran,* 133.

7. Ibid., 136.

8. Kazuo Miyagawa, "My Life as a Cameraman: Yesterday—Today—Tomorrow," trans. Linda Ehrlich and Akiko Shibagaki, *Post Script* 11, no. 1 (Fall 1991): 15.

9. Grilli, "Kurosawa Directs a Cinematic *Lear,*" sec. 2, 17.

10. In my article, "Literature and Film: A Review of Criticism," *Quarterly Review of Film Studies* 4, no. 2 (Spring 1979): 227–46, I evaluate the ideas of these critics.

11. Fleishman, *Narrated Films,* 198.

12. Marie-Claire Ropars-Wuilleumier, *Ecraniques: Le film du texte* (Lille, France: Presses Universitaires de Lille, 1990), 13.

Select Bibliography

"Akira Kurosawa." *Études cinématographiques*, no. 30–31 (printemps 1964).

Anderson, Joseph L. "Japanese Swordfighters and American Gunfighters." *Cinema Journal* 12, no. 2 (Spring 1973): 1–21.

Anderson, Joseph L., and Loren Hoekzen. "The Spaces Between: American Criticism of Japanese Film." *Wide Angle* 1, no. 4 (1977): 2–7.

Anderson, Joseph L., and Donald Richie. *The Japanese Film: Art and Industry*. Princeton: Princeton University Press, 1982.

Andrew, Dudley. *Film in the Aura of Art*. Princeton: Princeton University Press, 1984.

Andrew, Dudley, and Paul Andrew. *Kenji Mizoguchi: A Guide to References and Resources*. Boston: G. K. Hall, 1981.

Armes, Roy. *The Ambiguous Image: Narrative Style in Modern European Cinema*. Bloomington: Indiana University Press, 1976.

Arnold, Paul. *Le Théâtre japonais: Nô, Kabuki, Shimpa, Shingeki*. Paris: L'Arche, 1957.

Bakhtin, Mikhail. *The Dialogic Imagination*. Ed. and trans. Michael Holquist and Caryl Emerson. Austin: University of Texas Press, 1981.

——. *Problems of Dostoevsky's Poetics*. Ed. and trans. Caryl Emerson. Minneapolis: University of Minnesota Press, 1984.

Barthes, Roland. *Empire of Signs*. Trans. Richard Howard. New York: Hill & Wang, 1982.

——. *Image-Music-Text*. Trans. Stephen Heath. New York: Hill & Wang, 1977.

——. *Sade, Fourier, Loyola*. Trans. Richard Miller. New York: Hill & Wang, 1976.

——. "Theory of the Text." Trans. Ian McLeod. In Robert Young, ed., *Untying the Text: A Post-Structuralist Reader*. Boston: Routledge & Kegan Paul, 1981.

———. *Writing Degree Zero.* Trans. Annette Lavers and Colin Smith. Boston: Beacon, 1968.

Bazin, André. *The Cinema of Cruelty.* Trans Sabine d'Estrée. New York: Seaver, 1982.

———. *What Is Cinema?* Vol. 1. Ed. and trans. Hugh Gray. Berkeley: University of California Press, 1967.

Benedict, Ruth. *The Chrysanthemum and the Sword: Patterns of Japanese Culture.* New York: Meridian, 1974.

Bock, Audie. *Japanese Film Directors.* San Francisco: Kodansha International, 1985.

Bordwell, David. *Narration in the Fiction Film.* Madison: University of Wisconsin Press, 1985.

———. "Our Dream Cinema: Western Historiography and the Japanese Film." *Film Reader,* no. 4 (1979): 45–62.

———. *Ozu and the Poetics of Cinema.* Princeton: Princeton University Press, 1988.

Boyd, David. "*Rashomon*: From Akutagawa to Kurosawa." *Literature/Film Quarterly* 15, no. 3 (1987): 155–58.

Bradley, A. C. *Shakespearean Tragedy.* 1902. Reprint. New York: World, 1961.

Brecht, Bertolt. *Brecht on Theatre.* Ed. and trans. John Willett. New York: Hill & Wang, 1964.

Brooks, Cleanth. *The Well-Wrought Urn.* New York: Harcourt, 1947.

Browne, Nick. "Film Form/Voice-Over: Bresson's *The Diary of a Country Priest.*" *Yale French Studies,* no. 60 (1980): 233–40.

Brunette, Peter, and David Wills. *Screen/Play: Derrida and Film Theory.* Princeton: Princeton University Press, 1989.

Burch, Noel. "Approaching Japanese Film." In *Cinema and Language.* Ed. Stephen Heath and Patricia Mellencamp. Frederick, Md.: University Publications of America, 1983.

———. *To the Distant Observer: Form and Meaning in the Japanese Cinema.* Rev. and ed. Annette Michelson. Berkeley: University of California Press, 1979.

Buruma, Ian. *Behind the Mask.* New York: Pantheon, 1984.

———. *God's Dust: A Modern Asian Journey.* New York: Farrar, Straus, Giroux, 1989.

The Cambridge History of Japan. New York: Cambridge University Press, 1988–1990. Vol. 3, *Medieval Japan,* ed. Kozo Yamamura. Vol. 5, *The Nineteenth Century,* ed. Marius B. Jansen. Vol. 6, *The Twentieth Century,* ed. Peter Duus.

Cardullo, Bert. "The Circumstance of the East, the Fate of the West." *Literature/Film Quarterly* 13, no. 2 (1985): 112–17.

Caughie, John, ed. *Theories of Authorship.* Boston: Routledge & Kegan Paul, 1981.

Chang, Joseph S. "*Kagemusha* and the *Chushingura* Motif." *East-West Film Journal* 3, no. 2 (June 1989): 14–38.

Chang, Kevin K. W., ed. *Kurosawa: Perceptions on Life, An Anthology of Essays.* Honolulu: Honolulu Academy of Arts, 1991.

Chatman, Seymour. *Coming to Terms: The Rhetoric of Narrative in Fiction and Film.* Ithaca: Cornell University Press, 1990.

———. *Story and Discourse: Narrative Structure in Fiction and Film.* Ithaca: Cornell University Press, 1978.

Cohen, Keith. *Film and Fiction: The Dynamics of Exchange.* New Haven: Yale University Press, 1979.

Cohen, Robert. "Towards a Theory of Japanese Narrative." *Quarterly Review of Film Studies* 6, no. 2 (Spring 1981): 181–200.

Culler, Jonathan. *The Pursuit of Signs: Semiotics, Literature, Deconstruction.* Ithaca: Cornell University Press, 1981.

Daney, Serge. "Un ours en plus (*Dersu Uzala*)." *Cahiers du Cinéma*, no. 274 (mars 1977): 33–40.

Davies, Anthony. *Filming Shakespeare's Plays.* New York: Cambridge University Press, 1988.

Decaux, Emmanuel, and Bruno Villien. "Entretien avec Akira Kurosawa." *Cinématographe*, no. 88 (1983): 61–63.

Deleuze, Gilles. *Cinema 1: The Movement Image.* Trans. Hugh Tomlinson and Barbara Habberjam. Minneapolis: University of Minnesota Press, 1986.

———. *Cinema 2: The Time Image.* Trans. Hugh Tomlinson and Robert Galeta. Minneapolis: University of Minnesota Press, 1989.

Derrida, Jacques. *The Ear of the Other: Otobiography, Transference, Translation.* Trans. Peggy Kamuf. New York: Schocken, 1985.

———. "The Law of Genre." Trans. Avital Ronell. *Glyph*, no. 7 (1980): 202–29.

———. *Margins of Philosophy.* Trans. Alan Bass. Chicago: University of Chicago Press, 1982.

Desser, David. *Eros Plus Massacre.* Bloomington: Indiana University Press, 1988.

———. "Kurosawa's Eastern 'Western': *Sanjuro* and the Influence of *Shane.*" *Film Criticism* 8, no. 1 (Fall 1983): 54–65.

——. *The Samurai Films of Akira Kurosawa*. Ann Arbor: UMI Research Press, 1983.

Dostoevsky, Feodor. *The Idiot*. Trans. Constance Garnett. New York: Modern Library, 1935.

Eco, Umberto. *A Theory of Semiotics*. Bloomington: Indiana University Press, 1976.

Erens, Patricia. *Akira Kurosawa: A Guide to References and Resources*. Boston: G. K. Hall, 1979.

Ernst, Earle. *The Kabuki Theatre*. 1956. Reprint. Honolulu: University Press of Hawaii, 1974.

Fleishman, Avrom. *Narrated Films: Storytelling Situations in Cinema History*. Baltimore: Johns Hopkins University Press, 1992.

Foucault, Michel. *Language, Counter-Memory, Practice*. Ed. Donald F. Bouchard, trans. Donald F. Bouchard and Sherry Simon. Ithaca: Cornell University Press, 1977.

Frank, Joseph. *Dostoevsky: The Seeds of Revolt, 1821–1849*. Princeton: Princeton University Press, 1976.

——. *Dostoevsky: The Stir of Liberation, 1860–1865*. Princeton: Princeton University Press, 1986.

——. *Dostoevsky: The Years of Ordeal, 1850–1859*. Princeton: Princeton University Press, 1983.

Godard, Jean-Luc. *Godard on Godard*. Ed. Jean Narboni and Tom Milne, trans. Tom Milne. New York: Viking, 1972.

Goodwin, James. "Literature and Film: A Review of Criticism." *Quarterly Review of Film Studies* 4, no. 2 (Spring 1979): 227–46.

Gorky, Maxim. *The Lower Depths*. Trans. Alexander Bakshy. New Haven: Yale University Press, 1945.

Govaers, Hiroko, ed. *Le Cinéma japonais de ses origines à nos jours*. Paris: La Cinémathèque Française, 1984.

Grilli, Peter. "Kurosawa Directs a Cinematic *Lear*." *New York Times*, 15 December 1985, sec. 2: 1, 17.

——. "The Old Man and the Scene: Notes on the Making of *Ran*." *Film Comment* 21, no. 5 (September–October 1985): 48, 57–60.

Heath, Stephen. *Questions of Cinema*. Bloomington: Indiana University Press, 1981.

High, Peter B. "The Dawn of Cinema in Japan." *Journal of Contemporary History* 19, no. 1 (January 1984): 23–57.

Kawin, Bruce F. *Mindscreen: Bergman, Godard, and First-Person Film*. Princeton: Princeton University Press, 1978.

Keene, Donald. *Dawn to the West: Japanese Literature of the Mod-

ern Era. Vol. 2, *Poetry, Drama, Criticism*. New York: Holt, Rinehart & Winston, 1984.

Kinder, Marsha. *"Kagemusha." Film Quarterly* 34, no. 2 (Winter 1980–1981): 44–48.

Kirihara, Donald. "A Reconsideration of the Institution of the Benshi." *Film Reader*, no. 6 (1985): 41–53.

Kline, T. Jefferson. *Screening the Text: Intertextuality in New Wave French Cinema*. Baltimore: Johns Hopkins University Press, 1992.

Kobayashi, Hiroko. *The Human Comedy of Heian Japan*. Tokyo: Centre for East Asian Cultural Studies, 1979.

Komatsu, Hiroshi, and Charles Musser. "Benshi Search." *Wide Angle* 9, no. 2 (1987): 72–90.

Komparu, Kunio. *The Noh Theater: Principles and Perspectives*. Trans. Jane Corddry. New York: Weatherhill/Tankosha, 1983.

Kott, Jan. "The Edo Lear." Trans. Lillian Vallee. *New York Review of Books*, 24 April 1986, 13–15.

———. *Shakespeare Our Contemporary*. Trans. Boleslaw Taborski. New York: Doubleday, 1964.

———. *The Theater of Essence*. Evanston: Northwestern University Press, 1984.

Kozintsev, Grigori. *King Lear: The Space of Tragedy*. Trans. Mary Mackintosh. Berkeley: University of California Press, 1977.

Kristeva, Julia. *Desire in Language*. Trans. Thomas Gora, Alice Jardine, and Leon S. Roudiez. New York: Columbia University Press, 1980.

———. *Revolution in Poetic Language*. Trans. Margaret Waller. New York: Columbia University Press, 1984.

Kuleshov, Lev. *Kuleshov on Film*. Ed. and trans. Ronald Levaco. Berkeley: University of California Press, 1974.

Kurosawa, Akira. *Complete Works of Akira Kurosawa*. [In Japanese and English] Trans. Kimi Aida and Don Kenny. Tokyo: Kinema Jumpo Sha, 1971. Vol. 1, *Dodeskaden*; vol. 2, *Sanshiro Sugata* and *No Regrets for Our Youth*; vol. 3, *One Wonderful Sunday* and *Drunken Angel*; vol. 4, *Quiet Duel* and *Stray Dog*; vol. 6, *The Idiot* and *Ikiru*; vol. 9, *The Hidden Fortress* and *The Bad Sleep Well*. [The edition ceased publication after these volumes.]

———. *Ikiru*. Trans. Donald Richie. New York: Simon & Schuster, 1969.

———. *Ran*. Trans. Tadashi Shishido. Boston: Shambhala, 1986.

———. *Rashomon*. Ed. and trans. Donald Richie. New York: Grove, 1969.

———. *Rashomon*. Ed. and trans. Donald Richie. New Brunswick: Rutgers University Press, 1987.

———. *Seven Samurai*. Trans. Donald Richie. London: Lorrimer, 1970.

———. *Something Like an Autobiography*. Trans. Audie E. Bock. New York: Vintage, 1983.

McDonald, Keiko I. *Cinema East: A Critical Study of Major Japanese Films*. Rutherford, N.J.: Fairleigh Dickinson University Press, 1983.

Magny, Claude-Edmonde. *The Age of the American Novel: The Film Aesthetic of Fiction between the Two Wars*. Trans. Eleanor Hochman. New York: Ungar, 1972.

Malcomson, Scott L. "The Pure Land Beyond the Seas: Barthes, Burch and the Uses of Japan." *Screen* 26, no. 3–4 (May–August 1985): 23–33.

Manvell, Roger. *Shakespeare and the Film*. London: Dent, 1971.

Martin, Harris I. "Popular Music and Social Change in Prewar Japan." *Japan Interpreter* 7, no. 3–4 (Summer–Autumn 1973): 332–52.

Mellen, Joan. "The Epic Cinema of Kurosawa." *Take One* 3, no. 4 (March–April 1971): 16–19.

———. *Voices from the Japanese Cinema*. New York: Liveright, 1975.

———. *The Waves at Genji's Door: Japan through Its Cinema*. New York: Pantheon, 1976.

Metz, Christian. *Language and Cinema*. Trans. Donna Jean Umiker-Sebeok. The Hague: Mouton, 1974.

———. "*Trucage* and the Film." Trans. Françoise Meltzer. *Critical Inquiry* 3, no. 4 (Summer 1977): 657–75.

Miner, Earl, Hiroko Odagiri, and Robert E. Morrell. *The Princeton Companion to Classical Japanese Literature*. Princeton: Princeton University Press, 1985.

Miyagawa, Kazuo. "My Life as a Cameraman: Yesterday—Today—Tomorrow." Trans. Linda Ehrlich and Akiko Shibagaki. *Post Script* 11, no. 1 (Fall 1991): 5–19.

Morgan, Thaïs E. "Is There an Intertext in this Text?: Literary and Interdisciplinary Approaches to Intertextuality." *American Journal of Semiotics* 3, no. 4 (1985): 1–40.

Morrissette, Bruce. *Intertextual Assemblage in Robbe-Grillet from*

Topology to the Golden Triangle. Fredericton, New Brunswick: York Press, 1979.

———. *Novel and Film: Essays in Two Genres.* Chicago: University of Chicago Press, 1985.

Nichols, Bill, ed. *Movies and Methods.* Vol. 1. Berkeley: University of California Press, 1976.

Nolletti, Arthur, and David Desser, eds. *Reframing Japanese Cinema: Authorship, Genre, History.* Bloomington: Indiana University Press, 1992.

Nygren, Scott. "Doubleness and Idiosyncrasy in Cross-Cultural Analysis." *Quarterly Review of Film and Video* 13, no. 1–3 (1991): 173–87.

Pound, Ezra, and Ernest Fenollosa. *The Classic Noh Theatre of Japan.* 1917. Reprint. New York: New Directions, 1959.

Powers, John. "Kurosawa: An Audience with the Emperor." Trans. Audie Bock. *L.A. Weekly,* 4 April 1986, 45–47.

Prince, Stephen. *The Warrior's Camera: The Cinema of Akira Kurosawa.* Princeton: Princeton University Press, 1991.

Pronko, Leonard C. *Theater East and West.* Berkeley: University of California Press, 1967.

Raison, Bertrand, and Serge Toubiana, eds. *Le Livre de Ran.* Paris: Cahiers du Cinéma/Seuil, 1985.

Richie, Donald. "Dostoevsky with a Japanese Camera." In Lewis Jacobs, ed. *The Emergence of Film Art.* New York: Hopkinson & Blake, 1969.

———. *The Films of Akira Kurosawa.* Rev. ed. Berkeley: University of California Press, 1984.

———, ed. *Focus on Rashomon.* Englewood Cliffs, N.J.: Prentice-Hall, 1972.

———. *Japanese Cinema: Film Style and National Character.* Garden City, N.Y.: Doubleday, 1971.

———. "A Personal Record." *Film Quarterly* 14, no. 1 (Fall 1960): 20–30.

———. "Viewing Japanese Film: Some Considerations." *East-West Film Journal* 1, no. 1 (December 1986): 23–35.

Rimer, J. Thomas. *Toward a Modern Japanese Theatre: Kishida Kunio.* Princeton: Princeton University Press, 1974.

Ropars-Wuilleumier, Marie-Claire. *De la littérature au cinéma: genèse d'une écriture.* Paris: Armand Colin, 1970.

——. *L'écran de la mémoire: essais de lecture cinématographique.* Paris: Seuil, 1970.

——. *Ecraniques: Le film du texte.* Lille, France: Presses Universitaires de Lille, 1990.

Roskill, Mark, ed. *The Letters of Vincent Van Gogh.* New York: Atheneum, 1963.

Ross, Lillian. "Profiles: Kurosawa Frames." *New Yorker,* 21 December 1981, 51–78.

Roud, Richard, ed. *Cinema: A Critical Dictionary.* 2 vols. New York: Viking Press, 1980.

Sadoul, Georges. "Entretien avec Akira Kurosawa." *Cinéma,* no. 92 (janvier 1965): 75–83.

Sansom, George B. *A History of Japan, 1334–1615.* London: Cresset, 1961.

——. *The Western World and Japan.* New York: Knopf, 1949.

Sarris, Andrew, ed. *Interviews with Film Directors.* New York: Avon, 1967.

Sato, Tadao. *Currents in Japanese Cinema.* Trans. Gregory Barrett. Tokyo: Kodansha International, 1982.

——. "The World of Akira Kurosawa." Trans. Goro Iiri. *The Study of the History of Cinema* (Tokyo), no. 1 (1973): 79–96; no. 2 (1973): 81–96; no. 3 (1974): 79–96.

Seidensticker, Edward. *Low City, High City: Tokyo from Edo to the Earthquake.* New York: Knopf, 1983.

——. *Tokyo Rising: The City since the Great Earthquake.* New York: Knopf, 1990.

Shakespeare, William. *King Lear.* Ed. Russell Fraser. New York: Signet, 1963.

——. *Macbeth.* Ed. Sylvan Barnet. New York: Signet, 1987.

Shirai, Yoshio, Hayao Shibata, and Koichi Yamada. "'L'Empereur': entretien avec Kurosawa Akira." *Cahiers du Cinéma,* no. 182 (septembre 1966): 34–42, 74–78.

Silver, Alain. *The Samurai Film.* New York: Barnes, 1977.

Simenon, Georges. *Maigret's Memoirs.* Trans. Jean Stewart. New York: Avon, 1963.

Spiegel, Alan. *Fiction and the Camera Eye: Visual Consciousness in Film and the Modern Novel.* Charlottesville: University of Virginia Press, 1976.

Stam, Robert. *Subversive Pleasures: Bakhtin, Cultural Criticism, and Film.* Baltimore: Johns Hopkins University Press, 1989.

Svensson, Arne. *Screen Series: Japan.* New York: A. S. Barnes, 1971.

Tada, Michitaro. "The Destiny of Samurai Films." *East-West Film Journal* 1, no. 1 (December 1986): 48–58.

Tanizaki, Jun'ichiro. *In Praise of Shadows.* Trans. Thomas J. Harper and Edward G. Seidensticker. New Haven, Conn.: Leete's Island Books, 1977.

Tessier, Max. "Propos d'Akira Kurosawa." *Revue du Cinéma,* no. 408 (septembre 1985): 67–70.

Thompson, Kristen. *Breaking the Glass Armor: Neoformalist Film Analysis.* Princeton: Princeton University Press, 1988.

Tucker, Richard N. *Japan: Film Image.* London: Studio Vista, 1973.

Turgenev, Ivan. *Sketches from a Hunter's Album.* Ed. and trans. Richard Freeborn. New York: Penguin, 1967.

Turnbull, S. R. *The Samurai: A Military History.* New York: Macmillan, 1977.

Tynyanov, Yuri. "Plot and Story-line in the Cinema." Trans. Ann Shukman. *Russian Poetics in Translation,* no. 5 (1978): 20–21.

Ueda, Makoto. *Literary and Art Theories in Japan.* Cleveland: Press of Case Western Reserve University, 1967.

Ury, Marian, trans. *Tales of Times Now Past.* Berkeley: University of California Press, 1979.

Wright, Frank Lloyd. *The Japanese Print: An Interpretation.* New York: Horizon Press, 1967.

Yakir, Dan. "The Warrior Returns." *Film Comment* 16, no. 6 (November–December 1980): 54–57.

Yu, Beoncheon. *Akutagawa: An Introduction.* Detroit: Wayne State University Press, 1972.

Zambrano, Ana Laura. "*Throne of Blood*: Kurosawa's *Macbeth*," *Literature/Film Quarterly* 2, no. 3 (1974): 262–74.

Zeami. *On the Art of the No Drama.* Trans. J. Thomas Rimer and Yamazaki Masakazu. Princeton: Princeton University Press, 1984.

Film Characters

The Idiot [Hakuchi] (1951)

Film	Character Novel	Actor
Kinji Kameda	Prince Lyov Nikolayevitch Myshkin	Masayuki Mori
Denkichi Akama	Parfyon Rogozhin	Toshiro Mifune
Akama's mother	Rogozhin's mother	Mitsuyo Akashi
Karube	Lukyan Timofeyitch Lebedyev	Bokuzen Hidari
Tohata	Afanasy Ivanovitch Totsky	Eijiro Yanagi
Taeko Nasu	Nastasya Filippovna, Totsky's mistress	Setsuko Hara
Ono	General Ivan Fyodorovitch Epanchin	Takashi Shimura
Satoko, wife	Madame Lizaveta Prokofyevna Epanchin	Chieko Higashiyama
Ayako Ono, daughter	Aglaia Epanchin, daughter	Yoshiko Kuga
Noriko, daughter	Alexandra Epanchin, daughter	Chiyoko Fumiya
Jyunpei	General Aralion A. Ivolgin	Kokuten Kodo
His wife Nina	Alexandrovna Ivolgin	Eiko Miyoshi
Mutsuo Kayama, son	Gavril (Ganya) Ardalionovitch, son	Minoru Chiaki
Takako, daughter	Varvara (Varya) Ardalionovitch, daughter	Noriko Sengoku
Kaoru, son	Kolya (Nikolay) Ardaliono- vitch, son	Daisuke Inoue

The Lower Depths [Donzoko] (1957)

| | Character | |
Film	Play	Actor
Rokubei, landlord	Kostylyov, landlord	Ganjiro Nakamura
Osugi, his wife	Vassilissa, his wife	Isuzu Yamada
Okayo, her sister	Natasha, her sister	Kyoko Kagawa
Kahei, pilgrim	Luka, a pilgrim	Bokuzen Hidari
Sutekichi, thief	Peppel, the thief	Toshiro Mifune
The Actor	The Actor	Kamatari Fujiwara
The Samurai	The Baron	Minoru Chiaki
Otaki, peddler	Kvashnya, peddler	Nijiko Kiyokawa
Tatsu, bucket-maker	Bubnov, capmaker	Haruo Tanaka
Tomekichi, tinker	Klestch, locksmith	Eijiro Tono
Asa, his wife	Anna, his wife	Eiko Miyoshi
Osen, prostitute	Nastya, prostitute	Akemi Negishi
Yoshisaburo, gambler	Satin, gambler	Koji Mitsui
Shimazo, police agent	Medvedev, policeman	Kichijiro Ueda
Unokichi	Alyoshka, cobbler	Yu Fujiki
Tsugaru	The Tartar, longshoreman	Fujitayama
Thin man, companion to Tsugaru	The Goiter, longshoreman	Atsushi Watanabe

Rashomon [Rashomon] (1950)

Character	Actor
Tajomaru, the bandit	Toshiro Mifune
Takehiro, the samurai	Masayuki Mori
Masago, the wife	Machiko Kyo

Character	Actor
The woodcutter	Takashi Shimura
The priest	Minoru Chiaki
The commoner	Kichijiro Ueda
The police agent	Daisuke Kato
The medium	Fumiko Homma

Ikiru [*Ikiru*] (1952)

Character	Actor
Kanji Watanabe, Chief of Citizens' Bureau	Takashi Shimura
Mitsuo, his son	Nobuo Kaneko
Kazue, Mitsuo's wife	Kyoko Seki
Kiichi, Watanabe's elder brother	Makoto Kobori
Tatsu, Kiichi's wife	Kumeko Urabe
The maid	Yoshie Minami
Toyo Odagiri	Miki Odagiri
Ono, sub-section chief	Kamatari Fujiwara
Saito, subordinate clerk	Minosuke Yamada
Sakai, assistant	Haruo Tanaka
Ohara, assistant	Bokuzen Hidari
Noguchi, assistant	Minoru Chiaki
Kimura, assistant	Shinichi Himori
Deputy mayor	Nobuo Nakamura
City councilor	Kazuo Abe
Doctor	Masao Shimizu
Assistant	Isao Kimura
Patient	Atsushi Watanabe
Writer	Yunosuke Ito
Hostess	Yatsuko Tanami
Newspaperman	Fuyuki Murakami
Gang boss	Seiji Miyaguchi
Gang member	Daisuke Kato
Policeman	Ichiro Chiba
Housewives	Kin Sugai, Eiko Miyoshi, Fumiko Homma

Throne of Blood [Kumonosu-jo] (1957)

Film	Character Play	Actor
Taketoki Washizu	Macbeth	Toshiro Mifune
Asaji, his wife	Lady Macbeth	Isuzu Yamada
Yoshiaki Miki	Banquo	Minoru Chiaki
Yoshiteru, Miki's son	Fleance	Akira Kubo
Kuniharu Tsuzuki	Duncan	Takamaru Sasaki
Kunimaru, Tsuzuki's son	Malcolm	Yoichi Tachikawa
Noriyasu Odagura	Macduff	Takashi Shimura
Spinner prophet	Witches	Chieko Naniwa

Ran [Ran] (1985)

Character	Actor
Hidetora Ichimonji, the Great Lord	Tatsuya Nakadai
Taro, his oldest son, and heir	Akira Terao
Jiro, the middle son	Jinpachi Nezu
Saburo, the youngest son	Daisuke Ryu
Tango, Hidetora's retainer	Masayuki Yui
Ikoma, Hidetora's retainer	Kazu Kato
Fujimaki, a lord	Hitoshi Ueki
Ayabe, a lord	Jun Tazaki
Kyoami, Hidetora's fool	Peter
Lady Kaede, Taro's wife	Mieko Harada
Ogura, attendant to Taro	Norio Matsui
Lady Sué, Jiro's wife, daughter of a family Hidetora destroyed	Yoshiko Miyazaki
Kurogane, counselor to Jiro	Hisashi Igawa
Shirane, counselor to Jiro	Kenji Kodama
Naganuma, counselor to Jiro	Toshiya Ito
Tsurumaru, Lady Sué's younger brother, blinded by Hidetora	Takeshi Nomura
Hatakeyama, a commander of Saburo's troops	Takeshi Kato

Index